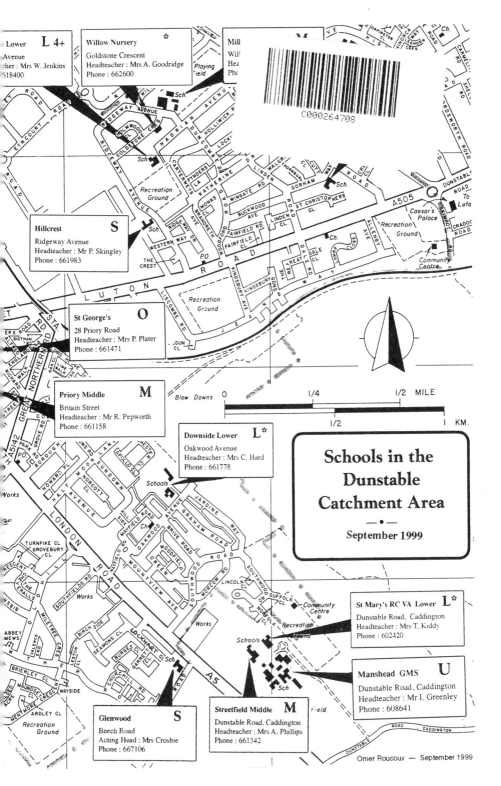

Lower **L 4+**
Avenue
...cher : Mrs W. Jenkins
...18400

Willow Nursery
Goldstone Crescent
Headteacher : Mrs A. Goodridge
Phone : 662600

Mill...
Will...
Hea...
Ph...

Hillcrest **S**
Ridgeway Avenue
Headteacher : Mr P. Skingley
Phone : 661983

St George's **O**
28 Priory Road
Headteacher : Mrs P. Plater
Phone : 661471

Priory Middle **M**
Britain Street
Headteacher : Mr R. Pepworth
Phone : 661158

Downside Lower **L✳**
Oakwood Avenue
Headteacher : Mrs C. Hard
Phone : 661778

St Mary's RC VA Lower **L✳**
Dunstable Road, Caddington
Headteacher : Mrs T. Kiddy
Phone : 602420

Manshead GMS **U**
Dunstable Road, Caddington
Headteacher : Mr I. Greenley
Phone : 608641

Glenwood **S**
Beech Road
Acting Head : Mrs Crosbie
Phone : 667106

Streetfield Middle **M**
Dunstable Road, Caddington
Headteacher : Mrs A. Phillips
Phone : 661342

Schools in the Dunstable Catchment Area
— • —
September 1999

Omer Roucoux — September 1999

PROUD HERITAGE
A Brief History of Dunstable
1000–2000AD

Vivienne Evans

Good Friday procession comprising 'Churches Together'.

To the People of Dunstable

First published November 1999
by
The Book Castle
12 Church Street
Dunstable
Bedfordshire LU5 4RU

ISBN 1 871199 19 0

Computer typeset by Keyword, Aldbury, Hertfordshire.
Printed in Great Britain by Redwood Books, Trowbridge, Wiltshire.

PREFACE

The end of the second Millennium is being built up as a huge event in our lives, yet in the spinning of the planets and the movement of the stars it has no context or meaning. This date is, in once sense, a creation of the Church, for it is the belief of Christians that Jesus Christ lived a human life on earth 2000 years ago and was yet Divine.

Dunstable has only been fully 'on the map' for the second of the Millennia since Jesus' time, but has had numerous significant 'moments' during the period, which this books helps us to explore and understand. The Christian faith has had a major role in the development of the town with its monastic foundations and its situation at a significant crossroads in the national communications network.

It has to be recognised that the Christian Church does not have a blemish-free history, and has much to be penitent over in terms of prejudice, intolerance and in-fighting. Yet out of its history we have been given the impressive architecture of the Priory and several other of the important buildings in the town.

In recent times Christians have begun to heal their internal divisions and to live and work together. I hope and pray that in the next Millennium we can continue to learn to live and work together – and even love each other! In so far as we are able to do this, we will be better able to serve the frail and needy of our town, offer wise counsel to those in authority and contribute more fully to the quality of life here. I hope and pray that we and our descendants can learn the lessons of history as Vivienne has vividly described them and add laudably to the progress of Dunstable through the third Millennium.

Graham Newton 　　　　　　　　　　　　　　　　*September 1999*
Rector of Dunstable

FOREWORD

Vivienne's book has uncovered the history of Dunstable from its foundation. Over the centuries the town has had good times and bad times but history has proved that however difficult things have been, success has always been waiting just around the corner.

Dunstable is just recovering from two decades during which it has suffered a serious loss to its manufacturing base. However, the tide has turned and success is waiting for us. I am delighted to report that we still have many manufacturing jobs and that a growing number of specialist high-tech industries are establishing bases on the Woodside Industrial Estate and Woodside Park. Last week I had the pleasure of opening the first shop of the White Lion Retail Estate and several more will be opening shortly. The Translink Rapid Busway, which is under discussion, will link Dunstable with Luton Station and, at a later date, continue up to the airport.

As a council we are proud of the recreational facilities which are available in the town and the hugely popular Charity Fireworks, Christmas Tree Carols Ceremony, the Carnival, the Sunday Afternoon Band Concerts and many other community events. The market is now back in its traditional place in the Square and I am delighted that the town is marking the millennium by building a new market cross.

As Mayor of Dunstable I see a great future for the town, one which the next generation will be proud to build on.

Tony Hawkins
Town Mayor of Dunstable

September 1999

CONTENTS

In the words of former County Archivist Pat Bell:
'Not every town was founded by a king'.

CREDITS

The books and magazines on lists that I have published before have all been of great help during the writing of this book. As always I have had a great deal of help from the staff at Bedford Central Library and Bedfordshire and Luton Archives and Records Service. The Dunstable Official Guide includes the 'Dunstable Book Collection' which is a comprehensive list of books and most of the specialist books used have been mentioned in the text. Two essential books on the subject of Dunstable's more modern history are Nigel Benson's *Dunstable in Detail* (The Book Castle 1986) and Richard Walden's *Streets Ahead* (The Book Castle 1999).

I am extremely grateful to my husband Lou, for his patience and for supplying most of the illustrations, also to the other people who have allowed me to use their work. I am also grateful to the many people who have shared their memories and research with me. In particular I must mention Omer Roucoux who helped in many ways and has kindly supplied the endpapers and Dora Godfrey who has shared her memories with all of us. I am particularly grateful to Dunstable Museum Trust who have helped financially with the preparation of this book. Also to my friend Adele because without her skills in interpreting my writing during the typing of this book it would never have been finished.

Thanks are also due to: Omer Roucoux for the photograph of Chew Schoolboys. David Fowler for permission to use the conjectural drawing of the Augustinian Priory. Ernie Hawes for the photograph of Dunstable's first police station. Dunstable Town Council for permission to use the picture of the Wall Painting and of Grove House. The family of the late John Gilbe for the drawing of the Dunstable Swan Jewel, from the booklet published by Dunstable Museum Trust. Andrew Leech for the conjectural drawing of the White Horse Inn from the booklet 'Henry VIII's Dunstable' published by the Worker's Education Association.

As always I have been dependent on the help, support and patience of the publisher, Paul Bowes.

Chapter 1

A Turbulent Century, 979–1100

Entry for royal manor of Houstone in the Domesday Book.

Overview

When the millennium opened England was a divided country; there were constant raids, often major attacks, by the Danes, England's petty kingdoms fought against each other and the Christian Church was divided. It was a lawless time when even quarrels between members of the various royal families could end in murder.

Part One
England and Bedfordshire in the Eleventh Century

Ethelred II (979–1016) had obtained the throne of Wessex following the murder of his brother Edward. He was supported by some of the other petty kingdoms (but not by Mercia) and his reign was punctuated by battles with the Danes during which he became so progressively unsuccessful that he acquired the name 'Ethelred the Unready'.

Eventually Northumbria and Mercia joined the Danish leader Sweyn, forcing Ethelred to flee to Normandy. In 1013 Sweyn was made king but still fighting continued. His son *Canute (1016–1035)* tried to hold the country together by force but was challenged by Ethelred's son *Edmund (1016)*, known as 'Ironside'. In 1016 they were persuaded to rule in tandem – Canute to hold the title of 'King' and Edmund to be 'Underking' of Mercia and Northumbria. However before the year was out, Edmund had been murdered!

Edmund's children Edwy and Edgar were exiled to Hungary, while Canute married Ethelred's widow, Emma, dismissed his foreign army and ruled as king of both the English and the Danes. He administered his united country with the help of four earls. The Earl of Mercia, Leofric, was an Englishhman whose wife would one day be known as Lady Godiva. During his reign he worked hard to bring peace and security to the country and to heal breaches within the church.

When he died in 1035, England had enjoyed twenty settled

years. However, following his death, his sons came near to dividing the country once more. *Harold I*, son of his first wife, ruled from 1035–1040 during which time he was suspected of the brutal murder of his half-brother, Alfred. He was succeeded by Alfred's brother *Hardicanute (1040–1042)*, son of Canute and his second wife Emma. He brought his mother and his younger brother, Edward, to join him in England, but this was another very short reign.

His brother *Edward (1042–1066)*, known as 'the Confessor' had grown up in Normandy. He was a quiet, pious man whose main fault may have been leaving too much power in the hands of his earls. He brought many of his councillors with him to England and on one occasion entertained his mother's great-nephew – William, Duke of Normandy. In the years to come William would insist that Edward had appointed him as the future king of England.

Bedfordshire Under Attack

Bedfordshire suffered very badly during the troubled years when the Danish raids became an invasion. Back in 886AD the king had tried to protect the bigger half of the country by giving the Danish leader a large part of eastern England. The line of 'Danelaw' was described as 'from the Lea to its source, from the source to Bedford and along the Ouse to Watling Street'. The Danes ignored the boundary and continued their raids to and fro across Bedfordshire. They became so confident that at one point they made Bedford their regional headquarters. However, they were forced back behind the line and the residents of both Bedford and Luton learned how to resist the raids.

Christianity Comes – and Goes

Another cause of distress was that the Danes were heathen and had no respect for churches or their property. Most of the villages had no resident clergyman and relied on St. Paul's Church, Bedford to supply them. However before the Danish raids had started, some Saxon king had given a house and a six hundred acre farm to one of the Mercian bishops. This was known as 'Bishops's-cote' [Biscot]; it may have been used as another 'minster' church supplying church ministers for south-west Bedfordshire. It was a valuable estate and one of the Danes may have taken it for his own use. Certainly it was lost to the church.

Peace came at last and long before the time that Edward (the Confessor) came to the throne, Bedfordshire had become a peaceful and prosperous agricultural county. It was administered for the king by a sheriff who lived in the castle at Bedford, on the north bank of the Ouse. St. Paul's was once more a respected minster church supplying clergy to most of the county and Luton had been given another church and another six hundred acre estate [later known as Dallow Manor]. Increasingly the land-owners were building churches on their own estates. On the royal estate at Houghton[Regis] sixty acres of land had been provided to support a church but in most other cases these new churches were the property of the land-owners and had no [taxable] land of their own. An example for which the paperwork has survived was at Studham. Around 1060 a widow called Aepelipa and her second husband, Oswulf, gave 'the land which is called at Stodham' to St. Albans Abbey, in memory of her late husband. They requested that the abbot should supply timber to build a church; this church was not entered in the Domesday tax report [1086] but there was a priest living at neighbouring Barwythe.

1066 And All That

The events of 1066 are well-known: the year opened with the death of Edward the Confessor on 5th January and ended with the coronation of William I on 25th December.

No sooner was Harold, Godwin's son, chosen to succeed Edward than William, Duke of Normandy raised an army to attack him from the south and Hardrada, King of Norway (a relation of Edward's) raised an army to attack him from the east.

Harold, who had previously been Earl of Wessex, only had a few months to try to consolidate his role as King of all England before the fighting began. On 25th September he defeated Harold Hardrada at Stamford Bridge, seven miles east of York. Less than three weeks later (on 14th October) he was killed during the Battle of Hastings. Recent studies suggest that he was struck down by the sword of a mounted knight, rather than by an arrow which pierced his eye.

The battle was over; the Saxon leaders withdrew to London and William, having gained control of both Sussex and Kent, marched his army almost to the River Thames. He then turned east, crossing the river at Wallingford. His army had reached Berkhamsted before the Saxon leaders invited him to become their king. Even then his army continued to ravage the country-side as they crossed part of Buckinghamshire, Hertfordshire and Bedfordshire. Not carrying any supplies, each night foragers scavenged widely to gather food and as a result, the countryside through which they travelled was so badly damaged that it still had not recovered twenty years later.

William (1066–1087) was crowned King of England in Westminster Abbey on 25th December (his wife was also crowned there about a year later). This was the first time that a coronation had taken place at the abbey. William and Matilda were very devout. They had supported the founding of many monasteries in Normandy. Provided it was loyal, William would strongly support the church in England.

His reign was far from easy. It took many years before he could truly reign as king of all England. However, by the time of his death on 9th September 1087, England was a settled and prosperous country. He was taken ill while visiting Normandy and although his elder son Robert was actively disloyal, William appointed him Duke of Normandy, while WIlliam (2) his next surviving son was designated King of England.

William II (1087–1100). Quite apart from fraternal jealousy, this situation caused many difficulties. Most of the great landowners owned land in Normandy and owed loyalty and support to Duke Robert, but they also owed similar allegiance

5

and support to King William for the land which they owned in England. The two brothers were soon at war!

Because of this division of loyalty, the expenses of war and William's extravagant lifestyle and because (unlike his father) he ignored the long-established laws and customs of England, he became unpopular.

It has never been firmly established who shot the arrow which killed King William while he was hunting in the 'New Forest' but a memorial in the Forest reads:

> 'Here stood the Oak Tree on which an arrow shot by
> Sir Walter Tyrell at a stag, glanced and struck King
> William II, surnamed Rufus, on the breast of which
> he instantly died 2nd August 1100.'

On that fateful day William's elder brother Robert was away on a crusade but his younger brother Henry was amongst the party in the forest. He did not wait to return to London but rode directly to Winchester where he was proclaimed king. England was ripe for development.

Part Two
Dunstable in the Eleventh Century

As it is well recorded that Henry I placed a town on Dunstable crossroads, it would therefore appear inaccurate to include it in this first century of the millennium but the evidence will show that there was a trading centre on Dunstable crossroads even before the Norman Conquest.

The Surrounding Countryside

By the time that the first century of the millennium had settled and become peaceful, South Bedfordshire had been recognised as valuable agricultural land. Much of it had been kept to provide food for the royal household [household manors] while some of it was rented out to provide an income, e.g. Caddington was let to a nobleman called Edwin. The area encompassed highly-populated villages, rivers, streams and watermills, meadows and downland for grazing sheep and most importantly many acres of arable land suitable for growing corn. These factors would be highly influential in the planning of the town of Dunstable.

At either end of South Bedfordshire the king held very large household manors. Both Leighton [Buzzard] and Luton had markets for the trading of local produce and each had a church. Adjoining Luton was the royal manor of Houghton, once the farm or village on the spur of the hill. Other pieces of land were used by the royal household to support its staff or as pensions. Edward gave Chalgrave to one of the chaplains that he had brought with him to England. This chaplain came from Lorraine and the 'Lorying' family of Chalgrave became generous patrons of Dunstable Priory. Queen Edith gave Sewell to 'her man Walraven'. The sheriff of Bedford Castle held land scattered over the county, some of which he let out to his officials.

Just as everything was really settled and men looked forward to passing on their well-cultivated land to their children, there was one more disaster! William's hungry army came marching into Bedfordshire and headed over Dunstable Downs looking for food. Twenty years later, it was reported in the Domesday Book that the value of Studham had fallen from £8 to £2 and that Barwythe [adjacent to Studham] from £3 to £1.50. The value of Totternhoe had reduced from £24 to £12.50 and four teams of plough oxen were missing. However as the royal manors were protected, Houghton remained undamaged.

It is most unlikely that either King Edward or King William ever visited Houghton and so it is possible that the same royal steward continued to live in the manor house and to administer the royal estate both before and after the Conquest. This situation may also have occurred in many other villages but the influential owners were no longer men and women whose families had held English land for several generations. They were foreigners who did not even speak the same language as their workers.

On the outskirts of what would become Dunstable was a natural chalk hill or watchtower known as Totternhoe. Far beneath it was an extremely valuable seam of building stone. William's civil servants kept the area of the quarry under the direct control of the king, having transferred it from the manor of Totternhoe. William had great ambitions for his new country and stone was essential. Walter of Flanders was made responsible for the watchtower and he built a small castle. The soldiers who camped there would not only guard the stone quarry but would keep watch over a very wide area, in case the Saxons tried to resist the Norman invaders. The castle was never used in anger and was allowed to deteriorate and fall down.

The Crossroads Called 'Dunstaple'

During the first century of the millennium there was no such place as Dunstable although it is likely that Dunstaple* with a 'p' was the name given to the crossing of the Watling Street and the Icknield Way. The deserted Roman town of Durocobrivis had long since crumbled away and the Saxon settlers had avoided the crossroads. By the opening of the millennium the land of Kensworth came up to the crossroads at what is now High Street South and West Street, Sewell lay between what is now West Street and High Street North and from the eastern side of High Street North, right across what we call Church Street to join High Street South was the royal manor of Houghton. Caddington was on the plateau at the top of the hill.

It is unlikely that the stewards of the three agricultural estates tried to bring their arable land right up to the crossroads. In addition to the threat of theft and damage, wells, ditches, cemeteries and rubble from the deserted Roman town would have made ploughing very difficult.

Land-owners or their stewards were responsible for keeping woodland cut back from the roads but this rule was often neglected. However although the rough, uncultivated ground around the crossroads was probably free of mature trees, there

* Dun = downland, staple = boundary post, or a market.

may have been a tangle of nettles, brambles and scrub.

The Turbulent Years

Nothing specific is known about the turbulent years when the Danes were living perilously close. The roads would have been far too dangerous for anyone to attempt to trade around the crossroads. Farming would have been a depressing occupation with the knowledge that not only did spoiled or stolen crops mean loss of income, but also loss of food for the family.

Saelig Houghton

It has been suggested that this was an early prefix for Houghton. 'Saelig' can be interpreted as holy or fortunate and there is evidence for this. The Manshead Archaeological Society have uncovered a Roman Christian site in a field to the east of Lords Hill. Even if it survived the unsettled period when the Saxons were still pagan, it would have definitely been lost during the Danish raids. However, it *may* have been during this period that the spring or 'well' at the foot of the present Bidwell Hill was developed as a Christian site. It is *just possible* that a pocket of continuous Christianity survived on what became the royal manor. St. Brigid was an Irish saint who died c.524. To strengthen the theory of a Christian site, it should be noted that as late as 1225 the road was referred to as 'Holewellehulle'.

Once the Danes were settled and had embraced Christianity it was safe to put up Christian buildings. Sometime before the Norman Conquest sixty acres were set aside to support a church. These acres ran from the village centre down towards the holy spring with the road (known as Bidwell Hill) as a boundary.

The Domesday Survey

The first time that we get any detailed information about the site on which Dunstable would soon be founded, is in the Domesday Book of 1086. When studying this we must remember that it was written as a tax report. Once the Christmas celebrations of 1085 were over, William consulted his council concerning the structure of his new kingdom. It was nineteen years since the Conquest and he was anxious to know how the shake-up in land ownership had worked out. What he really wanted to know was how much produce (or value) he was getting from his own household manors, who owned the rest of the land and whether the correct rents and taxes were being paid.

The Royal Manor of Houghton

To use this book as a way of interpreting the mid-11th century landscape and social history it is necessary to compare the statistics of one village with several others of the same size. Houghton was a prosperous agricultural estate but there were three factors which set it apart from other villages. One was that it had an exceptionally high population for the size of the agricultural estate: just under two hundred and fifty people living from approximately twelve hundred acres. It was a household manor which not only supplied food for the royal estate but had at one time produced pack-ponies and hunting dogs for the king. The inhabitants paid their taxes in gold and silver!

Traders Around the Crossroads?

The clerks who collected the information for the Domesday tax report had a set list of questions. They were undoubtedly troubled by local accents and there were no sections on the forms to allow for unusual circumstances. Socially a man was either a 'free' burgess [businessman] living in a recognised town and paying his taxes direct to the king or he was a tied agricultural worker who appeared as an asset on his employer's tax assessment.

When King William died in 1087, the monks who wrote his obituary noted that it was he who had made the roads safe enough for people to travel carrying money, without the threat of being robbed. By 1086 the sheriff had included Sewel in the royal manor, giving the residents of Houghton access to three sides of the crossroads. Had the men and women of Houghton been taking stalls and carts up to Dunstable crossroads during the settled period before the Norman Conquest and had they then had sufficient confidence in the stability of William's England to begin building permanent shops and houses?

King William II

This new landlord had a passionate need for money. He was unlikely to interfere provided his tenants paid the very high rents imposed by the sheriff's brother, Ivo Tallboys, whom he had appointed to the post of steward. So at the end of the first century of the new millennium, Dunstaple crossroads was already being used for trading and was ripe for development.

Chapter II

A Century of Progress, 1100–1199

Conjectural view of Dunstable Priory drawn by F. A. Fowler.

Overview

During this second century of the millennium Henry I, youngest son of William I, reigned for nearly thirty-five years. For Bedfordshire this was a time of peace and increasing prosperity. In a matter of a few years a business centre was planted on Dunstaple crossroads, a palace was built and a group of Augustinian canons settled nearby. A new town was laid out beside the village of Biggleswade and it is probable that Bedford received its first charter.

Henry lost his son and heir in a tragedy at sea. As a result, England was disrupted by civil war. Henry's nephew Stephen reigned for nineteen troubled years, followed by his great-nephew, Henry II. This second period of thirty-five stable years gave Dunstable the opportunity to develop its national and international trade. These survived even when Henry's son, Richard (who reigned for the last ten years of the century) spent more than nine years

Part One
England and Bedfordshire in the Twelfth Century

King Henry I (1100–1135)

Henry's first major act was to take control of the exchequer; he employed mercenary soldiers and sailed for Normandy. By the end of 1106 Robert was a prisoner in Cardiff Castle and Henry was both King of England and Duke of Normandy. Now it was time to build up trade between England and the continent and to re-build England's prosperity.

It followed that to increase trade, especially exports, it would be necessary to devise a new system where more burgesses could have specialist markets and three day fairs to encourage traders to gather from a much wider area. New towns would be needed.

The shiretowns and a handful of places such as the king's manor of Houghton had independent churches with land for their support but most other places had only a small wooden church owned by the Lord of the Manor; very few villages had their own clergyman.

Many more churches and ordained priests were needed. King Henry took the lead in these and other plans for the modernisation of the country. Aware that part of his brother's unpopularity had been due to his ignoring the old Saxon customs and laws, Henry had a long list of these drawn up and agreed to keep to them. England was entering a period when the climate was kind to farmers, which helped to improve the country's prosperity.

When he set out for Normandy in early 1120, Henry had recently lost his first wife, but he had a seventeen year old son, William, newly married to the daughter of the Count of Anjou. He must, therefore, have been reasonably confident that if anything befell him, his policies would be carried out by his son. On the journey back to England, the ship carrying William sank in deep water and he and many others were drowned and although Henry remarried, he fathered no more legitimate children. Worried about the succession, he persuaded his church and secular leaders to swear an oath of support for William's sister, Matilda.

Henry died during a visit to Normandy in 1135; Matilda was with him, together with Henry's favourite illegitimate son whom he had elevated to the title Earl of Gloucester. As soon as he heard the news of his uncle's death, Henry's nephew Stephen (who was also abroad at the time) swiftly returned to England. The barons were grateful for the opportunity to appoint a male ruler and with Matilda still in Normandy, they agreed to crown Stephen.

King Stephen (1135–1154)

The reign appeared to start well in Bedfordshire. Stephen spent his second Christmas in Dunstable before sailing for Normandy. However, as we shall see below, on his return things went very wrong indeed. Even before the civil war started, Stephen attacked Bedford Castle!

The Civil War

Matilda's half-brother, Earl Robert of Gloucester, brought an army to England and there was fighting in many parts of the

15

country. *Matilda* was a very imperious lady and made herself unpopular by ruling without consultation or discussion. Her coronation was delayed and eventually the people of London chased her out of the city. Earl Robert continued to fight on her behalf until he himself was captured. He was released in exchange for King Stephen, but died soon afterwards. When Matilda left England in 1146, there were hopes for a peaceful settlement.

Sometimes referred to as 'the Empress' because her first husband had been the German Emperor Henry V, Matilda's second husband was Geoffrey, Count of Anjou. Their son, Henry, was only two when his grandfather died but in January 1153, already holding the titles Duke of Normandy and Count of Anjou, he brought an army to England.

After several sieges, battles, damage and distress, the two armies faced each other across the River Thames at Wallingford. Advisors on both sides persuaded the two leaders to avoid a pitched battle and eventually it was arranged that Stephen would declare Henry his heir.

Stephen died while visiting Dover on 25th October 1154 and Henry was crowned in Westminster Abbey on 19th December.

King Henry II (1154–1189)

By this time Henry had married Eleanor of Aquitaine and was so powerful that England was once more a peaceful and economically successful country. He ordered the destruction of the mercenaries' castles and quickly restored law and order. Previously the courts of justice had been in London; they were out of touch, over-crowded and justice was only available to the wealthy and influential. Henry instigated the system of itinerant judges who travelled around six circuits.

Henry's struggle with Thomas à Becket was part of his wider intention to reduce the power of the church which he felt had far too much influence over secular affairs. He deliberately chose his friend and loyal companion to be the new Archbishop of Canterbury, but was horrified when Thomas completely changed his style of life and transferred his devotion and loyalty to God and God's church here on earth.

Henry and Eleanor had four sons who grew up to be both disloyal and irresponsible. The more they tried to persuade or even force Henry to share the responsibilities of his great inheritance, the more the king was convinced that he should keep control in his own hands. Two of the sons, Henry junior and Geoffrey died during these troubled times. The disloyalty of his sons marred the last years of Henry's life, which ended in 1189.

King Richard I (1189–1199)

Richard spent most of his ten-year reign overseas, quite often on crusades. The cost of these campaigns caused financial hardship, especially when, following his captivity in the early 1190s, it was necessary to raise an extremely large ransom. During his long periods of absence England was very much neglected.

In this way a century which began with one Henry and every hope of a peaceful and prosperous future ended with the son of a second Henry and the prospect of oppression and yet more distress.

The Civil War in Bedfordshire

Bedford was attacked even before the civil war began. Unless there was any question of disloyalty to the Crown, it was the custom in England that having paid a fine to the king, a man might pass his estates to his heir. When Simon de Beauchamp (hereditary constable of Bedford Castle) died, his heir was his grandson Miles. Stephen formally agreed but later changed his mind. He wanted Bedford Castle for one of his supporters, but Miles defended it, forcing Stephen to mount a siege which lasted for five weeks. During the distressing years of civil war which followed, it twice more changed hands.

Two years later it was Luton's turn to suffer. Part of the vast estate which had been provided to support the newly-appointed Robert Earl of Gloucester was the royal manor of Luton plus the church lands of both Luton and Houghton. When Robert was fighting against Stephen in 1139, his estates were forfeit and Luton was given to Robert Waudari, one of Stephen's mercenary officers. Soldiers from both castles terrified the neighbourhood. Eventually Luton Castle was peacefully demolished, but in 1153 (before Stephen made his settlement with the young man who would soon be King Henry II) Henry not only stormed Bedford Castle but also plundered and set fire to the town!

A Good Recovery is Made

Bedfordshire made a good recovery during the long reign of Henry II and as agriculture prospered, the heavy taxes of Richard's reign may not have caused too much distress. Matthew Paris, the chronicler from St. Albans Abbey, described Luton as 'a place abounding with parishioners and richly endowed'. Allowing for the varying sizes of the different communities and the standards of the day, this statement was probably true for much of Bedfordshire.

Part Two
Dunstable in the Twelfth Century

Although King Henry was crowned during the first year of the century, it was another six years before Robert was captured and Henry was free to concentrate on the economy and welfare of England.

On inheriting the royal manor of Houghton, Henry automatically became owner of one of the most important crossroads in the country. The combination of excellent corn-growing soil, grazing on the Chiltern Hills, the prosperous community in the village together with access to these four main roads made Dunstable crossroads the ideal site to promote a new business centre.

At this stage of England's history the social structure of the country was still based on what is known as the 'feudal system'. The people who physically worked in the fields and cowsheds were classified as part of the land-owner's estate. At its simplest, the king owned everything: some estates he kept for himself and for the support of his household, some were let to his personal knights, while others were given or let to his archbishop, bishops and monasteries or let to his main landholders in return for pecuniary rents of services. This was a very efficient system; any category of food, fuel, horses, hunting dogs or other household need could be transported to the royal household whenever and wherever they were required. The household cavalry was provided for, as were those church leaders assisting in the country's administration. Income would be generated by the letting of estates, the tenants being responsible for the repair and upkeep of roads and bridges, and not only the supply of staff for the king's castles but also both the supply and training of his soldiers.

In addition to this system, in a very few places, there were groups of burgesses or businessmen. They were independent of the feudal system and paid their taxes direct to the king and were the only people allowed to be merchants, travelling around the country and arranging exports. More of this type of town would be needed and where better than Dunstaple crossroads on the royal manor of Houghton?

Therefore in 1106 or very soon afterwards, a proclamation was sent all over England inviting businessmen to settle along these four wide roads. Surveyors laid out burgess plots at the commercial rent of one shilling per acre. This was not to be a feudal community with its market for the sale of local produce, but a group of businessmen with a promise that they would share the same freedoms as those trading in London. It was also announced that Henry was to have a palace built to be used when he and his family travelled in this part of the country. The quieter northern side of East Street [Church Street] was chosen for the nine-acre site and the palace was built, decorated and furnished in time for Henry to stay there in 1109. Although there are no clues to the size of the building, it was a very large house-party. By that time there must have been a well-settled town with a prosperous, respectable population because for each dignatory and his family who stayed at the palace of 'Kingsbury', there were probably six or seven clerks, chaplains and senior servants lodging somewhere in the town.

The church at Houghton was going through a difficult time. The income from the valuable farm, which should have been used to pay a clergyman, was going to a senior civil servant. So although no records have survived, the wealthy businessmen of Dunstable were presumably using a temporary church on the site of the present Priory.

When Henry and his queen first came to stay in Dunstable the Order of Augustinian Canons was still new in England. During this visit clerks prepared formal papers for Henry's signature, granting Queen Matilda the right to arrange for canons from the original Augustinian house at Colchester to travel to Holy Trinity, Aldgate and to establish another such house on that site. This was probably Henry's first visit to his new town and he no doubt met some of the newly-settled businessmen, discussing potential problems concerning the burgesses, their businesses, the shortage of land, the management of the market and the lack of a school and a suitable church.

In addition to being ordained priests, Augustinian canons were educated men; many of them were from families familiar with estate management, marketing and assisting the king in the administration of the country.

Shortly after this visit, Henry arranged for the same two men who had been overseeing the building and the organisation of the new Augustinian house in London to travel to Dunstable with orders to oversee the founding of another house opposite his palace.

The Augustinian Canons Come to Dunstable

However, Augustinian houses were not just training schools for priests; their main work was to pray for the king, their patrons and for the busy secular world. They also took on various other important roles, e.g. the care of the sick, of shrines and of travellers. In the first instance the Dunstable house had the responsibility for travellers but as the years went by they had to care for many sick travellers who remained in Dunstable and also for the shrine of St. Fremund.

The Prior was given Control of the Town

Cutting, dressing, carting and building with Totternhoe stone was a slow process, and it would have taken several years to complete the domestic buildings and a small section of the church. However, by 1131 there were enough resident canons settled into their Augustinian routine for Henry to hand over to them the town, the market, the schools, the manor court and complete control over the businessmen who lived there. To help support the Priory he made three important gifts; one of these was the valuable stone quarry at Totternhoe and another was woodland grazing at Houghton Buckwood, [now part of Markyate, given to Houghton by Henry I in compensation for the loss of land around the crossroads] plus a share of the common grazing at Houghton, Totternhoe, Kensworth and Caddington.

The reference to 'schools' is interesting; Geoffrey de Gorham (who became Abbot of St. Albans in 1119) may have started a school in Dunstable as early as 1110. He left Dunstable to become a penitential monk when valuable gowns which he had borrowed from the abbey and intended for use in a play, were lost in a fire. It is probable that the play was the first miracle play to be performed in England and possible that the fire was a local protest against the event. With the departure of de Gorham, it is likely that the school was continued either by the canons or some other capable people.

Following their king's example, both the rich and the poor made gifts to the Priory. Many of these gifts were in South Bedfordshire but they also received land and property in several other counties. Although individually they followed a vow of poverty, as a house they became important landowners. However, they would never become wealthy. Apart from their main responsibilities, holding up to eight services a day in praise of God and praying for the souls of their patrons, they took on full financial responsibility for the welfare of travellers.

When Henry handed over the town into their care, he made their responsibilities quite clear. The deed started with the words:

'Know ye that for God and my health and the souls of William my son and Matilda [,] the Queen my wife have given to the Church of the Blessed Peter of Dunstable which I have founded in honour of God . . .'

As his son William had died in 1120 and his first queen,

Matilda, in 1119 'the Queen my wife' referred to his second wife.

Within the first few years of the start of the next century, the Priory opened a hospital for lepers and other sick people on the southern boundary of the town and took over a second hospital on the boundary of Hockliffe. They ran an almonary for poor travellers, a hostel (now Priory House) for wealthier travellers and the Prior's own house was used to provide accommodation for the Pope's legate and for the Archbishop of Canterbury, bishops and others of importance. They were also responsible for the care of the aged and sick in their own community and in other parishes where they held land.

Another great expense was the provision of churches in the many outlying parishes for which they were responsible, e.g. Studham, Totternhoe and Harlington – Houghton Regis was the responsibility of St. Albans Abbey.

The actual size of the palace of Kingsbury is not known, but it was chosen for the king's great Christmas 'court' (or formal houseparty) in December 1122, when again the large numbers must have overflowed into the town. It is tempting to think that the reason for choosing this venue was that the first stage of the church building had been completed. They rode out of Dunstable on January 1st for a hunting-party at Berkhamsted Castle. In 1136 King Stephen held his Christmas court at Kingsbury*. Towards the end of his reign, Stephen returned again to Kingsbury. Following the peace treaty with Matilda's son, Henry on 13th January 1154, a large ceremony was held at Oxford. Soon afterwards Henry and Stephen had a quieter business meeting at Kingsbury and it was probably then that the small castle at Luton was taken down.

The businessmen of Dunstable took advantage of the consolidation and progress experienced during Henry II's reign to establish the town as one of the leading new towns of the 12th century. At the Priory they also consolidated and progressed and ended the century in such a strong position that two years into the new century they were able to attract one of the foremost scholars in the country to take up the post as prior.

---

*   Some sources give 1137 but 1136 seems more likely.

Chapter III

The Introduction of Magna Carta, 1199–1307

The surviving Eleanor Cross near Northampton; the one at Dunstable was carved and decorated by the same artists. Drawn by L. P. Evans.

Overview

This century covers the reign of three kings – King John who was the great, great, grandson of William (known as the Conqueror), John's son, Henry III, whose reign spanned five and a half decades of the century and John's grandson, Edward, whose reign included seven years of the fourth century of this millennium.

For the business centre on Dunstable crossroads it was a particularly successful century. Despite the civil wars and the disruption caused to both church and trade during the reign of King John together with the constant fighting on the English borders and overseas, Dunstable prospered.

The Augustinian priory became a highly respected monastic house while also becoming wealthy in property, if not in income. The first prior of the century was blessed with such skills of diplomacy that he was constantly called upon by the Pope, the King and the Archbishop of Canterbury to act as peacemaker.

The damage caused locally, nationally and internationally to traders and also locally to farmers was partly compensated by long periods of good weather. Businessmen from Dunstable bought raw materials, such as wool, hides and corn and cleaned and prepared them for sale – grading and repacking for distant markets or overseas. Some Dunstable merchants also acted as agents for the king and as tax-collectors when wool was ready for export.

Travellers from all over the country broke their journeys at the various hostels provided by the Priory. The acquisition of their own shrine brought even more visitors into the town. The combination of a wealthy business community and a lively 'tourist' trade meant that by the end of the century Dunstable had what was probably one of the largest retail centres in this part of England.

Part One
England and Bedfordshire in the Thirteenth Century

King John (1199–1216)

The youngest of Henry II's sons grew up surrounded by disloyalty and took advantage of Richard's absence to behave in a similar manner himself. When he actually became king, the autocratic and insensitive way in which he manipulated the feudal system caused great concern and bitterness. The fact that he first offended and then defied the Pope resulted in a seven year 'interdict'. During this period churches were closed; weddings and burials took place in the porch and only immediate family could enter the church for baptisms.

The Fight for Magna Carta

By the summer of 1213, John had ridden roughshod not only over church affairs but also over all branches of secular life. He had broken so many promises that civil war seemed certain. Then it was remembered that John's great-grandfather, Henry I, had a list compiled of the Saxon customary laws of England, which he had signed at his coronation. Could the list be found and could John be persuaded to sign it?

Henry's list was found in the archive of St. Albans Abbey and on 4th August 1213 the church leaders, the great landowners and the mayor (or steward) plus four men from each royal town (including Dunstable) met for a conference at the Abbey. The list was read out by the Archbishop of Canterbury, approved by the listeners and so John's representative, the Earl Marshal of England, agreed to take the document to John and to advise him to sign it.

The well thought out scheme also failed and it was only when John was forced, by the presence of an opposing army, that he finally signed the great charter at Runnymede.

Bedfordshire Gets Involved

The sheriff, William de Beauchamp, was one of the barons who organised the struggle to persuade King John to sign the great charter. Most of the other Bedfordshire landowners not actually employed by King John also took part. When, after all their efforts, King John ignored the charter, they once more raised an army against him. He responded by sending soldiers under his mercenary officer, Falkes de Breauté, to attack Bedford Castle. It held out for a few days but fell on December 2nd, badly damaged during the attack. Falkes was ordered to repair and strengthen the weakened building. Taking stone from Bedford churches, timber from Warden Abbey and later using force to steal money from St. Albans Abbey added to both Falkes and the King's unpopularity. Dunstable with its four main roads suffered once again from the repeated visits of soldiers. In addition to the usual theft and careless damage, there were also deliberate attempts to sabotage property.

King Henry III (1216–1272)

Then quite suddenly towards the end of 1216 King John died and his nine year old son was crowned. The barons knew that the men appointed as advisors to the young king were sympathetic to their cause so they disbanded their army, most of whom returned home. When in 1217, the justices visited Dunstable collecting signatures in support of the young king, the people must have hoped that everything would be peaceful once more. However, Falkes refused to relinquish Bedford Castle and, not having any military duties, he and his soldiers caused much distress across Bedfordshire, particularly between 1220–21 when they built a second castle at Luton.

In 1223 King Henry instructed Falkes to dismantle the Luton castle and when the King's travelling judges visited Bedford, the people of Luton presented a long list of charges for damage. Both this court and the one held during the following summer were ignored by Falkes, causing the judges to give him a final warning to appear before them when they sat at Dunstable three weeks later.

An Outrage at Dunstable

The court opened at Dunstable Priory on June 10th 1224 and included on the list were twenty-two complaints from Luton. Falkes failed to appear yet again but a message was received to say that his brother, William, had sent soldiers to capture the judges!

The court was quickly disbanded but Judge Henry de Braybrook was captured and thrown into the dungeon of Bedford Castle. His wife begged the young king to rescue him and Henry quickly summoned soldiers, together with men with equipment to meet him at Bedford on Friday 21st June.

The Men of Dunstable Storm Bedford Castle

Towers were built and siege engines called 'cats' were put in place to shelter underground diggers, slingers and crossbowmen, while manganols were used to throw great boulders to damage the castle walls. The attack had begun! Possibly because the outrage took place at the Priory, the men from Dunstable appear to have led the attack on Wednesday 14th August. Several of them were killed but the survivors 'acquired horses with harness [plus armour], oxen, bacon, live pigs and countless other plunder'.

The description of the breaking of the siege included in the Annals of the Priory is so detailed that either the writer must have been present or he must have questioned the soldiers closely on their return. This is one of the best accounts of breaking a medieval siege to survive and illustrate English history.

Henry's standard was hoisted to the top of the tower, the wife of Falkes de Breauté, the captured judge and many other prisoners were released, but the soldiers were hung on a series of gibbets. Falkes was brought before the seventeen year old king and sent into exile, leaving the monarch to begin a long and mainly peaceful reign.

Simon de Montfort

Encouraged by their ruler, major building work was under- taken at the monasteries and cathedrals, including Westminster Abbey. Dominican and Franciscan friars were welcomed to England, while Henry spent lavishly on projects which were not always approved by his great landowners. In 1265 Simon de Montfort, Earl of Leicester, invited these landowners, together with representatives from other sections of society, to meet him at Oxford. It was suggested that a system of consultation with not only the landowners but also representatives from counties, cities and boroughs should take place at regular intervals in the form of a 'parlez' or discussion with the king. Following this meeting, which is accepted as the first Parliament, there were yet more battles. Simon de Montfort died at the Battle of Evesham, but the idea of parliaments lived on and were soon held regularly.

As the years went by, Henry gradually retired and after a difficult start, his very capable son, Edward, took over his duties.

King Edward I (1272–1307)

Born at Westminster in 1239 Edward was in his mid-twenties in time to head his father's army to victory at the Battle of Evesham in 1265.

He had been named after Edward the Confessor and spoke fluent English. He was away on a Crusade when his father died but on his return sent officials around the country to ensure that it was being governed correctly. There were very few complaints about the organisation or management of Bedfordshire and none about Dunstable.

Convinced that the future lay in the formation of a united national group of states, Edward aimed to build up a union of such states and to persuade Welsh and Scottish princes to accept him as overlord. So although his reign led to a strong national feeling, conducive to building up cultural and economic success, there was a constant need of money and men to supply his armies.

A New Form of Taxation

By the end of the century Edward wanted to introduce a new form of taxation which would include a much wider cross-section of the population. This involved a detailed valuation of various commodities in store or in business premises, also luxury items in the home. From all these details we can see that Bedfordshire in general and Dunstable in particular were ending the century in an economically healthy and, in some cases, really prosperous condition.

Part II
Dunstable in the Thirteenth Century

Prior Richard de Morins

In 1201 a brilliant young scholar at Merton Priory, Richard de Morins, was sent to Rome by King John to negotiate with the Pope. This interrupted his preparations for ordination, but by the time of his return to England, Prior Thomas of Dunstable Priory had resigned and somehow, perhaps through the influence of the king, he was invited to become the next prior. He finished his training, was ordained and took up the position in Dunstable. Although he was frequently called away from the Priory to carry out diplomatic roles for the king, the papal legate and the Archbishop of Canterbury, his years as prior were particularly successful ones for the Priory. Lay brothers were installed, a gaoler appointed, a curate to help with the services in the parochial end of the church and another to act as warden of the leper hospital. A few years later (1225) he persuaded one of the businessmen to financially support Dunstable's first resident vicar. Steps like these released the canons to attend services more regularly and to spend more time in private study. In particular from 1202 to 1242, canons from the Priory kept the book known as the Annales of Dunstable Priory (which, as one of England's treasures, is kept in the British Museum). Also surviving from the start of this century is a long list of accounts and rents and from the end, some tracts describing various events connected with the Priory. Somehow, perhaps by offering payment, Morins persuaded a church at Cropedy (Salop) to part with the bones of St. Fremund, thought to be a Saxon saint. The bones were reverently brought to the Priory and housed in a specially constructed shrine. Their presence was advertised, attracting many prilgrims travelling to St. Albans to stay overnight at Dunstable so as to visit the shrine. Soon word spread that miracles were occurring at the shrine and many specific pilgrimages to Dunstable were planned.

King John Gave Kingsbury to the Priory

It was customary in most monasteries for the abbot or prior to live in a separate (often very comfortable) house. In a town like Dunstable, where accommodation had to be provided for many very important visitors, the prior's lodging may have been very comfortable indeed. On the other hand, Kingsbury palace which was nearly one hundred years old, may have been cold, uncomfortable and in need of repair. In 1203 King John stayed in Dunstable, maybe at the prior's house, after which he arranged that future royal parties would stay at the Priory and in return he gave them the palace of Kingsbury. It is described as 'houses' – plural, so it is probable that these were let out to the more prosperous businessmen. John also granted the Priory the privilege of holding a three-day fair from the 10th to the 12th of May.

Others followed John's example, presenting the Priory with valuable houses and land.

The Bishop of Lincoln Dedicated the Priory Church of St. Peter

In 1207 a special altar was dedicated to St. Fremund just before the interdict closed all the churches. By the time that it was lifted in 1213 the great Priory Church (considerably longer and higher than it is today) was finished. The Bishop of Lincoln came to Dunstable for a solemn dedication and the whole town would have taken part in the great celebration which followed. It must have been a terrible shock when, nine years later, a freak storm blew one of the great towers down, destroying the north-west corner of the buildings. The two very different doors on the west front of the church are evidence of the storm.

Visitors Were a Great Expense

The year after the visit of the Bishop of Lincoln, the Archbishop of Canterbury stayed at the Priory, and King John returned the following year. In 1217 and for several centuries following, the king's itinerant justices stayed at the Priory and held their court there.

It is doubtful that the official church visitors offered payment for either their own accommodation of that of the large 'households' which accompanied them. Royal parties left 'gifts' which, nevertheless did not compensate for the empty storerooms left on their departure. However it was the costs involved in providing care and accommodation for the poor and sick travellers which kept the Priory poor. So many distressed people visited that on one occasions they were described as 'laying about the town'.

Administering the Town

To exploit their estates and to produce as much income as possible, in 1221 the Prior's steward together with the businessmen, produced what are thought to be the earliest surviving byelaws in the country: the market stalls were to be taken down at sundown, the roads were to kept clean, and no blood, offal or manure was to be left in the street!

Despite this co-operative effort and the fact that the businessmen made generous gifts to the church of the Priory, the 1220s were marred by a long dispute between these same men and the Prior. Both wanted complete freedom to run the town as they saw fit. It was 1230 before a compromise was reached. By the time that Prior Richard de Morin died in 1242, the canons and the burgesses were once more working to build up Dunstable's trade. In the future there would be weak and strong priors, long periods of good weather and times of famine, yet during de Morins' forty years as Prior he had laid down such a sound financial basis not only for the Priory but also for the town that both remained known and respected throughout the country.

Before de Morins' appointment, Henry I, Stephen and Henry II each made several visits to Kingsbury. After his arrival John and Henry III made several visits to the Priory, while Edward I stayed on so many occasions that he even discussed the possibility of having a suite of rooms built there for his private use.

Tournaments Took Place in Dunstable

These were not popular with the early Norman kings, as large gatherings of armed knights created the perfect opportunity for plots against the Crown. However, by the reign of Henry III they were an accepted way of training knights for combat. The sites needed to be close to both a good road network and to a large amount of varied accommodation. It was also essential to have available about half a mile of flat, wide, rough land. The first recorded tournament at Dunstable was held in 1232 and although at least another twenty-five were planned over the next hundred years, many of them were cancelled for reasons of security.

Two or occasionally three barons would challenge each other or sometimes they challenged 'all-comers'. Between forty and fifty knights would attend to support each of the leading combatants, accompanied by an entourage of about ten servants of various social standing, together with a least three horses for the knights plus mounts for their servants. Some stayed at the Priory, some in the town and many in a previously erected 'tent town'. Groups of about forty to fifty mounted combatants would face each other and, over a period of many hours, the 'affray' would move to and fro over the allotted half mile site. This almost definitely took place along the flat area presently known as Jeansway and beyond, while the onlookers would have stood or sat on wooden stands on the top of the hill.

This was a colourful and exciting spectacle to experience and undoubtedly brought money in to the town, but the followers, 'groupies' and petty criminals who followed the combatants have been compared to a football crowd!

The Order of Dominican Friars

By the middle of the century, when the businessmen of the town were working together with Prior Simon of Eaton to make best financial use of the visitors streaming into and through the town, a potentially divisive situation arose.

Earlier in the century, an Augustinian canon called Dominic who lived in Spain realised that although, as an individual he was 'poor', the wealth of his house interfered with his ability to communicate with and help the poor. After much thought and prayer he started a new order, to become known as Dominican Friars. They would follow the words of Christ and not just be individually but also communally poor. The order did not aim to build elaborate and ornate churches or to provide hostels for travellers, but to support people spiritually and to help the distressed. To enable them to fulfil these aims, it was necessary for them to beg for alms, which meant that they must settle in communities of thriving businessmen. It follows that one way of judging the prosperity of a medieval town was whether or not it had a friary.

The Dominican Friars Come to Dunstable

The Prior was very worried when in 1259, actively supported by Henry III and Queen Eleanor, the Dominicans settled opposite the Priory. Their site is now called Friary Field. The Prior bitterly resented their intrusion and there are several references in the Annales to their disagreement. The most violent was a scuffle which ended when the Prior, one of the canons and several townsmen broke into the Friary, 'assaulted and wounded' three of the friars, threw one of them into the pond and put the other two in prison! It hardly seems possible that the Prior would have become personally involved in violence but that was the charge at the official enquiry.

Until the friars came to Dunstable most people from the town and local villages made their gifts to God via the Priory but after 1259 these gifts were divided. The people liked the friars who owned no property apart from their own house and three cottages on their boundary and who did not interfere in the running of the town.

The Dominican house in Dunstable was small but very much respected. Their church of St. Mary was about the size of the remaining Priory Church and faced onto High Street South.

Queen Eleanor's Funeral – and Crosses

The frequent visits of the king's judges, their official staff, the many people connected with each case, many of whom came from outside Bedfordshire, together with the crowds of onlookers made another profitable spectacle.

However, the crowds which accompanied the great and solemn funeral procession of Eleanor, wife of Edward I, probably attracted one of the largest gatherings of that or most other centuries.

Eleanor had died in 1290 while staying at Hardby near Lincoln. Edward led the procession back towards London and on the night of Monday December 11th they rested in Dunstable. Surrounded by candles, the coffin stood on a table before the altar and throughout the night the canons knelt in prayer. The senior members of the community and local landowners queued to pass quietly by and pay their last respects. The rest of the townspeople and hundreds from the surrounding villages knelt by the roadside as the following morning the coffin was slowly drawn out of the town.

In remembrance of this important occasion in 1311 a great cross was erected on the crossroads. In recent memory a plaque was mounted on the wall of a nearby bank.

A Prosperous Town

The valuation for the tax of 1297 showed that by the end of the century there were one hundred and twenty-one families who were rich enough to be taxed, suggesting a population of about five hundred and eighty prosperous people plus a large number of non-taxpayers.

There were: 10 tanners, 9 dealers in skin, 4 blacksmiths, a carpenter, a tiler, a carter, a brewer, 5 butchers, 5 fishmongers, a poulterer, 2 bakers, a fruiterer, a spicer and a man who made candles.

Chapter IV

A More Difficult Century, 1307–1399

Back view of Middle Row showing original roof line plus the encroachments.

Overview

This century is covered by the reigns of Edward I's son and grandson, both called Edward and his great great-grandson, Richard. In 1376 the death of his great-grandson, Edward, known as the Black Prince, not only disturbed the succession but also led to continual disputes which would overshadow most of the following century.

The fourteenth was a difficult century for Bedfordshire. It started and ended with unpopular kings, dissatisfied landowners and troubled politicians riding to and fro across the country, stirring up trouble. As a result there was a breakdown of law and order, tournaments were forbidden and trade on the crossroads suffered very badly. Both kings ended their reign imprisoned by men who should have been helping them to run the country. Additionally Edward's reign was divided by a period of desperately cold wet winters which virtually brought trade to a standstill and eventually led to famine. Richard's reign, which suffered spells of less severe bad weather, had the major disruption of the so-called 'Peasants' Revolt'. It was not, however, peasants but the businessmen of Dunstable who stormed the Priory gates.

Between these two difficult periods just one king, Edward III, covered the central fifty years of the century. His policy of law and order, nationalism, pride in one's country and the cult of St. George greatly improved the 'feel-good factor', trade and prosperity, but his years of fighting in France were a constant drain on both the economy and manpower. However it was the 'Black Death', the disaster which hit Bedfordshire and the rest of England in 1348, which overshadowed life in the town and at the Priory for many years to come.

Part One
England and Bedfordshire in the Fourteenth Century

King Edward II (1307–1327)

Edward's son, Edward II, followed his father seven years into the new century. He has been described as a 'country squire of the best type'. Estate management, sports, theatre, poetry and socialising with his friends were of more interest to this young man than continuing his father's attempt to control the Scots. Unhappily married and destined to choose unsuitable friends, the final blow must have come when his wife joined with his dissatisfied earls to drive him from the throne. Forced to retire in favour of his young son, Edward was murdered in 1327.

The great natural disaster which took place during Edward's reign was made worse by lack of good government. In 1310 the very long spell of good weather which had led to a great improvement in basic mediaeval agriculture, came to an end. It was not short spells of extreme cold which eventually led to a national famine but very long spells of cold, wet weather.

In both 1314 and 1315 the seed corn planted in the autumn rotted in the fields. No cottagers and very few farmers had spare grain for a second sowing. These were the two years recognised as a national and international famine, but in Bedfordshire, as in many other places, the disaster continued for at least another three years. Poor harvests resulted in a shortage of wheat and therefore bread, barley and therefore beer. However, worse was to follow. Food for the livestock was not only in short supply but of such poor quality that a year or two later, the cows and sheep were too weak to resist infection, leading to their loss in very large numbers.

Because these natural disasters took place during the period of weak government experienced during the reign of Edward II, there was no help filtering down from the national government. Imported corn bought to relieve starvation was impounded and sold on the 'black market'.

King Edward III (1327–1377)

This Edward was only fourteen when his father's enemies put him on the throne. Within a year of his coronation he married Phillipa of Hainault and their exceptionally happy marriage lasted for the next forty years. At first he was unable to govern as he would have wished because of the unfortunate influence of his mother and her friends. Once he was able to take control, he restored law and order, made the roads safe for travellers and encouraged trade both at home and overseas. He curbed the power of some of the great landowners (including the monasteries), and reformed parliament.

Whether it was provocation by the Count of Flanders and the King of France or whether it was a further stage of Edward's nationalistic spirit, from 1338 there was a long series of battles overseas, sometimes referred to as 'the Hundred Years' War'. Taxes were raised and men compulsorily recruited but such great victories as Cresy in 1346 and Poiters in 1356 fanned the heady feeling of national success. Local landowner, Sir Nigel Loring of Chalgrave was the hero of a naval battle at Sluys. After the political unrest and the years of agricultural disaster experienced during the previous reign, the people of Dunstable needed a strong stimulant for recovery. In the days of mediaeval agriculture and health-care, it took a long time to recover from a serious spell of bad weather. Not only was health affected at the time but it had a serious effect on population numbers in the future.

The Black Death

Although the devastating illness known as the Black Death did not appear in Bedfordshire for another thirty years, it is probable that the very high death-rate was aggravated by on-going malnutrition. The black boil-like swellings from which the disease took its name are symptoms of Bubonic Plague. Over the centuries although many people have died from the epidemic, the total on these occasions was not even fifty per cent of the patients affected, so it seems likely that there were two or three separate infections attacking simultaneously.

Background

During the autumn of 1347 a terrible disease spread across Europe. It arrived at Melcombe Regis (Dorset) during the summer of 1348 and rapidly fanned out across England. Some places escaped but it was extremely widely spread with towns and villages situated along a main road most likely to suffer. The high death-rate devastated society; from a lack of clergy to bury the dead and a lack of local and national administrators down to a lack of men and women who were able to plough and tend the stock.

It took many years for the country to recover from such a widely-based disaster and Bedfordshire must have suffered very badly. This desperate outbreak of disease started twenty years into Edward's reign, when the country was already in debt due to his need for funds to support the army. The shortage of labour following the numerous deaths caused a major disturbance in what remained of the feudal system. Harsh legislation was brought in to defeat attempts by estate workers to escape from their tied positions in search of a life of comparative freedom. Estate owners were forbidden to illegally tempt them by offering wages above the controlled rate and people who had 'escaped' were punished and returned to their original employers. Merchants, exporters and wholesalers were struggling to find produce to sell; retailers had lost their customers and had far fewer goods to sell. The 'feel-good factor' was completely forgotten! Matters were made even worse when Edward's success in France began to fail and international trade became increasingly difficult.

A Sad End to the Reign

The Queen died in 1369 and Edward's son and heir died in 1376 after a long wasting illness. This meant that the heir to the throne was a ten year old boy. What started as a most successful and popular reign, uniting the country and promoting justice at home and trade abroad, closed with a dangerously long period of neglect.

King Richard II (1377–1399)

Richard was in his eleventh year when his grandfather died. Legally he was the direct heir to the throne but on the sidelines there were, amongst others, his uncles, John [of Gaunt], Duke of Lancaster, Edmund, Duke of York and Thomas, Duke of Gloucester. Thomas was only twenty-two but the other two were in their mid-thirties, while John had a ten year old son, Henry.

While Richard was still a boy, the country was ruled by a council. None of his uncles were on this council, but the Duke of Lancaster held the important position of Steward of England. His mainly unsuccessful attempts at reform during the end of Edward's reign had made him very unpopular with sections of parliament, the church and the City.

The Peasants' Revolt

In 1381 a number of problems came to a head and led to a revolt by a small but wide section of the community.

The Feudal System
The neglect at the end of King Edward's reign plus the confusion when England was run by the council led to widespread dissatisfaction. Following the 'Black Death' and the severe shortage of labour which followed, many farm workers tied to the feudal system described above were able to gain their freedom. Those who were strictly held back and refused what had become common freedoms, longed to be allowed to move on to more enlightened estates.

Religious Belief Causes Problems
During Edward's reign John Wycliffe had been Master of Balliol College, Oxford, from where he became a well-known scholar and preacher. Part of his message was that the clergy should not encourage worship of God via the saints and in particular via statues or paintings of saints, because it was too easy for the uneducated to start worshipping the saint or even the statue. By 1381 he was translating the Bible into the vernacular so that people could read Christ's teaching for themselves. Also during the 1370s a priest called John Ball (who had been ejected from his living in York) was walking the countryside, preaching a similar message and pointing

out the contradiction of Christ's message of poverty compared with the wealth of the bishops and abbots. He was also concerned that people should themselves pray to God and not feel obliged to pay a priest to make their private prayers for them.

An Unpopular Tax
In addition to the above, a new form of taxation had been introduced – instead of taxing property and stored goods, individual people were targeted in a head or poll tax. This was particularly hard on large families who had just sufficient income to be included and tax-payers.

The Revolt in London
These are just three of the subjects of dispute which combined caused thousands of people, mainly from Essex and Kent, to come streaming into London. They were joined by groups from the large Benedictine-owned towns such as Bury St. Edmunds and St. Albans. The demonstration got out of control, people were murdered and a great deal of property was damaged, including the house of John of Gaunt.

King Richard to the Rescue
The young king was only fourteen and still had to rule with his council, but he quickly summed up the dangerous position. He summoned the leaders of the different groups to take their people to the smooth fields [Smithfield] to the north of the city where, having listened to their grievances, he promised that these would be investigated; if they returned home they would all receive pardons for their part in the revolt.

Their main demands were:
1. that agricultural workers should receive wages, pay rent and not have their lives totally dominated by their employers – having to work as and when ordered to pay for their homes and land;
2. that businessmen in the monastically-owned boroughs could organise their own business affairs and that all free men should have access to fairs and markets.

It Ended in Disaster

The leaders of the revolt accepted Richard's word and streamed out of London. However he was forced to withdraw his promises and we will find in Part Two that it was in St. Albans that the revolt ended in disaster.

Once Richard was able to rule alone he tried to make peace amongst those in authority, but his relations with the House of Lancaster, i.e. his uncle, John of Gaunt and cousin, Henry Bolingbroke broke down and Henry was sent into exile.

The Death of John of Gaunt

When Gaunt died in 1399, his heir Henry was in Paris, but another Henry, Bishop of Lincoln, a son of his second marriage to Catherine Swinford, joined the long, slow funeral procession back to London. It passed through Dunstable on its way to spend the night in St. Albans Abbey and there was a rumour that the Abbot might refuse to accommodate them for political reasons. The Bishop decided to wait behind at Dunstable Priory. Messages were sent to King Richard and friendly replies were received but the Abbot was not reassured, so the coffin was kept at the gatehouse. As a son of the Duke, the Bishop did not receive permission to enter London and remained in Dunstable. Eventually it was arranged for the Bishop of London to take the funeral service and a group of monks agreed to accompany the coffin into London. Only after his father's body had departed was the Bishop able to travel on to St. Albans. Rightly or wrongly, Richard took the great estates of the Duke of Lancaster into his own hands after the funeral. During the previous few years, Richard had become increasingly unpopular and when Henry Bolingbroke came to England with an army to demand his inheritance, many of the large landowners supported him. Together they forced Richard to give up the throne and they imprisoned him in Pontefract Castle, where he died the following year, either starved or murdered.

This was a century in which two kings were murdered, there was a famine, an extremely serious plague and a political and religious revolt. Yet such evidence as we have suggests that at the end of the century, Bedfordshire had not suffered as much as might have been expected.

Part Two
Dunstable in the Fourteenth Century

It was noted above that at the end of the last century the presence of successful wholesalers, the Priory, the pilgrims and travellers had helped Dunstable to become a thriving retail centre. A less detailed tax assessment for 1309 points to the fact that Dunstable was, by that date, bigger and even more wealthy. Then, at the end of the decade, when the unusually kind weather which England had enjoyed for most of the thirteenth century began to come to an end, Dunstable began to decline.

In the next surviving tax record of 1332 not only had the number of people wealthy enough to pay tax dropped sharply but also the value per person tax raised. In other words, less people were sufficiently affluent to be included in the tax and, in modern parlance, those that did pay were mainly in a low tax bracket.

A Dunstable Tournament

In 1308, a year that may have been at the height of Dunstable's prosperity, a major tournament was held. It sounded quite innocent; Sir Giles Argentein [of Wymondham in Hertfordshire] challenged 'allcomers' to meet him at Dunstable. The very large number of people involved in such tournaments has been noted. On this occasion we know that there were nearly two hundred and fifty knights taking part. If each one was accompanied by only five friends and servants, the total number of official visitors would have been approximately one thousand, two hundred and fifty. Adding a large number of sightseers, entertainers, pedlars, beggars, pick-pockets and camp followers would bring the number to over two thousand! Space also had to be found to tie up, if not stable, as least five hundred tournament horses plus riding horses, cart-horses, pack ponies and others.

The population of Dunstable at that time is unknown. One hundred and seventy paid tax in 1309, which would suggest over eight hundred people living in the more comfortable houses. If the large number of cottages which lined the courtyards behind the big houses along the main roads is included, there must have been at least another eight hundred residents. For the week or so of the tournament the population of Dunstable must have doubled.

The Dunstable Armorial Roll

With such large numbers of riders taking part in the tournament, the umpires and spectators needed help to identify them. So the combatants had banners and wore large cloth badges depicting their coats of arms. Beautiful hand-painted lists of knights' names and their coats of arms were made. These were fragile and have long ago disappeared but amazingly two Dunstable Rolls, which were perhaps copied around 1600, have survived. In her 'History of Bedfordshire' Joyce Godber has a reproduction of the first page for 1308. The decorated title tells that the tournay was held in the town of Dunstable during the second year of 'Edward, son of Edward' [II]. This, together with the second survival, 1334, is in the British Museum archive.

Tournaments Cause Problems

This was the only tournament held in Dunstable during Edward's reign. In June 1309 all tournaments were forbidden but this did not stop the great earls from trying to get dispensations. Tournaments were arranged at Dunstable in 1312 and 1319 but both were forbidden. The great tournament of 1309, sponsored by Sir Giles Argentein, becomes less innocent when we discover that he was a loyal follower of the Earl of Gloucester. By studying the Roll we can see that it was not just Sir Giles, his brother John and friends against the rest but – the Earl of Gloucester, his followers and several other earls with their followers in one group, the Earl of Lancaster and his large band of about seventy-seven knights in a second group and the 'commune', another seventy-seven apparently independent knights in a third group. These *may* have been divided and used to balance the other two sides. If so, this could have been a potentially dangerous situation.

While so many of the earls were present in Dunstable, King Edward was travelling to the coast to meet his friend, Piers Gaveston, who had earlier been sent home to Gascony. His re-appearance in England tested the loyalty of the earls, which is why Edward did not risk them gathering at the tournament in large groups of armed supporters.

Despite the Dunstable tournament being forbidden in 1312, the town still got involved in a violent scandal. Streams of armed men marched through the town and then, led by the Earl of Lancaster, arrested Piers Gaveston and took him back to Warwick where he was put to death. Edward was still with Gaveston when he surrendered, causing a delicate constitutional situation. On their way back to London, the great landowners and their numerous armed followers stayed in and around Dunstable while they decided what to do.

Dunstable's Members of Parliament

During the previous year Dunstable had been summoned to send two representatives to parliament. They were summoned again in 1312 but either the cost was too high or they thought it was too politically dangerous. Somehow they managed to ignore the summons and Dunstable has never since had its own representatives in Parliament.

Famine Across England

From 1312 onwards the weather deteriorated and there was a breakdown of both normal agricultural routine and of marketing. It is unlikely that anyone in Dunstable died from starvation, but the shortage of both money and food must have caused a great deal of distress.

Unwelcome Royal Visits

Although Edward II travelled through Dunstable there is no record that he stayed at the Priory. During the period when loyalty to the King meant disloyalty to the powerful Queen and her friends, the burgesses were probably grateful for his absence. In 1322 St. Albans was threatened by armed men because the abbey had entertained the King! However in 1326, when the Queen and her followers had raised an army to force Edward's abdication, the Prior was obliged to entertain her and several of her noblemen.

During September 1327, travellers into Dunstable began to whisper that Edward had been murdered. All too soon this proved to be true. Desperately worried about the economic situation, the Dunstable wool merchants rushed off to York to the young King Edward III and his advisors. The market began to improve but around 1340 bad weather and the fighting in France led to another crisis in the wool trade. However the travel trade was soon prospering.

Two Important Tournaments

The young Edward III loved tournaments; in 1329 he sponsored such a large meeting that there was no room at the Priory to accommodate all his party. In 1297 the richest man in Bedfordshire had been wool merchant, John Durrant. He may have lived at the old palace of Kingsbury. By 1329 he had been dead for many years and his house was neglected. Edward ordered its repair to house the overspill of his party. A team of carpenters, tilers and plasterers worked for over a week at between 4d (1.75p) and 6d (2.5p) per day to mend the houses around the courtyard plus some of the outhouses [stables]. Other men were employed to repair the lead gutters. By this date the type of tournament was changing. The great melées or mock battles would soon be replaced by jousts. It is possible that various knights tilted against each other within the Kingsbury courtyard while spectators watched from the surrounding houses or from specially constructed stands. A contemporary account of the Dunstable tournament of 1341 records that:

> 'a great juste [was] kept by King Edward at the towne
> of Dunstable with other counterfeited feats of warre,
> at the request of diverse young lords and gentlemen
> whereat both the king and queene were present with
> the more part of the lords and ladies of the land.'

The Black Death

Although a great deal is known about the effects of this terrible illness in some parts of England, little is known about the situation in Dunstable. In St. Albans forty-seven our of the sixty resident monks died while in Luton there were four new clergy in three years. All that is known about the Dunstable outbreak is recorded in the Annales. Regular entries ended in 1297 but one of the later, occasional entries was for 1349. In this terrible year when the residents of the town on the crossroads may well have witnessed the death of up to a third of the population, the writer noted that the people of the town had 'made themselves a bell and called it Mary'. This bell can be seen today, mounted on an inside wall of the church.

Inns Were Opened in Dunstable

It is not known which prior (or when) decided that the traditional accommodation provided by the Priory needed to be increased. By 1353 St. Albans had seven hostels in addition to the accommodation within the Abbey precincts. In Dunstable part of the present *Priory House* (which was the main hostel) is thought to date back to the 13th century. The road (A5) has been repaired so many times since the foundations of the building were laid that it is now necessary to descend two steps to reach the front door! A few doors along *The Saracen's Head* which has been partially rebuilt at least once, is also approached by descending two steps. This may have been built originally in the same century. Once there were too many travellers for them all to stay at the Priory

Hostel, the Prior must have opened a hospice or inn on the other side of their main gate. The choice of name reflected the number of travellers who were soldiers or pilgrims on their way to the Holy Land.

Another very early inn was built off the end of High Street North, jutting out onto the crossroads and running down East [Church] Street towards Kingsbury. It was called *The White Swan* into the 17th century when it became known as *The Red Lion*. The owner in 1381 was Thomas Hobbes, who at that time was the burgesses' representative.

The Peasants' Revolt

By the time that Richard II came to the throne, most of the agricultural workers originally tied into the feudal system mentioned above had become free men. However, on the great monastery-owned estates the workers were still strictly controlled. In Houghton Regis and in several other villages some of the workers were free while others, on the Dunstable Priory estates were tied. This was bound to cause dissatisfaction.

Religious Beliefs could be Dangerous
A totally different cause of dispute was the approach to worship. Followers of John Wycliffe must have been regular travellers through Dunstable and as many Dunstablians were able to read, they were probably well-informed. Those that travelled to distant markets may have heard the very brave Reverend John Ball preaching against the practices of the Established Church. Although the townspeople had their own clergymen, they were appointed by the Prior or his staff and some of the businessmen may have resented their spiritual dependence on the Priory. One observation made by John Ball was the gap between the words of Jesus concerning poverty and the wealth of the religious houses.

Although with hindsight we know that the canons lived quite frugally, compared with the Dominican friars, they appeared very wealthy. Because of this, many Dunstablians greatly respected the friars.

The Poll Tax

The very poor residents of Dunstable would have been below the cut-off tax band and although no one likes taxes, the poll tax may not have caused too much distress in the business community.

The Real Cause of the Revolt in Dunstable

We have noted that, back in the 13th century when Henry I gave the businessmen the freedom of the burgesses of London and then gave the Prior complete control over the town, there was bound to be trouble. Nevertheless, by the middle of the 13th century they had agreed to work together. Whereas St. Albans Abbey had been in dispute with its tenants several times during the 13th and 14th centuries, in Dunstable relationships had been reasonably good, but in 1381 matters came to a head!

The Revolt in St. Albans

The leaders of the revolt accepted Richard's word and streamed out of London. The group from St. Albans, watched by business-men from Dunstable who were trading in the market, arrived home, storming the gates of the Abbey demanding their rights. Various abbots had treated the burgesses of the town like servants of the Abbey. The free farmers of Barnet and Redbourn had been treated as though they were tied workers. These acts of servitude had been enforced by charters which were kept in the Abbey.

Tenants from other estates round Bedfordshire and Hertfordshire joined the crowds at the Abbey gates and refused to withdraw until all the charters were handed over and burnt, which eventually happened on Sunday June 16th. After the celebrations, everyone returned happily to work, not knowing the council in London had cancelled both the freedoms and the pardons issued by King Richard.

In under a fortnight a trial had opened in St. Albans and the ring-leaders arrested. In just over a month John Ball had suffered the terrible death of being hung, drawn and quartered and the three local leaders and twelve others had all been publicly hanged and were left hanging in chains.

The Revolt Came to Dunstable

As related above, very large numbers of men and women had gathered in London, but relying on the promises of the young king had later returned home. The chronicler at St. Albans Abbey described the crowds of 'peasants' who stormed the abbey gate and broke open the gaol. When he goes into more detail we can tell that the people at the gate were not peasants, but townsmen from Barnet, farmers from Redbourn and the businessmen of St. Albans. A scribe at Dunstable Priory recorded:

> that it was June 17th when the men of St. Albans returned from London;
>
> that it was market day and that some of the Dunstable traders were at the market;
>
> that they returned to Dunstable led by 'Thomas Hobbes, the worthless mayor [leading burgess] who accosted . . . Thomas Marshal, the Prior to whom he had previously never spoken';
>
> that Hobbes pretended that he carried a message from King Richard ordering the Prior to 'grant the townspeople a charter of liberty as they had from Henry I';
>
> that reluctantly the Prior thought that the safest thing to do was to replace their charter but that once he heard that the revolt in St. Albans had been cruelly broken, he took it back.

Finally the scribe recorded that unlike the others, the Prior of Dunstable did not sentence any of the townspeople to 'punishment by bloodshed' and the report ended with a request that the mercy shown by Prior Thomas Marshall should not be forgotten. It took some years but the reforms did gradually take place. In Dunstable they may have come more quickly because the revolt ended with less bitterness.

In 1300 Dunstable was at its economic peak, but even after this difficult century, it was still an important business centre.

Chapter V

Seven Kings and a Civil War, 1399–1509

Dunstable Swan Jewel, drawn by John Gilbe.

Overview

During this very disturbed century six kings (not including the uncrowned thirteen year old King Edward V) sat upon the English throne!

It had been noted that the death of the Black Prince in 1376 not only disrupted the direct line of the throne but also left the regal line open to dispute for over a hundred years. When the century opened, Henry IV, son of the Duke of Lancaster [John of Gaunt] had taken the throne from his cousin Richard II by force. Henry's son, Henry V, followed his father but died prematurely when he was only thirty-five. The long reign of his son, Henry VI (a further descendant of the Duke of Lancaster) was punctuated by a series of battles, known as the 'Wars of the Roses' and died naturally in 1471, ten years after the death of his son at the Battle of Tewkesbury.

Following this victory Edward, Duke of York was crowned King Edward IV and reigned for over twenty years. However, with the mysterious deaths of his sons (the 'Princes in the Tower'), the monarchy was once more in dispute. The princes' uncle, Richard, Duke of Gloucester, became King Richard III but despite his efforts to unite the country, too many people suspected him of involvement in their deaths, so two years later he was challenged by an indirect Lancastrian, Henry Tudor, descended from John of Gaunt and his second wife, Catherine Swynford. The two opposing armies met at Market Bosworth, where Richard was killed. So a century which had seen so many changes, including a most distressing civil war, concluded with the first fifteen years of the more settled Tudor dynasty.

Throughout all these upheavals, Bedfordshire fared much better than might have been expected. Civil wars of this period bore little resemblance to the horrific events which take place today, having more in common with a game of chess! Kings, queens and prospective monarchs, supported by various knights and bishops with their soldiers [pawns] moved about the country [the board] taking castles and sometimes towns trying to trap members of the opposing royal family or their representatives.

Castle-owners defended them against the opposition, there were sieges, many soldiers and civilians were killed and wounded and damage was done to the town or inside and outside the castle, but only to a limited area. Sometimes there were major battles where very large numbers of soldiers were killed and wounded and where surrounding farms and villages were devastated, but again serious loss of life was restricted.

Economically the great damage to the country was the breakdown of law and order. This meant that the roads were unsafe, markets suffered and, quite often, exports came to a standstill. In addition to its damaged trade, Dunstable, standing on two main roads, also suffered from the continual passing through of soldiers. Both sides tried to recruit or press-gang men to join their armies, they commandeered or stole horses and other supplies and forced townsmen to transport their baggage on to the next town.

Part One
England and Bedfordshire in the Fifteenth Century

King Henry IV (1399–1413)

Born on April 3rd 1367 at Bolingbroke, Lincolnshire with two English parents, Henry felt that Richard, rather than he, was the usurper, but many people disagreed. He was never recognised by the King of France (who was related to Richard by marriage) and trade suffered as a result. Not only did the Scottish king refuse to accept him, but there were also rebellions in Wales and the north of England.

One contentious subject which Henry decided to tackle early in his reign was the spreading of something which the church regarded as heresy. Wycliffe had died in 1384 but before his death he had completed his English translation of the bible. His ideas of a more personal, less clergy-dominated form of religion was spread right across the area of the Thames and Chilterns by his converted followers of Lollards. Although there were individuals and small groups of converts in many parts of England, the new movement was most successful in areas where there were communities of trade and craftspeople.

A law was passed in 1401 ordering that anyone who should 'teach, preach or write' without permission from a bishop or who was against the church of Rome should be burned to strike fear into others! The first Lollard was publicly subjected to this ordeal in that year, with more than twenty others suffering the same fate during the following few years because they refused to accept that during the mass the bread and wine did not actually become the body and blood of Christ.

By 1406 Henry was suffering perhaps from leprosy (thought today probably to have been a form of nervous eczema or venereal disease) which gradually worsened, affecting his judgement in state matters. He resisted the attempts to persuade him to pass the crown to his son, so although young Henry took much responsibility, it was not until the death of his father in 1413 that he was crowned.

King Henry V (1413–1422)

Although the young Henry set out to heal the breaches which dangerously damaged the country during his father's reign, the worst of the Lollard atrocities took place in 1414. Very heavy taxes were also raised to pay for the war against France, but the successes Henry enjoyed, e.g. Agincourt, increased his popularity and opened up trade between the two countries. While in France he became ill and a doctor was sent from England, but in July 1422 while trying to lead his troops in battle, he was too ill to sit on his horse and finally died on August 31st, probably from a very severe form of dysentry. Apart from the loss of a young, successsful and popular king, the problem for England was that his heir was only a baby.

Probably due to Shakespeare's play, Henry is remembered as the king who, in 1415, won the battle of Agincourt. It is less well known that both he and his father were great patrons of the arts. He enjoyed both listening to and playing music. One of the leading musicians of the day was 'John of Dunstable'.

King Henry VI (1422–1461)

Henry V's brothers were to become Regents of England and France and Richard Beauchamp, Earl of Warwick was to be tutor to the young king. In April 1445 when he was twenty-three, a marriage was arranged with the sixteen year old Margaret of Anjou. Unlike the quiet, pious Henry, Margaret was fiery and tempestuous.

Five years later Henry became distressed and mentally confused and Margaret took over the control of the country. He quickly recovered and in 1453 a son, Edward, was born but the bouts of mental illness kept recurring and became more serious, causing Richard, Duke of York to be made Protector temporarily in 1454, as the noblemen did not like the forceful Queen Margaret. Each time Henry recovered and took back the throne, Edward's Yorkist supporters felt strongly that he should resign permanently in favour of Edward. This was resisted by Lancastrian Margaret who planned to be Regent on behalf of her son. Almost by accident in 1455, this competition for control of the country led to *the first Battle of St. Albans*.

Both parties, supported by groups of soldiers, were approaching the town from different directions when confused and deliberately withheld letters of negotiation led to violent bloodshed. Both sides were shocked by the loss of life; Henry was wounded and taken into the Abbey to be cared for. Subsequently he agreed that the Duke of York should become Protector again if he himself became incapacitated. Had Henry been mentally well enough to conduct his own negotiations with the Duke, all might have been well. As it was, the remorse following St. Albans soon faded and other battles followed.

In December 1460 Margaret had a great victory at *the Battle of Wakefield* and Richard, Duke of York, was killed. His son, Edward, was now Duke of York but he was living in exile and could not claim his father's estate. He returned to England with a small army, enlarged by the many people who joined him as he crossed the country. The battles continued! *The second Battle of St. Albans* (see below) was won by the Lancastrians but the Council refused to accept Margaret, Henry or their son, Edward.

King Edward IV (1461–1483)

Although the Council proclaimed Edward as king there was still a large Lancastrian army waiting in the north of England. Prince Edward was now eight years old and they were anxious to preserve the Lancastrian line. Further battles followed and in 1470 the mentally ill King Henry was reinstated to the throne. However, the following year the Lancastrians were beaten at *the Battle of Barnet*. Shortly afterwards *the Battle of Tewkesbury* was bitterly fought until with the arrest of Queen Margaret and the eighteen year old Prince Edward, the Yorkist cause was settled. So bitter were the feelings on both sides that to make themselves completely safe, Prince Edward was murdered and Henry, already confined to the Tower, was found dead in his room. Margaret of Anjou was also strictly confined to the Tower until eventually she was ransomed by the King of France.

Peace at Last

A terrifying number of people of all social classes had died to make the throne secure for Edward. Even when his enemies were at last defeated, there were less serious disputes between his own and his wife's families. These turbulent years masked the social and cultural events of his reign but like his predecessors, Edward was a patron of the arts, encouraging the new skill of printing and giving much work to William Caxton. He is also credited with starting the first postal service. In 1482 horsemen were based at relays of twenty miles along the road to Scotland to carry official despatches. Politically he kept complete control over the country, but when he died on the 9th April 1483, the country was once more in turmoil. Edward's queen had a very large family referred to collectively as the 'Woodvilles'. They were very unpopular with the traditional Yorkists. When he died, Edward's sons, Edward and Richard, were being cared for at Ludlow by his brother-in-law, Sir Richard Woodville (now Lord Rivers). He appointed twelve year old Edward as king and his brother, Richard, Duke of Gloucester, as Protector.

King Edward V (1483)

The coronation was provisionally arranged for May 4th. Richard (the late king's brother) arranged to meet the princes and Lord Rivers (his brother-in-law) at Northampton on 29th April but when he arrived, they had moved on to Stony Stratford. They eventually met and travelled slowly into London. On May 4th the princes rested at the Bishop of London's palace and then Edward was moved into a comfortable suite of rooms at the Tower. His brother was soon to join him.

Outside the Tower rivalry, bitterness and violence grew. The coronation was repeatedly postponed. Richard first extended his authority until Edward came of age and then, apparently to halt violence, decided to rule in his own name. Questions asked about the welfare of the princes living in the Tower might have been regarded as treason.

King Richard III (1483–1485)

Even if Parliament had decided against accepting the twelve year old Prince Edward as king, there were many other people with a legal right to have been considered. Of these, after less than two troubled years, it was Welshman, Henry Tudor, whose small army challenged Richard at Bosworth. Richard was killed and according to tradition, his crown was rescued from a thorn bush and placed on Henry's head by Lord Stanley. A local addition to this story is that William Cantilupe, owner of Eaton [Bray], remained loyal to Richard and therefore lost his estates while Sir Reginald Bray, who would soon give his name to the village, was fighting alongside Stanley.

King Henry VII (1485–1509)

Although Henry had taken the crown by force he could claim a distant connection with Edward III through both his mother and his father. At this time Prince Edward and Prince William may still have been alive in the Tower. There is no proof that Richard had had them killed – in fact there is evidence that he did not. Also there were several other contenders for the throne and Henry needed to establish a legal claim. The Lancastrian party recognised him as a descendant of John of Gaunt and to appease the followers of York, he married Elizabeth, daughter of the late Duke of York and sister of Prince Edward and Prince Richard.

Part Two
Dunstable in the Fifteenth Century

Royal Visits Continue

During the first thirteen years of this century and during the three or four years that went before, there were numerous unofficial visits as royal parties rode to and fro across the country. Richard II broke his journey here in February 1397 and again in May and June 1398. It has always been assumed that these overnight stops were at the Prior's House, but when the eighteen year old Prince Henry stopped overnight in November 1405 on his way back from Wales, his lodging place was described as the *Old Royal Palace*. Also when he was returning north a month later, his lodgings was recorded as *Kingsbury*.

Although Prior Thomas Marshall did not retire for a further eight years, he must have been already approaching seventy. Maybe Henry thought that he would be more comfortable at Kingsbury or that he could avoid waiting for mass and could get back on the road more quickly the next morning! Prince Henry stayed again on the night of 3rd December 1408 but once he became king he was frequently out of the country and recorded visits have not been found.

Some Wealthy Businessmen

We do not know what use the various priors made of the building complex which comprised the old palace. It has been assumed that John Durrant, the richest man in Bedfordshire at the time and a great benefactor of the Priory, lived there in the thirteenth century. He died in 1297, two of his sons went to Oxford before becoming priests, and nothing more has been found relating to this family. No doubt some other rich merchant rented Kingsbury from the Priory.

Although we know less about individual residents in the early years of this century, the gentlemen mentioned later in the chapter were probably already in business. Sir Thomas Chalton of Dunstable became a member of the Mercers Company, Sheriff of the City of London and in 1449, Lord Mayor of London. When there was a dispute concerning the will of merchant John Holm in 1414, it was of sufficient importance to reach the King's Court at Westminster. Merchant Laurence Pygot (who would later be a founder-member of the Fraternity) was co-executor. Richard Anable* who made his will on 23rd April 1453, had a brother William who was also a founder-member of the Fraternity. A later John Holme was executor of Anable's will which included land in Dunstable and elsewhere in Bedfordshire and Hertfordshire. He had several silver cups, mazers (probably carved wooden cups) and spoons. His wife Margaret and his son and heir Richard were well provided for, his second son, William and daughter, Alice were both to have 'a complete bed with brass pot and dish, basin and hand-ewer with six silver spoons'. Another wealthy Dunstablian of the early 15th century was Thomas London ('of Dunstaple'), maltman, who was probably trading to innkeepers up and down Watling Street.

By this time the English wool trade had altered. Less wool was being exported and the buyers, including some from Dunstable, may have moved their offices to London, while the smelly business of tanning was now less likely to be sited in town centres. However, there was still at least one specialist workshop dealing with the production of white leather; on March 3rd 1411, John George, tawyer*, of Dunstable was summoned to the King's Court at Westminster to answer a charge of having 'broken a park of the Prior of Dunstaple and taken sixteen deer worth £20' back in 1408. The park cannot have been in Dunstable, but it may have been on the Priory estate at Wadelow (Toddington) or at Segenhoe (Ridgemont).

The Cost of Hospitality

The Priory was desperate to retain its many estates, to help provide free care and accommodation for all the poor and sick travellers, maintain the almonary, two leper hospitals and the large number of squatters camping around the town. Wealthy gentlemen, e.g. Richard Anable, helped financially and in his will asked to 'be buried in the church of St. Peter at Dunstable'. As was usual at that time, he left a small gift to compensate for any tithes he might have 'forgotten' and also towards church repairs. Each clergymen (including the two Fraternity chaplains – see below), received a small gift. To make sure his departure towards heaven was helped by a great wave of prayer, his executors were ordered to distribute three shillings and fourpence (16.7p) amongst the poor on the day of his death.

It was often the practice to bequeath money for the poor or to help mend the roads. However, much to their distress, the canons lost many potential bequests to the Dominican Friary. When the foundations of this church of St. Mary was excavated in 1995, a coffin and several skeletons were found. In 1408 an extremely wealthy lady, Radegund Becket, requested that her body should be buried 'in the church of the Friar Preachers of Dunstapul'. She left them a really valuable red silk gown (possibly for the celebration of the mass) and other important gifts.

---

*   A skilled leather worker.

Henry VI and his son were aware of the financial problems from which the Priory suffered. In December 1406 it was arranged that two pipes of red wine would be delivered to celebrate the Easter mass. This would also have given Henry the assurance that he would be remembered in the canons' prayers. When Prior John Marshall died on October 12th 1413, the king's stewards took the profits from their estates until the new prior was elected. Although legal, this was a great financial burden, so that when the tax collectors were officially informed of the appointment of John Roxton as prior on January 26th, there was a delay of only three days before they were ordered to return the payments, due to 'the great expenses of [the] church and [the] houses of the priory'.

Musician – John of Dunstable

We know the names of the people who are mentioned above because when they made their wills or appeared in court they were still living or based in Dunstable. Once a businessman moved away to live permanently in London or at a port like Bristol, rather than John 'Durrant' or John 'Young' he became known as 'John of Dunstable'.

This was the case with internationally-famous musician, John of Dunstable. The date and place of his birth have not been recorded, but he was sufficiently mature and successful to be asked to write the music for the great service held in Canterbury Cathedral in 1416, to celebrate Henry's victory at Agincourt. It is known that Henry sponsored the careers of several musicians and he may well have started Dunstable on the road to fame. However, Henry's younger brother, John, Duke of Bedford, is usually named as his patron. There is a gap in our knowledge of the early years of Dunstaple's* life and although there is no proof, it seems likely that he received his education at the Priory and perhaps even became a chorister. If so, Prior Marshall could have pointed him out to Henry on one of his visits to the town.

---

*   This is the way his name is usually spelt.

Another way in which Dunstaple may have been noticed by royalty was through St. Albans Abbey, where a local man, John Bostock (known as John of Wheathampstead) became abbot in 1420. He himself was a well known scholar who had met Humphrey, Duke of Gloucester (King Henry's youngest brother) at Oxford University and often invited him to visit the Abbey.

Dunstaple was also a renowned mathematician and astronomer. At least one of his manuscripts (which he probably illustrated himself) is in Emmanuel College, Cambridge. When he died, Wheathampstead wrote an epitaph where he recorded that Dunstaple had 'a secret knowledge of the stars'.

When Henry V died, the Duke of Bedford was appointed head of the regency council; he often had to travel abroad, and was accompanied by Dunstaple, which explains why most of his manuscripts are still in continental collections. When a previously unknown piece of work was found, quite by chance, in Estonia, it proved to be one of the most important finds so far. As a result, a disc of the Orlando Consort playing the Agincourt piece and the newly-found Gloria was released a few years ago by a small Northampton-based label, Metronome. Dunstaple died on Christmas Eve 1453, but it is not known where he was buried.

In the 20th century he was described as 'England's most successful musical export before the Beatles'! Certainly in the 15th century his music was extremely influential across Europe.

The Relationship of Gown and Town

Although the businessmen of Dunstable were forced to hand back their new charter of freedom in 1381, during this century they gradually gained control. Recruitment was no longer so easy for the monastic houses and there were more charities to which people were giving their alms. The universities and private schools were gradually taking over as suppliers of education, although famous scholars like John of Dunstable may well have started their education in the Priory school.

Skilled physicians like John of Gaddesden were offering medical help to those who could afford his fees but although leprosy had almost been eradicated, in England, the Priory hospitals were functioning for local people and for travellers. Prior Roxton was still both landlord and Lord of the Manor of Dunstable, controlling the Wednesday and Saturday markets and the May (10th–12th) and August (9th–12th) fairs. He therefore expected all those who worked in the town to attend his manor courts and the 'commuters' to attend when they were at home. However, absentees were no longer heavily fined and the Prior's officials worked hard with the businessmen to organise and promote the town.

In 1392 the townspeople had been allowed to use part of the monastic nave for their services in addition to the traditional north aisle, both of which they had to maintain. They had their own clergymen who were employed by, but were not themselves, members of the Priory.

The Poor Educational Standards of Some Vicars

One of the reasons that both John Bell in the 14th century and the Lollards in the 15th found support for their criticisms of the Established Church was the very low educational standards of many clergy. The men who originally built the parish churches provided land for their support and also arranged for *all* their tenants and workers to donate a tenth [tithe] of their crops and livestock to support the clergymen. By 1381 most of the church land and tithes had been given to various religious houses, while the *vicars* who lived within the community received a small house [vicarage], a piece of land [glebe] and the *small tithes*, such as milk, honey, eggs and perhaps even fruit and vegetables. With such humble expectations, it was difficult to attract educated, eloquent preachers, so it therefore became the custom for rich men, e.g. William Dyve of Sewell, to get permission to found a *chantry* and to put a number of rents aside to pay for their own family priest. Quite often there was an element of charity involved. Dyve made up a large package of rents (including that from the White Swan [Red Lion] on Dunstable crossroads) to support a chaplain to sing mass daily in a chapel within All Saints

Church, Houghton Regis, while a second chaplain was to sing mass at his private house at Sewell and six poor Houghton Regis boys were to receive free education at a school in East [Church] Street, Dunstable.

The Fraternity of St. John the Baptist

It was not feasible for each rich man within the town to have a private chantry, so during the 15th century it became the custom to found a *Fraternity* or brotherhood. In 1442, Laurence Pygot (described as a wool merchant on his brass in the Priory Church), William Anable, Henry Martell and others bought a licence from King Henry VI to enable them to employ a priest to say masses for the souls of King Henry, his family and the members of the newly-formed brotherhood. They dedicated the Fraternity and their altar in the Priory Church to St. John the Baptist.

In addition to the religious activities of the brotherhood, there was also a social aspect. At least once a year there would have been a great feast. Their main charity was an almshouse or hostel which stood in West Street (near the present site of the bus stops) and provided accommodation for four of their own members who had fallen on hard times and for six poor travellers. It is possible that they may also have taken over the Priory almonary and their school.

Henry VI Visits Dunstable

Henry VI was still a young man when he granted the licence for the Fraternity. During the early years of his marriage and before the fateful first Battle of St. Albans, he frequently visited the Priory. Although the records show overnight stays on 11th July 1437 (on the way to Leicester), 23rd July 1450 (returning from Kenilworth Castle) and 14th September 1451 (*en route* for Leicester and Coventry), there was a longer stay in 1452 (between 18th and 21st February) and there may have been other unrecorded occasions. The next recorded visits were during the terrible years of the civil war.

The Wars of the Roses

Although none of the battles during the Wars of the Roses took place in Dunstable, the constant movement of soldiers caused the usual financial and social distress. The troops taking part in the first Battle of St. Albans in 1455 approached that town from the south and east, but after the fighting was over, many of the wounded and destitute men would have to come to the Priory seeking medical and financial help to get them home.

During the next few years there were several more serious battles. King Henry must have been aware of the many important people who passed through and stayed in Dunstable, so it is not surprising that he paused in the town to issue a proclamation 'The king commandeth that no manner of man of this township of what craft or mystery [special training] he be of, be adherent or drawing to any lord, to aid or go with him'. The poor king was frequently mentally ill and both sides tried to keep him with them as a sign of their authority. He stayed in Dunstable (presumably at the Priory) on the nights of 24th–25th February 1460 and 19th January 1461.

It was a desperately difficult time for both sides; money and supplies were short and the soldiers were exhausted and disspirited. Henry was soon too ill to take any further part in the actual fighting, but Queen Margaret continued on behalf on their young son. After a victory at Wakefield she hastily recruited more men in Yorkshire and despite the shortages of both food and supplies, speedily marched them south, following a route similar to the line of the present A6 road. The Duke of York planned to intercept them just north of St. Albans, where his army lay in wait with trenches dug out in the area of Sandridge. On hearing this, Queen Margaret led her tired and hungry men off to the west, coming through Dunstable. According to contemporary chronicles they 'came down suddenly to the town of Dunstaple robbing all the countrie and people as they came'. Waiting for only a brief rest and allowing the soldiers to take what food they could find, the officers returned them to the road. Under cover of darkness they caught the Yorkist army by surprise, having marched from the west, along the equivalent of the A5 route. Quite unprepared to fight on that side of the town, the Yorkists were soon forced to withdraw and as a result, Margaret had such a resounding victory that she wanted to march straight on to London. However, it took some time for her officers to round up their men, who were, by that time, completely out of control. Many of them, drunk on a mixture of excitement and stolen alcohol, were looting and vandalising the town. Eventually most of them set out to march south but the London businessmen, having heard what took place in St. Albans, erected barriers to exclude them from the city. Margaret and a group of officers were allowed entry but her wild, undisciplined army was sent back to camp to live off the land in and around Dunstable.

The Dunstable Swan Jewel

The events above *may* be connected with one of Dunstable's great unsolved mysteries. In 1965 the Manshead Archaeological Society was excavating the known site of the Dominican Friary (Grid ref: TL 019217). During the evening of Friday 16th July a young teacher, Miss Maxene Miller, picked up a piece of jewellery which she assumed had been dropped by the last person digging in that trench. Other more experienced diggers recognised that it was made of gold and took it to the police station! From then on there was a great deal of speculation but more of the exciting story unfolded at the coroner's court held in October. First the site director, Mr Les Matthews, gave evidence about the Friary dig and the finding of the brooch and then Mr John Cherry MA, assistant keeper of the Department of British Medieval Antiquities at the British Museum was called. At that stage he gave evidence of the date the piece as around 1400 and told of its great historic value. At a later meeting Mr Cherry explained that this particular swan with its crown and chain and one crooked foot was the badge of the Swan Knights. Some months later, the British Museum paid £4,800 for the one-and-a-quarter inch high jewel. It is one inch long, with a three-and-a-quarter inch chain. It is described as 'moulded in gold in the round' but one reason for the very high price by 1966 standards was that the feathered parts of the bird were covered in white enamel. This technique, known as 'white enamel *en-ronde-bosse*' was being practised in Parisian workshops around 1400. The other reason for the museum's anxiety to own the brooch was that it was the first one of its type ever found in England and can now be seen displayed in a prominent position in the medieval jewellery collection.

How Did the Jewel get to Dunstable?

Although some of the tournaments held in Dunstable were rather like practising military manoevres, others were great loyal social gatherings. On these occasions the prizes were often valuable trinkets with a royal connection. Several of the kings who visited Dunstable were members of the Swan Knights, e.g. Henry V who used the emblem as his badge (these are discussed in detail in the booklet 'The Dunstable Swan Jewel'*). However, one very likely connection is Margaret of Anjou's army. Her uncle, the Duke of Berry used a swan as his crest and when Margaret was recruiting in 1459 on behalf of her son, the Earl of Chester, she:

> 'made her sone called the prince give a livery of
> swannys to alle the gentelmenne of the Countie
> and many others thorought the lande; trustying
> thorough thayre streyngthe to make her sone
> king'.

The badges that the soldiers wore so that they could be recognised in battle were more like those worn by footballers, but senior officers or members of the royal family may well have worn a valuable badge in their hats. From these facts we can conjure up all sorts of speculations, especially before and after the second Battle of St. Albans.

---

* Evans, V. 1982 Dunstable Museum Trust.

The End of the Century

The chapter started with a flurry of royal visits and reference to some of the businessmen who may have been prepared to entertain them. At this time these businessmen were only just beginning to gain control over their own town.

By the end of the century they were not only equal partners with the Priory but were also preparing to take over some of their charitable duties and although they had been keeping the body of the church in a reasonable state of repair, by this time the roof of the nave was becoming dangerous. We shall find that, at the start of the next century, the members of the Fraternity undertook a restoration of such magnitude that we would find difficult even today.

Chapter VI

The Tudors – A New Beginning, 1509–1603

Conjectural reconstruction of the White Horse Inn, drawn by Andrew Leech.

Overview

The descendants of the victorious Henry Tudor dominated the whole of this century. It therefore follows that much space has been dedicated in this book to the amazing changes, nationally and locally, which took place during that time.

For the first nine years Henry VII continued to rule with strength, severity and efficiency, allowing his son in 1509 to inherit a secure, peaceful and wealthy country. Henry VIII was not quite eighteen when he came to the throne and during the thirty-eight years of his reign England experienced changes which influenced the rest of the millennium. Between 1533 and 1543 Henry separated England from the Church of Rome, became head of the church in England and closed all the religious houses.

Initially his youthful charm, energy and enthusiasm was extremely exciting, but his popularity (which had helped to unite the country) quickly turned to concern and bitterness when the taxes needed to pay for his ambitious schemes were introduced. Because of this, many people welcomed his great religious reforms, hoping that not only would the taxes be relieved, but also that wealth would be redistributed. As Henry grew older, his failing health, his disastrous marriages and his genuine concern about the lack of an heir led to the irrational behaviour which caused people to dislike and fear him.

The second half of the century was shared by Henry's three children. Jane Seymour's son, Edward VI, was only ten when he inherited the throne and although his health deteriorated during the five and a half years of his reign, he supported his council when they brought in the Church of England.

His elder sister Mary (daughter of Catherine of Aragon) was a devout Catholic. Her conviction that it was her religious duty to return England and all its people to the Church of Rome led to many atrocities being carried out in her name. She died of ill-health when she was only forty-two.

Her early death brought Edward's younger sister, Elizabeth (daughter of Anne Boleyn) to the throne. This intelligent twenty-five year old young lady was anxious to return to the Protestant church, but she worked carefully, having learned the lesson of tolerance. Age and infirmity caused her high standards to slip by the end of her long reign, but for over forty years England was governed both wisely and well.

Part One
England and Bedfordshire in the Sixteenth Century

King Henry VIII (1509–1547)

During his long reign both Henry's character and attitude to kingship changed completely. Although he is renowned for the number of his marriages, his reign covered so many important events that it is prudent to divide it into three sections.

Introduction

During the summer of 1501 Henry VII and his advisors completed their plans for a political marriage between his sixteen year old son, Arthur and the fifteen year old princess of Aragon. Arthur's health was already causing concern and so it was his ten year old brother, Henry, who early in October, rode off the Plymouth to meet the young Catherine. Once the wedding celebrations were over, Arthur and Catherine rode off to the prince's castle at Ludlow and Henry returned to his studies. Five months later Catherine rode sorrowfully back to London; Arthur had died of a consumptive illness.

Rather than allow Catherine and her valuable dowry to return to Spain, a new betrothal was arranged in June 1503 – this time with the young Henry. It was intended that the wedding ceremony would take place in three years, but as things turned out, they were forced to wait for nearly six.

Even though Arthur's ill-health had prevented the consummation of his marriage, the pope's permission was needed

71

before Henry could marry his brother's widow. While they were waiting for his decision, circumstances in Spain had altered, Catherine was no longer as wealthy and politically important as had been hoped and Henry VII changed his mind. Although his feelings were of no importance while his father was alive, the young Henry waited only six weeks after his death in April 1509 before marrying *Catherine* at Greenwich Palace, with Archbishop Warham of Canterbury officiating.

1. Youth and Enthusiasm

Henry's early policies were popular and the extravagances of the court were ignored. When Henry and Catherine lost both a still-born daughter and a two month old son in the first two years of their marriage, people genuinely mourned with them.

Whereas his father had tried to avoid involvement with the power struggles on mainland Europe, Henry longed to join in. The opportunity came in 1512 when he attempted an invasion of France, despite warnings by his more cautious ministers and early military failure. It was with great relief that the people of England shared in the treaty celebrations which opened at St. Paul's on Sunday 3rd October 1518.

Between the unpleasant episodes of these first nine years, Henry and his court enjoyed a lively and expensive social life of music-making, dancing and pageantry, together with more active sports, hunting and jousting. Catherine was encouraged to accompany him on all these pleasant duties and despite suffering at least two more miscarriages, she was safely delivered of the future Queen Mary on 18th February 1516. This did not, however, prevent Henry from openly conducting several extra-marital affairs. During the spring of 1519 Elizabeth Blount gave birth to a son, Henry Fitzroy.

2. The Middle Years

By this time Henry VII's accumulated wealth had been squandered away and heavy taxation had alienated both Parliament and the people. His church policy was more successful. Having previously considered himself a moderate reformer, Henry was shocked and dismayed by the writings of Martin Luther. The booklet which he wrote in response ('The Assertion of the Seven Sacraments') so pleased the Pope that he rewarded Henry with the title 'Defender of the Faith'.

By the end of this period Henry was preparing to separate the legislative powers of the church from Rome's authority. We will find below that it was events which took place in Dunstable in 1533 which caused a total separation. Meanwhile, encouraged by Thomas Wolsey, Henry proceeded to close the small religious houses. It was said that any house with an income of less than £200 per year could not afford to support itself and carry out the spiritual duties intended by its patron. In practice the closures added greatly to Henry's income! There were few active protests because of the people's jealousy of the apparent wealth of the monasteries. Despite this, large groups marched south from Lincolnshire and parts of Yorkshire to demonstrate their disapproval; the growing movement becoming known as the Pilgrimage of Grace. It was brutally crushed by Henry's soldiers and the fact that the orders came from the King personally did nothing to dispel the increasing fear within the people.

Henry's domestic life and his enjoyment of sport became even more passionate, but although he had a succession of mistresses, his affection for and support of Catherine appeared unchanged. He was, however, genuinely worried about the succession. He had a legitimate daughter and an acknowledged but illegitimate son, but Catherine's health had been ruined by the constant miscarriages and the safe arrival of a son and heir seemed unlikely. Meanwhile Catherine herself was only too aware of these things and also the increased attention paid by her husband to the young, healthy and beautiful Anne Boleyn.

For over six years *Anne Boleyn* resisted the royal advances – it was marriage or nothing. Eventually, however, Henry was able to convince her that because Catherine had been previously married to his brother, Arthur, he could by-pass the Pope by having his marriage annulled in England. Once this decision had been made, events raced ahead. Henry and Anne were secretly married, she became pregnant and Catherine was sent away from court. Ten days later, the pregnant Anne was crowned queen; the future Queen Elizabeth was born two months later! All might then have been well had it not been for enemies of the Boleyn family convincing Henry that Anne had been unfaithful – she was executed on 19th May 1536.

The day after Anne's execution Henry announced his engagement to *Jane Seymour*; they were married ten days later and Prince Edward was born in October 1537. At last Henry had a son and heir, but so great were the celebrations that no one noticed Jane was dying of puerperal fever.

3. The Downward Slide

The closing of the small religious houses had helped Henry's economy, but not sufficiently to get him out of trouble. From 1535 onwards threats and bribes gradually persuaded the larger religious houses to 'surrender' both their houses and their property. When the small houses were closed, the inhabitants were able to move to larger, more efficient houses. Now they were turned our into the secular world with only very small pensions to support them. Officials supervised the removal of any valuables and the breaking of the bells and other metals, which were taken away and used for armaments. They were also supposed to supervise the removal of the roof so that there was no opportunity for the residents to return.

Within a year the Court of Augmentation was administering vast estates in every county and Henry was a very rich man. His excuse for retaining all this wealth was his intention to use some of it to establish new schools and colleges and some to divide thirteen over-large bishops's sees. In practice it was left to his son to make most of the educational improvements and apart from six new diocese, the rest (including Lincoln) had to wait for several centuries.

By this time Henry had moved cautiously ahead with his plans for religious reform. An English translation of the Bible was to be chained in every church, but Henry was worried about the use to which they were being put. Although he was happy to promote the idea that the creed, commandments and Lord's Prayer should

be taught in English, he was strongly against the Ana-baptists*
and people who read the Bible and then questioned the teaching
of the church. In April 1539 he persuaded Parliament to pass The
Six Articles which enforced the continuation of such matters as
the traditional liturgy and the celibacy of the clergy. He also
backed the practice of allowing wealthy individuals and
fraternities to pay for private chaplains to celebrate masses on
their behalf. Throughout this last phase, Henry's domestic life
continued to cause him distress and to build up fear and
resentment within the court. After the death of Jane Seymour
Henry remained single for two years, but there were problems
abroad and Thomas Cromwell was anxious for a
politically-suitable marriage. Henry agreed to marry the
thirty-four year old *Anne of Cleeves* but when she was brought to
England, Henry was shocked by her looks, clothes and general
appearance. They were, nevertheless, married at Greenwich on
6th January 1540, but by July Henry had persuaded the church
authorities to annul the marriage. Cromwell was executed at the
end of the month and Henry married the young and beautiful
Catherine Howard. Despite her charm and vivacity and the
happiness which Henry had in his marriage, 1541 started as a
difficult year both at home and abroad. Henry's health suffered
but he was better by the end of the summer and publicly displayed
his love and pride in his beautiful young bride. Then in November
disaster struck yet again. Catherine was found guilty of adultery,
was accused of treason and was beheaded on 13th February 1542.

Eighteen months went by before Henry married for the sixth
time. On 12th July 1543 he married *Catherine Parr*, a thirty year
old widow; sufficiently tactful and caring to remain in favour
with Henry, she managed to avoid the extreme jealousy of his
different courtiers. She brought Henry's three children back into
the family circle and during the last years of his life improved
their relationships. Despite the fact that his long and eventful
reign ended with fighting in both Scotland and France, his
domestic life was stable and happy until he died four years later.

---

*   The movement which would later be known as Baptists.

King Edward VI (1547-1553)

Although Henry had separated the church from Rome and introduced the use of English into parts of the services, he did not have any intention of allowing any further changes. Amongst both his church and secular leaders there were men who bitterly resented the break with Rome and others who were looking for ways to change England into a fully Protestant country.

Before he died, Henry set up a council of sixteen men and, as Edward was only nine years of age, his maternal uncle, Edward Seymour, was made Protector. Young though he was, Edward fully understood that his councillors wanted to complete the Reformation. The Latin mass book was banned and replaced by the Book of Common Prayer and Henry's Six Articles were replaced by another list of forty-two which were prepared by the Archbishop of Canterbury, Thomas Cranmer.

During the centuries when England had been part of the church of Rome, parishioners had not been encouraged to make regular, commemorative prayers on behalf of their loved ones who had died. They usually made small payments to the parish priest and asked him to pray for them. Some people bequeathed small (even very small) pieces of land so that the rent money could be used to remind the priest to continue praying year after year. The rent money may have been intended to pay for a candle to be lit each year at the statue of a favourite saint.

In 1545 an Act of Parliament had granted Henry the income from these small chantries, but it had never been put into practice. Within the first year of Edward's reign, the grant was renewed and a commission set up to carry out a survey with the intention of selling all the land and paying the proceeds into the King's treasury. Archbishop Cranmer was hoping to use this money to increase the pay of the poor clergy, but he was unsuccessful.

One of the big changes instigated by the reformed church was that parishioners should be educated and encouraged to pray for their own loved ones. It was therefore thought unnecessary to pay a priest to carry out this service and that statues could lead to idolatry. Logically, therefore, these chantries were regarded as unnecessary and possibly dangerous. Continuing with this line of thought, the far more wealthy fraternities were also unnecessary and their estates should be taken over by the Crown. Further enquiries during the early years of Edward's reign led to the complete closure and confiscation of them all. Where it had been found that the richer chantries or fraternities included a charitable (usually educational) clause in their foundation, arrangements were made for it to continue.

Planning for the Future

Edward appears to have agreed completely with his advisors' wish to reform the church, but apart from this, his five-and-a-half years on the throne must have been very unhappy. His health deteriorated and his Council quarrelled bitterly amongst themselves.

The Council's main concern was, once more, for the succession. It was obvious that Edward would not live long enough to take over the kingdom. According to Henry's dying instructions, Mary was next in line for the throne. If that happened, the total Reformation package would collapse. It was known that Protestant Elizabeth would never go against her father's wishes and lead a revolt against her elder sister, but there were several Protestant second cousins. John Dudley, Earl of Warwick (later Duke of Northumberland) who had succeeded to the role of Protector, had decided to manipulate the young Lady Jane Grey as his preferred candidate for the throne. In an endeavour to retain control over the country, he arranged her marriage to his son, Lord Guildford Dudley.

While the young king drifted in and out of consciousness, the Duke of Northumberland encouraged him to nominate Lady Jane Grey as his heir, for the good of the Protestant church. Edward eventually died on 6th July 1553 and Jane was proclaimed queen.

Queen Mary (1553–1558)

Daughter of the devout Roman Catholic Catherine of Aragon, Mary was in no doubt that it was her duty to become queen, to use her royal powers to restore the church of Rome and re-open the monasteries and nunneries as quickly as possible. She therefore refused the invitation to be at Edward's bedside, withdrew from her castle at Hunsden, Hertfordshire and by the time of his death had already joined her Roman Catholic friends and supporters. It soon became obvious that attempts to enthrone Jane were bound for failure and she was abandoned by both her own father and her father-in-law. Mary rode into London on 3rd August, accompanied by her sister Elizabeth and her once step-mother, Anne of Cleeves. They were received with general rejoicing and having appointed a new Council, Mary gradually began her policy to restore the 'old religion'. Jane and her husband were kept reasonably comfortably within the Tower and initially Mary was prepared to accept that Jane's role had been one of a puppet for her ambitious father.

Mary's advisors assured her that the Roman Church could never be peacefully restored while there was a Protestant figurehead who could be manipulated by other resurgents. Jane and her husband were eventually executed on the 12th February 1554 and on the 25th July Mary fulfilled her great ambition to marry Philip of Spain. This was against the recommendation of many of her advisors and was very unpopular in the country.

Her health began to suffer, Philip spent ever-increasing long periods in Spain and she became increasingly suspicious of her advisors, even her sister Elizabeth. After five difficult and unhappy years she died on 17th November 1558.

Queen Elizabeth (1558–1603)

Elizabeth was at Hatfield when Mary died. Three days later, 20th November, the Councillors arrived from London and met in the Great Hall with many noblemen who had travelled from miles around. She appointed her Privy Council carefully, including some who had supported her sister Mary and made Protestant William Cecil her Secretary of State, charging them all to take great pains for her and for her realm. Most of them must have been hoping and praying that, with the coronation of this new young queen, the horrific burnings of Mary's reign would come to an end. With the best of intentions, Elizabeth's family had handed down to her a divided country.

Elizabeth appealed to them all, according to their degree and power, to be of assistance to her, so that together they could make a good account to Almighty God. It was a moving and encouraging speech and when Elizabeth set out for London in three days' time, she was accompanied by over a thousand people. She received a rapturous welcome and everyone awaited her coronation. Mary was buried with full Catholic rites on 14th December and the Latin mass (with some parts read in English) continued as the only official legal service. Although it was known that Elizabeth was still attending mass, it was anticipated that there would soon be a change in legislation. The news that she had challenged the Roman ritual within her own chapel on Christmas Day soon spread across London, giving further encouragement to her Protestant subjects, but the young queen knew she must move very carefully.

She had only been two-and-a-half when her mother, Anne Boleyn, was executed and nine when the same happened to her step-mother, Catherine Howard. During her twenty-five years, other members of her family, friends and servants had suffered the same or even worse fates. Intelligent and educated, she was aware of the waves of fear, mistrust and even revolts that had followed each new atrocity. She herself had been declared illegitimate by her father and, many years later, by her brother. Her sister had sent armed soldiers out to Ashridge House to arrest her and, despite her ill-health, had taken her to London where she had been imprisoned in the Tower. Although not in the dungeon and only there for a month, Elizabeth never forgot the fear, isolation and sense of helplessness she felt during that time.

Land enclosure and difficult weather conditions were still causing great poverty and distress, vagrancy was on the increase and the country would not be easy to govern. Determined as she was to bring back Edward's Protestant church, she must be careful to avoid any violent objections which could escalate into a revolt. She was also aware that there were still distant relations who could be used as figureheads to lead organised rebellion.

The overriding principle of religion that she wanted to introduce was that men and women were responsible for their own salvation and could build up their faith by reading the scriptures and hearing them expounded by reformed preachers. This would mean that there would have to be an increase in the number of educated clergy who were able to both preach and teach. However, she had no intention of removing the authority of the bishops and archbishops, thus allowing the selection and appointment of clergy to slip into the hands of local lay people. Nor was she about to allow people to absent themselves from their parish church if they disapproved of the teaching of their minister or were unlucky enough to have a minister who was unable to preach.

Apart from the many influential families who might resist the break with Rome, Elizabeth was aware that there were others who might soon be opposing her. Across the country there was a growing number of 'dissenters' who would like to see the Protestant Church reformed or even replaced by a locally-based, more spontaneous form of worship. Neither she nor her ministers wanted to enforce the Protestant Church by an undercover search for dissenters of either persuasion, followed by the burning of heretics, so a national church into which the moderates of both sides could be accommodated was introduced. Although some things from the medieval church were retained, it was a reformed Protestant body in doctrine and everything moved forward with care. Five Protestants who had previously lost their seats in the House of Lords were re-instated and the Roman Catholic bishops were replaced by Protestants. Before the first Parliament closed, a slightly amended Book of Common Prayer and Articles (as first introduced by King Edward) was part of the national form of worship. Protestant dissenters (extremists) were tolerated, provided they regularly attended their parish churches and did nothing to disturb the services. Roman Catholic families who kept their own household chaplains, disguised as Latin teachers, were fined but never tortured. However, Roman Catholics coming in from overseas were seen as a potential threat to the throne. When priests from France were known to be moving secretly around the country in 1580, there was a period when, once again, men were declared heretics, accused of treason, tortured and hung for their faith.

The Queen Receives Proposals of Marriage

Something else that Elizabeth witnessed as a young girl was the rivalry and bitterness which sprang up between families when one or another became related to the reigning monarch. She had also witnessed the unhappiness and often uselessness of political marriages, made with partners from overseas. One after another, suitors were introduced and, for various reasons (often connected with religion), she cheerfully or sadly sent one after another on their way.

Mary Queen of Scots

One of the most worrying and distressing of the different problems which Elizabeth had to solve was that of her relative, Mary Stuart. There were political and religious as well as humane reasons as to why she should or should not have come to Mary's aid while she was still in Scotland. When Mary took refuge in England in 1568, the eyes of the world were upon her as Elizabeth was forced to make impossible difficult decisions. In Scotland (as in other countries), people were divided as to whether Mary had been implicated in the murder of her husband. There were also issues concerning religion and Elizabeth was frequently reminded that Mary might be seen as a contender for her own throne.

For six years she waited, took advice and watched the political situation in Scotland and elsewhere. When at last she was presented with proof that Mary really had been involved in a plot against her, Elizabeth ordered her execution. It is said that even then she sent a message to withdraw the order, but that it arrived too late.

The End of a Tumultuous Century

Elizabeth's support of the Protestants in the Netherlands, the Portugese and her execution of Mary, Queen of Scots, led to fighting with Spain. The glorious success of the Armada and other less spectacular victories united rather than divided the country. The discoveries of the explorers such as Sir Walter Raleigh would open new trade routes and markets, so that a century which opened under the strong dynamic rule of King Henry VII witnessed the unbelievable changes brought about by his son and grandchildren, ended with the peace and prosperity brought about his youngest granddaughter.

Part Two
Dunstable in the Sixteenth Century

A New Roof for the Priory Church

As far as the people of Dunstable were concerned, this century opened as the previous one had closed – the need to raise money to pay for the new roof of the Priory Church! The strong economy which supported their home and overseas trading plus the rapidly increasing travel market, probably made this a suitable time for such an ambitious project. At that time the roof was nearly twenty feet higher that it is today and there were clerestory windows below the roof line. The major scheme was to lower the roof and to insert windows into what had been the triforium openings.* Work of this proportion also involved redesigning the western gable end. It is not known who carried out all this work, but it could have been a team brought together by a master mason from the Totternhoe quarry.

---

* Well-illustrated details of the scheme can be found in the Priory Church booklet written by John Lunn and with important new photographs by Omer Roucoux.

Once the Dunstablians realised that the time had come to have an entirely new roof they probably took time to seek advice and to learn what others had done in similar situations. Earlier in the century, a major restoration of St. Albans Abbey involved lowering a roof, adding new windows and giving a new illuminated aspect to the buildinig. They completed the work with twenty angel busts, each supported on a bracket along the line where the new roof rested. Ten of the angels had crossed hands and ten were holding shields.

It is likely that this great piece of work may have inspired the Dunstable businessmen, as when their work was finished they also paid to have carved wooden figures mounted in similar positions.

The Wooden Carvings in the Roof

The fourteen carvings are twenty-seven inches (700mm) high and twelve inches (300mm) wide. From floor level it was apparent that they were not angels, but when photographer Omer Roucoux managed to get close enough to take detailed pictures, it was obvious that they were not canons either. All but two two of the effigies (portraying secular gentlemen) are attired in ankle-length tunics covered by cloaks and are holding shields, one of which sports the earliest version of the Dunstable arms yet discovered.*

Who Are the Figures Carved in the Roof?

It is known that the parishioners raised the money for the new roof and among the surviving wills of the period, both John Hudley and Nicholas Purvey (whose families were connected with the Fraternity) each left £2 towards the project. Our knowledge of the period suggests that it could only have been a group from the Fraternity who undertook such a complex and expensive undertaking.

It would therefore seem likely that at least ten of the figures

---

*   These figures are illustrated in the booklet 'Mediaeval Carved Wooden Figures in the Roof of the Church'.

in the roof represent their committee, the two figures differing in dimension and dress *perhaps* representing the schoolmaster and one of his pupils?

The Fraternity Register

Surviving wills illustrate the wealth of a group of Dunstable residents, while surviving pages from the Fraternity's register, which was kept on a yearly basis, shows the group to be quite large. Its members came not only from all over Bedfordshire and Hertfordshire, but also from places where the Dunstable merchants traded – the most distant being the port of Hull.

The Register pages for 1506–1508 and 1522–1541 are housed in Luton Museum. There are eighty-three parchment leaves and most years open with a page which has a wide gold border filled in by a professional illuminator, with capital letters in either blue or red also usually being filled in, but sometimes overlooked and still blank today. The illustrations include miniature portraits of the officers and their wives, while on one page is a picture of their patron saint, St. John the Baptist, with his severed head and his emblem (the lamb of God) being portrayed on other pages.

The year 1506 began with an introductory sentence:

> 'Thes ben the namis of the brethren and sisters made in the tyme of Master William Grene president of this fraternite of Saint John baptist. Wardenyns of the same fraternite In the yer of owre Lorde god' 1506.

It is possible that the pages 1509–1521 are not missing but that the Fraternity was so desperate to raise the money for the roof, that they decided to save money on scribes and illuminators. 1522 starts with the sentence:

'This boke was newe made in the vigill of Seynt John baptist at mydsomer in the yere of oure lorde god'.

Familiar Dunstable names such as Burr, Bennett, Fossey, Peddar and Crawley were included in the register, as were the prior, sub-prior and various canons.

The Fayrey Pall

One of the wealthy Fraternity families was the Fayreys. John (a member of the Mercer's Company in London) owned property in Dunstable and may have originally opened the White Hart in High Street North. A brass in the Priory Church commemorating the lives of John's parents, Henry and Agnes Fayrey, and dated 1515, is now in the Victoria and Albert Museum.

John himself commissioned an extremely beautiful and valuable rich red velvet funeral pall (coffin cover), with dark purple sides, all richly embroidered. Although it is thought to have originated in Florence, the embroidered panels were added in England, as while the illuminators and embroiderers could have been connected with the priory, both craftsmen and women are known to have travelled around the country taking commissions for their specialist work.

Gold (silver gilt) threads and brilliantly-coloured silks were used to portray the elaborate clothes and headdresses and the two identical long-side panels feature a number of figures. In the centre of each panel is the depiction of St. John the Baptist, standing on a small mound of rocks and grass and wearing a short gold tunic and gold cloak lined with red silk, a halo above his head. He appears to be preaching, his hand raised in benediction, to a group of fourteen men, led by a figure identified as Henry Fayrey facing him on his right and thirteen women led by Agnes Fayrey on his left. It is assumed that the other figures are members of the Fraternity. The two shorter sides are not identical. At one end John the Baptist is standing preaching while at the other he is kneeling in prayer, while John and Mary Fayrey kneel facing him.

When the Fraternity was closed the pall was lost, but in 1891 it was returned to the care of the rector of the Priory Church. For many years it was known as the 'best' pall and hired out at 6d (2.5p) per funeral. In living memory it was displayed in a glass case in the church but eventually the Parochial Church Council realised that it was at risk and for safety it was given to the Victoria and Albert Museum, where it is on permanent loan.

Dunstable During the Reign of Henry VII

In the 13th–14th centuries Dunstable was a leading trading and wholesaling centre dominated by the Priory, while in the 18th–19th centuries it was a well-known travel centre with the businessmen running their own affairs, in consultation with the representatives of the Crown. Changes were beginning to take place during the reign of Henry VII:

1. as we have seen, the Fraternity was already taking over much of the control and organisation which had previously been the Priory's role;

2. although many of the members of the Fraternity were still traders and wholesalers (several dealing in wool and cloth), their businesses were so widespread that some of them had offices and warehouses in London, leaving gaps in Dunstable High Street which were quickly taken up by entrepreneurs in the travel industry.

Thomas Bently, who is described as 'Yeoman of the Crown' in contemporary documents, may have amassed his capital while serving in some administrative capacity. He was sufficiently rich and influential not only to persuade the Prior to sell him a prime site in North Street, where he built *The White Horse Inn* to such a high standard that it was suitable for Henry VIII to use on his journeys, but also in 1528 to become president of the Fraternity. His will indicates how well a high-class innkeeper would have dressed. In addition to his everyday clothes, there is mention of black satin doublets, a blue jerkin and gowns trimmed with velvet and lined with taffeta.

On the other side of the road, John Fayrey rented *The White Hart Inn* from the Prior. On the island of buildings in the middle of the road (known as Whites Lane), Richard Denton, warden of the Fraternity in 1528, rented a smaller house known as *The Lyon*. In South Street the Prior's bailiff, Adam Hilton (warden in 1525) may have already been renting *The Saracen's Head*.

However it was not only the innkeepers who made money. The presence of the Priory, the Fraternity and the high-class inns made it possible for musician Robert Foster to run a business large enough to warrant taking and training apprentices. There was also a great deal of work for blacksmiths, wheelwrights, saddlers and general workshops for those who could carry out quick repairs to damaged coaches, traces and leatherwork. Much money could be made by people prepared to risk their capital and hire out horses. Travellers changed horses every few miles; a 'postboy' (who worked for the owner) accompanied the customer and took the tired horse back to its stable, while the traveller continued on a fresh horse. Apart from the inns there was a great need for beer-houses. The above-mentioned *Lyon* (and *The Peacock* which stood nearby) may have been two of Dunstable's 'cookhouses' or restaurants.

We Can Actually See Portrayals of Some 16th Century Dunstablians

It is not always easy to find out about the population of a town in the early 16th century, but as has been noted above, in Dunstable we are particularly fortunate. *The Fraternity Register* gives us long lists of names with tiny portraits of some of them, the embroidery on the *Fayrey pall* gives the most careful portrayal of their formal clothes and illustrations of members of the Fayrey family and some of the senior members of the Fraternity. The *wooden carvings* which may be of a slightly later group, illustrate the different facial features and their marginally different gowns. These may be connected with their London companies or the robes which they wore when it had been their turn to be president or warden.

The surviving brasses sometimes show their features and clothes but at other times follow the fashion of portraying them in their shrouds! *The surviving wills* of this period also illustrate the wealth of some of these families. Thomas Anlaby had already set his sons up in business, provided generously for his wife in his will and was still able to provide each of his three daughters with a dowry which included enough furniture, linen and fittings for them to fit out a kitchen and bedroom at the time of their marriages.

87

Robert Dermere owned the small inn in the Middle Row called *The Cross Keys* and a neighbouring house, described as standing 'in the mid of the street against the Frerys [Friar's] gate . . .' This was probably a butcher's shop because he also owned a barn and a slaughterhouse at the back in Halwyke Lane.* He owned five other houses and had a 'tenture' at the west end of Dunstable. This was probably a yard or paddock where newly-milled or dyed cloth was stretched and weighted over wooden frames so that it dried flat and even. People of this financial background sent their children to school. Richard More instructed his wife to send his grandson to school and, later in the century, Elizabeth Ames provided for the education of her son William. The Fraternity chaplain, William Newton (who died in 1500), left one penny to each poor scholar. Because he lived in a house owned by the Fraternity, he does not mention property in his will, but was able to leave a generous amount of money and to pay for a most elaborate funeral.

There were many wealthy people living in Dunstable at this time and no doubt several of them helped in the organisation of national events and trade. Probably the most significant of these was George Cavendish, elder brother of William, who married Bess of Hardwick. In 1524 George's father died and he became an extremely wealthy young man. The following year he became President of the Fraternity and at some point married Margaret, widow of Richard Pinfold of East Street, whose brass is in the Priory Church. There are miniature portraits of George and Margaret in the register. Their two families came from nearby villages in Suffolk and he returned there after her death.

Circa 1520, George became a gentleman usher to Cardinal Wolsey, remaining loyal throughout his fall from popularity and writing the respected biography 'The Life and Death of Cardinal Wolsey'. He also built up a substantial agricultural estate in and around Dunstable and probably bought Kingsbury from the Prior as a suitable home for his family. When Wolsey died in 1530, King Henry offered Cavendish a position at court but (probably

---

*   Later known as Chapel Walk.

wisely) he chose to return home. Henry paid the wages he was owed and gave him a cart and six horses to bring his belongings back to Dunstable.*

Dunstable is Involved in the King's Weighty Cause

In the booklet 'Henry VIII's Dunstable' I described a theoretical visit which King Henry could have made to Dunstable. Royal progresses could involve the feeding and accommodating of up to two hundred people, in addition to the locals who came to the town as sightseers, entertainers, thieves and supplicants.

There is no written evidence that King Henry VII made any official visits to Dunstable, but his policies had helped the economy of the town and no doubt there was grieving at the time of his death. During the weeks that it took the young Henry to take over the country and marry his long-standing fiancée, the inns would have been hotbeds of gossip. As the years passed there would have been rejoicing at the successful birth of the Princess Mary and a sharing of the grief and concern on the death of the other babies. No doubt travellers, coming from Court, would have passed on the gossip concerning Henry's infatuation with the beautiful young lady-in-waiting, Anne Boleyn. They would have heard, grumbled and argued about the Pope's refusal to annul Henry's marriage to Catherine and probably considered themselves well-informed. However, it must have come as a great shock to learn that secretly Henry's friends and supporters were about to open a court of enquiry at the Priory. How soon they knew is pure conjecture, but the innkeepers must have been forewarned to reserve all their best beds well before 10th May 1533, the day that the enquiry opened. Henry himself did not stay in the town – in fact the story had been spread that he knew nothing about it. Catherine, on the other hand, had been asked to give evidence. She refused and spent the time before, during and after the enquiry under house arrest at Ampthill Castle.

---

* This research was carried out by John Lunn and appeared in Bedfordshire Magazine Vol. 26 No. 207.

Prior Markham acted as host and possibly chairman, the newly-appointed Archbishop of Canterbury, Thomas Cranmer, controlled the discussion and steered it in the way that he intended it to go. The main members of the panel were the Bishops of London, Winchester and Bath. However, there were other powerful observers and witnesses staying in the town, as well as large numbers of clerks, scribes, grooms and personal servants.

Events had moved quickly during the preceding year. One part of the preparation was that the clergy had been presented with a document setting out that in future church court legislation should (as with the secular courts) require the King's approval and would derive this authority from the sovereignty of the King. The other part was that a deputation visited Catherine (already at Ampthill) on 9th April to notify her that Henry had now 'married' Anne, who was pregnant!

The court assembled in the Lady Chapel of the Priory Church (i.e. the eastern end) on Thursday 8th May and on the 9th messengers rode to Ampthill to request that Catherine should attend the enquiry. She refused and on the Saturday afternoon, the first full meeting was held. The Bishops of Lincoln and Winchester were present, but not 'Master' Bryan or the Duchess of Norfolk, who had accompanied her husband and Bryan* to confront Catherine with the news. Nor was Lady Guilford. As one or two other necessary witnesses were also absent, the meeting was postponed until Wednesday. A letter dispatched by the clerk after this abandoned meeting hoped that, as a result of later meetings, 'the matter shall [should] succede according to the King's expectations'.

Throughout the next day, the full assembly and their servants probably took part in the various public services. By this time the news of Henry's 'marriage' was public knowledge and whoever took the services would have had to make the embarrassing decision of whether to pray for the soul of one queen, while the other was living just a few miles up the road!

---

*   Sir Francis Bryan was the King's steward at Ampthill and was involved in the plans to annul the marriage from the very beginning.

By Monday morning Bryan had arrived and it was decided not to wait for the two ladies. A commission was sent to gather evidence from London.* That night the clerk wrote that Cranmer had 'handled himself well and very uprightly without eny evydent cause of suspicion to be noted in him'. Cranmer wrote secretly to King Henry that as Catherine had refused to attend despite, as Mr Bryan had witnessed, receiving a full explanation of the circumstances and need for the enquiry, he hoped to finish more quickly than planned.

There are no records of further meetings until the Friday when general business was covered. Then on Saturday 17th May the king's representative, Dr Trygonnell, was invited to speak and a call was made requiring any representative of Queen Catherine to identify themselves – no one came forward. Finally the written evidence was examined.

Once again the clerk's letter to Cromwell gives away the deceit of the enquiry. Writing in advance he states that Cranmer *will*** notify the king's representative to attend on Friday 23rd May 'when sentence will be given** in the king's favour'. Cranmer wrote to Cromwell bringing him up to date with the proceedings, congratulating himself on the success of the enquiry so far, but warning him to keep matters secret for the time being. He wrote:

> For if the noble lady Catherine should – [hear rumours of]
> this matter in the mouths of the inhabitants [of Dunstable]
> or, by her friends or council hearing – a great bruit
> [clamour] and voice of the people in this behalf [might stir
> her to delay the court] which peradventure [she would]
> not do if she shall here [hear] little of it.

Needless to say, master-minded by Cranmer, everythng proceeded as planned. There was one last short meeting on the Friday which, according to the clerk, ended at 10am. Sentence of divorce was then given in open court.

The clerk must have immediately rushed a letter off to

---

*   It appears the these two ladies were actually trying to avoid the court
      because they were both loyal to Catherine.
**   The italics are mine, not in the original letter.

Cromwell, arranging for the messengers to travel 'post', changing to fresh horses at St. Albans and Barnet.

Cranmer himself wrote a more formal letter to King Henry:

Please yt yow highness to be advertised that this 23rd day of this present month of May, I have given sentence in your Grace's great and weighty cause . . .

The letter goes on for several sentences, including a reference to the second marriage and a request to know the king's pleasure concerning 'the same matrimony' and 'the time of the coronation'. It was signed and dated 'From Dunstaple the 23rd day of May [1533]'. So it was over; gradually the bishops and officials rode away leaving the people of Dunstable to return to their usual routines. Catherine was moved from Ampthill to Buckden and then on to Kimbolton, where she died in 1536*.

Henry Became Head of the Church – in England

The decision to defy the Pope and decide the king's 'weighty cause' in Dunstable was a public declaration that England was no longer a member of the Roman Catholic Church. The break was tidied and made formal by an Act of Parliament in 1534. Shortly after this, clerks came to Dunstable (as well as to every other town and village) requesting all the civil officers, the clergy and all the various monks to sign and witness their loyalty to Queen Anne and accepting Henry as head of the church.

Royal Visits Continue

Back in 1508, Henry VII had obtained the castle and the great hunting park at Ampthill. Henry VIII loved hunting and travelled to Ashridge and Ampthill as often as possible. Another reason for his frequent journeys was that he had a great fear of infectious diseases. Without fully understanding the cause of the infection, he did know that, by the end of the summer, London was a dangerous place to

---

* A booklet by Mr John Lunn, containing these letters is on sale at the Priory Church. It is of interest that within these letters Dunstable is spelt both with a 'b' and a 'p'.

stay. He would make a circular tour towards one of his hunting parks and once safely settled there with his house-party, would remain partially isolated. Official visitors would be kept waiting in Dunstable or in Ampthill town to prove that they were not carrying infection.

Although there is no record of Catherine actually staying in Dunstable, she probably did rest at the Priory. Henry himself had taken Anne Boleyn to Ampthill the year before her marriage, but Princess Elizabeth was born in September 1533 and by September 1534 Henry was in love with Jane Seymour! Once more there was turmoil in the court. Henry married Jane in 1536, but she was not able to accompany him in 1537 as she was resting at Windsor prior to the birth of Prince Edward. This was the visit when Henry broke with the royal custom of staying at the Priory. Early in August Prior Markham heard that the royal party was on the road travelling north and hastily ordered the suite of royal rooms to be prepared, only to discover, to his horror, that when the King's steward rode into the town to make the final preparations, he rode straight past the Priory on his way to visit Thomas Bentley at the White Horse Inn. The possible reason for this was that Henry's policy to close the religious houses was well under way and it was feared that Markham may have embarrassed the monarch with a confrontational argument.

Markham quickly wrote a letter and sent it back along the road to Archbishop Cranmer, begging him to speak to the King to assure him that the Prior's humble rooms were at his disposal. If, however, the King chose not to use them, the Prior hoped that Cranmer himself would stay with him.

Henry and his party stayed in Dunstable on the nights of Thursday 9th and Friday 10th August, then hurried on to Ampthill where he stayed for six days, before riding on to another hunting park at Grafton Regis, returning to Dunstable for the weekend of 1st and 2nd September. Whether he went hawking on Dunstable Downs on these occasions is not recorded, but it is known that he enjoyed the sport.

After this visit Henry was frequently in or around Dunstable. One well-recorded stay was in September 1543 when he was travelling with his last wife, Jane Howard and Catherine's daughter, the twenty-seven year old Princess Mary, whose expenses records have survived. As they arrived at the entrance to the town they were welcomed by the Prior and probably the president and officers of the Fraternity. Princess Mary left a purse of money which was to be distributed to:

The King's Boys (choirboys)	7s.6d (38p)
The King's Minstrels	£1.5s.6d. (£1.27)
The Officers at the Threshold	£4
The Escort Guard	£4.14s.10d (£4.74)

The last in the list were probably members of the militia and volunteers dressed up for the occasion, while the 'officers' may have been senior members of the Fraternity who would have received 'alms' on behalf of the town's charities. The first two entries, however, suggest that with the town receiving so many royal visits, small sums of money were given to the Prior to ensure that the king was provided with good music during his visits.

Dunstable's Loyalty to Catherine and Mary?

Although it is most unlikely that the results of the great enquiry in 1533 were ever pinned on the church door, quite accurate 'leaks' must have spread through the town on a daily basis. Nationally people backed Catherine rather than the unpopular Anne Boleyn. The only information that survives about feelings in Dunstable is that Catherine was supported by the influential George Cavendish and that the clerk who was keeping the Fraternity Register, felt unable to completely obey the royal command to remove her name from their register and replace it with Anne's. At the top of the prayer list he erased Catherine's name but then left the resulting space blank. He left her badge of the split pomegranate undamaged, in its original place in the margin.

The Marian Pillars
Over the vestry door on the north side of the High Altar in the church today are ten beautiful wooden banisters, each with different motifs carved all round. Rails at the top and bottom link

them together to form a screen. Although they are thought to date from the reign of Queen Mary (1553–58), the split pomegranate and other symbols of Queen Catherine can be seen clearly. It has been suggested that they were placed in the church (in some other position) by order of Queen Mary when she was trying to restore Roman Catholicism. However it has been noted that the Fraternity had recently used a most excellent wood-carver to complete their restoration work. *Maybe* when Catherine's grown-up daughter made her first formal visit to the town, the carving of these discreetly loyal rails was ordered to in some way atone for the fact that the town had played host to the annulment of her mother's marriage, leaving her illegitimate.

The Dissolution of the Dominican Friary

Not a great deal is recorded about the friars but it is known that:
1. They were greatly respected not only across the county but also in distant places.
2. They received frequent gifts from kings, queens, church officials and lay-people, both rich and poor.
3. That because of their own responsibilities, the canons were very jealous of this popularity and financial support.
4. With financial help from Edward III they were able to host a three-day Provincial Chapter from 15th–18th August 1332.
5. One wealthy lady buried at their Church of St. Mary has been mentioned above. In 1344 Hawise, wife of Sir Richard Hoo, was also buried there. It is known that builders disturbed skeletons in the graveyard and that archaeologists uncovered a lead coffin and twenty-two skeletons.*

They must have been prepared for closure in 1536, when orders were given to close the small houses, but later the friaries were exempt and they survived until 1538. As they did not bring a dower to their house, friars were not paid pensions, so it is impossible to trace them, but no doubt they found jobs and support amongst their families and friends.

---

* For the history and archaeological report by the Manshead Archaeological Society, see their magazine, number 16.

The Dissolution of the Augustinian Priory

There was no single Act of Parliament ordering the closure of the larger religious houses. Depending on the seniority, character and ability of their leaders, they gradually made plans and negotiated terms. Together with a handful of the biggest and most powerful in the country, the Priory held out to the very end. Markham surrendered his house on 31st December 1539 and it was officially closed on 20th January 1540, by which time he had not only made plans for himself but also for his canons. He retired to a small house in South Street where he remained until he died in September 1561 and was then buried at the Priory. He had received a pension of £60 per year, while the canons had much smaller sums. However, as they were all ordained, most soon found jobs as clergymen.

Dunstable After 1540

The names of some of the canons, the jobs which they found and a complete survey of the town in 1542 is included in the book 'Dunstable with the Priory, 1100–1550'.*

The Dominican Friary

As soon as he could after the closure, Robert Ingworth, Bishop of Dover, rode into Dunstable to supervise the removal of the church roof and the start of the demolition of the domestic buildings. He was also supposed to check that any precious metals from the altar plus all the lead from the windows and roof were carefully packed on carts to be sent to the official collectors in London. However, when he wrote to Thomas Cromwell he admitted that he had arrived too late, that some of the valuables had been stolen before he arrived and other pieces had been taken in lieu of outstanding debts. On 8th May 1539 Thomas Bentley of the White Horse signed an agreement to rent the site of the friary 'with all buildings, gardens, orchards, lands and

---

*   Evans, V. published by The Book Castle 1994.

grounds within [the] site and precincts of same House—' and agreed to pay £2.4s.8d a year for the next twenty years.

It is probable that he intended to convert the site and damaged buildings into a stable yard and paddocks. It had different uses over the centuries; at one time it was known locally as 'the Butts' and may have been used for training the militia. Part of the land was still used for grazing within living memory and the site managed to resist the increasing pressure for building land until the 1980s.

However, Bentley did not acquire all the buildings. Evidence appeared that William Marshall, a wealthy Bedfordshire land-owner had become a type of corody-holder at the Friary. Tenant might be a better description, except that he was probably responsible for the conversion of the buildings which became his 'retirement home'.

He had died just before the drawing up of the rent list so that his heirs (his daughter and her husband, Roger Lee) were responsible for the rent. Geoffrey Chamber, the king's accountant, separated this property from the rest of the friary and it was described as:

'a kitchen near the friars' kitchen plus a great chamber, two small chambers and a stable standing together as one block just inside the main gate'.

These rooms stood somewhere near the Square and were probably made of Totternhoe stone. Two centuries later they were still referred to as 'the Marshalls' Lodging'.

A Cathedral for Dunstable?
Although by the middle of January the canons had all departed, Dunstable was one of the few priories which had not been instantly destroyed. It had long been realised that the diocese of Lincoln was far too large and difficult to administer. The Priory with its grand and well-maintained church sitting on two main roads with access to both, was in an ideal position to become a new cathedral.

Priory House
Because of the delay, Richard Greenway, Usher of the King's

Chamber, was made 'Keeper' of the 'mansion, chief messuage and gardens'. This probably means Priory House and the great courtyard with its barns, stables and other buildings. Detailed estimates were made for the new bishopric but the money slipped away and the plans were abandoned. Had Queen Mary lived longer she might have tried to have the buildings repaired and the Priory re-opened. She let the mansion and grounds to Sir Leonard Chamberlain – one of her key supporters. As it was, the buildings crumbled and local people stole a vast amount of the stone. Eventually the mansion and grounds were put up for sale and were purchased by two Dunstable innkeepers, one of whom was Henry Bennell. Richard and Elizabeth Ames [or Aves] bought it soon afterwards, but this may have been a family arrangement. When widow Elizabeth Ames made her will in 1590 she referred to her daughter, Elizabeth and son-in-law, Roland Bennett. Her daughter Agnes and son-in-law, Richard Pudsey, were to receive [the use of] for four years 'two parts of *the site of the late monasterie or priory* of Dunstable' and of the five-acre Duff [Dove] House Close and double duff house adjoining the Priory. They were to use the profits from the two parts of this valuable asset to care for and educate her young son, William. The third part was 'to remain to the queens majesty during the minority of the said son William'.

This may have been a way of ensuring that Queen Elizabeth's officers cared for William's education and future prospects. She describes the house in which she is living (possibly Priory House) as having a big, well-furnished hall open to the roof with a central fireplace and hanging cooking pots. It was lined with expensive wainscot, as was the parlour, but the master bedroom, over the parlour, was lined with painted cloths (wall-hangings).

The Priory Church of St. Peter

Because the people of Dunstable had for several centuries supported and repaired their section of the church, it was transferred to the people of the town. It has continued ever since as the parish church of Dunstable.

The Rectory, the Church Land and Great Tithes

When the priory closed, the bailiff, Adam Hilton, agreed to pay 13s.9d per year for the use of the church land with 'all tithes of corn and hay and fees connected with the cemetery'.

Lordship of the Manor and Profit from the Fairs

In addition to the use of the church lands, Adam Hilton also rented this position on the agreement to pay £7 per year for the profit which he expected to make from the market, fairs and manor court. He paid an extra £1 per year for the tolls from the market.

The Almonry of St. John the Baptist

Nothing more is heard of the almonry which was behind [west of] the market running back towards West Street. The Almshouse which belonged to the Fraternity was in the same area but described as 'West Street'. This may be a re-building of the same charity house. In addition, after the closing of the Priory, a house further up West Street was provided for the use of the parish.

Kingsbury

It has been assumed that George Cavendish had bought this estate from the Prior before the Dissolution, as it does not appear in the rent-list. After the death of his wife, Cavendish returned to Suffolk and nothing more is heard about the history of this house until after 1600.

Ownership of the Town

Although Hilton had the right to administer the town, it was actually owned by King Henry and as such it became part of the great scattered royal estate known as the Honour of Ampthill. In most cases the king's steward was anxious to convert these properties into cash and several of the Dunstable businesses were rapidly sold. However, parts of the town remained in royal possession until 1870.

The Reign of Edward VI

From later evidence it would seem likely that the parishioners of Dunstable welcomed the English Bible and Book of Common

Prayer, but they may not have welcomed the closing of the Fraternities. The officers and members of St. John the Baptist had played such an important part in building up the prosperity of the town and were undoubtedly helping fellow member, Adam Hilton, to keep it running smoothly. Nevertheless it was closed, as was the Houghton Regis chantry. There was no reference to a Dunstable school* but the Houghton School in East [Church] Street where John Couper was teaching 'VI pore folkes children' was allowed to continue.

The Reign of Queen Mary

The death of the sad young king was kept secret for the first few days to give more time for the 'wheelers and dealers' to carry out their plans. Although most of the action then took place in East Anglia, the various pieces of news probably reached the Dunstable inns remarkably quickly. It seems likely that the people of Dunstable would have been very anxious to learn if Roman Catholic Mary or Protestant Jane would be their next queen. In May 1533, the annulment of Henry's first marriage was followed by the break with Rome and from then on, changes came with increasing rapidity. As they waited to hear who would become their next queen, they may have looked round their town with wonderment.

The Start of the 'Modern' Town

The Augustinian canons, whose institution had been part of the town for over four hundred years, had gone. The Priory buildings were empty and crumbling and the great courtyard and Priory hostel [House] were in private ownership. Across South Street, the Dominican friars had also left, their large and imposing church of St. Mary had been taken down and the buildings around their gate were now (or would soon become) an inn, with the domestic buildings either demolished or being used as stables. In West Street the Fraternity's meeting house, chaplain's house

---

* What may have been the Priory school in South Street was probably kept going by a private teacher.

and possibly almonry were also in private hands and had become dwellings or small businesses. In East Street, the Houghton Chantry School did remain, but the house where their priests once lived had become an inn, known as *The King's Head* (later *The White Horse*). The original inn which once stood on the site of *The Bull* (North Street) may also have been established at this time. It was probably built on land previously owned by the chantry and its original name was *The Prince's Arms*.

Amidst all these changes, the Priory Church of St. Peter still stood proudly looking out over the town. Inside, the rood and rood cross had been taken down as had the one or two statues. The Bible chained to the lectern was in English and the service was now based on the Book of Common Prayer, but nevertheless, the church itself still stood as a sign of stability in a changing world. God was still waiting to welcome the people of the town and passers-by.

Dunstable Without Priory or Fraternity

Until the 15th century Dunstable had been dominated by the Prior and his staff. From the mid 15th century, members of the Fraternity had helped and gradually taken over responsibility for organising town life. By the time that Queen Mary came to the throne, both had been closed.

Parish Responsibility

Travellers brought not only money into the town but also problems. The care of the roads had traditionally been a manorial responsibility. As part of the agricultural routine, the Prior's steward had sent men out to fill the pot-holes and break up the stones. New landowners across the country were not always doing this. As more people travelled, the roads deteriorated by no one accepted responsibility for mending them. A new form of administration had to be found.

Legislation instigated during Queen Mary's reign not only provided a new way of repairing the roads but also introduced a new system of *Parish Responsibility*. Parish officers, backed by the magistrates at the Quarter Sessions would form a national network. Men elected at the parish meeting would take over from the Fraternity. In Dunstable these were probably members of the same families.

Repairing the Roads

Two men known as *Surveyors* or stone wardens were elected at the Easter vestry to supervise the parish roads for the next twelve months. It was their job to identify the most urgent work and supervise its completion. It was intended that materials were donated from local sources, while the Act provided labour by making it compulsory for every man to work for four days each year on the roads of his parish.

In Dunstable, with its four main roads, this was only partially successful. At Houghton Regis, with a network of local roads plus several main roads and Puddlehill, it was impossible.

Caring for Poor Travellers

Back in 1536 it had been ordered that a collection should be made after church on Sunday to help to support the poor of the parish. The church wardens would then distribute this money as they thought best. During Edward's reign this was strengthened by instructing ministers to include a plea for charity in their Sunday sermons.

These measures might have been successful in Dunstable – had it not been for the poor and sick travellers. Throughout the centuries, distressed people had made for Dunstable, squatting around the town and seeking help from the Priory. They still came but now there was no almoner to aid them. If the church wardens used the alms collected in the church, nothing would remain for the townspeople.

Poverty Becomes Even More Serious

The Sunday collections were both unpopular and unsuccessful so at last the new parochial network was implemented. In 1572 it was decided that collectors or *guardians* should be appointed at the Easter vestry and empowered to collect *poor rates*. Each person's property was valued, the guardians would assess the money needed and then balance it by their calculation of the poor rate. It was a thankless task and the guardians were trapped between those who claimed to pay too much and those who felt that they did not receive sufficient support. Their position was made even worse in Dunstable, as the town collection had to help not only local people fallen on hard times but also visitors passing through the town.

Some relief came to Dunstable in 1601 when it was established that a pauper's birthplace was his/her true 'home' and that if he/she became destitute, he/she should be removed to that parish. However this was very difficult to administer and even more difficult to carry out.

The Roads Continue to Deteriorate

The road improvements of 1555 had not been successful and in 1563 the four days spent working on the roads were increased to six. Despite the fact that this was backed up by more strict legislation, it was still not successful, so in 1575 it was decided to use a 'property value assessment' to levy a *road rate*.

Queen Elizabeth – 'the Most Illustrious of Tourists'*

Queen Elizabeth moved about her kingdom even more than some of her predecessors. There were no religious houses where she could receive free accommodation, so she chose to 'invite' herself to stay at many different country houses instead of staying at inns. As she travelled with a party of at least a hundred and fifty people, even the newly-built Toddington manor house (which she visited in 1563) could not have housed her entire retinue, many of whom must have lodged in Dunstable. Woburn, which she chose to visit in 1572, was not really prepared for a royal visit, so again some of the party may have waited in Dunstable.

---

*   Tinniswood, A. A History of Country House Visiting.

The First Sign of Religious Dissent

As has been noted in the first chapter, Queen Elizabeth had tried to make the national church suitable for moderates. There is no evidence that either the clergy or the people of Dunstable behaved in any way which as likely to cause offence but during the first few years of the following reign, we will find the the minister at the Priory, John Richardson, was in trouble for refusing to conform.

Merry England!

Queen Elizabeth died three years into the next century. The upheavals which took place during the reign of her father and brother were long past, the town had settled down again and was moving forward. We will find in the next century that it was the innkeepers who had come forward as leaders and organisers and that the town was ready to receive the great rush of travellers which would build up in the years to come.

Chapter VII

The World Turned Upside-Down, 1603–1688

Detail from the hunting scene painted c.1600 now on the wall of the Nationwide Building Society, High Street North.

Overview

This century has to be divided into four quite separate sections:*

1. The first two Stuart kings, *James I* and *Charles I* ruled (as they thought they should) on the assumption that they had been appointed by God. They ignored the customs of England, which went back before the Norman Conquest and had been written down in the 13th century as the Magna Carta.

2. For many different reasons a large section of Parliament (backed by many of the great landowners) rose in battle against their king. During the *Civil War* Oliver Cromwell rose to Lieutenant General.

3. After the war *Oliver Cromwell* refused to allow his supporters to make him king but eventually accepted the title of *Lord Protector*. A wise and intelligent man, his years in control were marred by royalist sympathisers on the one hand and extreme radicals on the other.

When he died in 1658 there was no logical successor waiting to take over. Although his son Richard was persuaded to accept the title, he was grateful for the chance to resign less than a year later.

4. By this time some of the families who were strong supporters of Parliament realised that the time had come to restore the monarchy, so the late king's son was brought back to England and proclaimed *Charles II*. He made his entry into London on the 29th May 1660, his thirtieth birthday. With him came many of his royalist friends and supporters, who had shared his exile. Some of these had once held positions of authority and before the country could settle down there were breaches to be healed and old scores to be settled.

Things did eventually settle and ran reasonably smoothly for many years. However, just as in the 1630s, the country was divided by matters of religion. In a country which prided itself on its Protestant form of religion, Charles married Roman Catholic Henrietta Maria of France. What was even worse, having no

---

* The fifth section of the century, William and Mary, has been held over to Chapter 8.

surviving children, Charles' heir was his brother James, also a Roman Catholic, Charles died in 1685 and his brother was crowned *James II*.

Although Charles had no legitimate children, he had a much-loved illegitimate son to whom he had given the title Duke of Monmouth. Having been loosely and innocently involved in an attack against Charles and James, he had been sent into exile. After the coronation of his Roman Catholic uncle, he was persuaded to lead what became known as the Pitchfork Rebellion*. This was soon brought to an end but in 1688, James' son-in-law, William of Holland (known as the Prince of Orange) arrived with an army. There was no need for a battle as James left England and went to live in France.

William and Mary reigned together from 1689 to 1694 and following Mary's death, William ruled alone for a further eight years.

Bedfordshire had a very difficult time during the Civil War, with some of the people who were strongly against the established church suffering for their religious convictions both before and after the conflict. Before they left Holland, William and Mary insisted that they would be sympathetic to those 'who had a tender conscience' for their religious beliefs.

Part One
England and Bedfordshire in the Seventeenth Century

James I (1603–1625)

Queen Elizabeth died unmarried on 24th March 1603 while in her seventieth year and the forty-fourth year of her reign. Although the Tudor dynasty appeared to die with her, Henry VIII had had two sisters, both of whom had descendants.

---

*   The Battle of Sedgefield.

Elizabeth lay critically ill for some weeks and to discuss the subject of her successor while she was still alive was treason. Much secret plotting and planning went on behind closed doors and as soon as it was known that she had finally died, Sir Robert Carey set off to bring James swiftly back to London. James, however, made no attempt to hurry, stopping at various country houses to enjoy the hunting. While he was staying at Hinchinbroke House, near Huntingdon, he was approached by sixteen Puritan ministers from Bedfordshire and Hertfordshire who were anxious for his support in their efforts to reform the Church of England. Scotland was a Presbyterian country and these men were hoping that James would help them to introduce similar principles into the English church. He received them politely and then slowly made his way towards London. Because James' mother had been Roman Catholic, English Catholics were also hoping he would support them.

James held a conference at Hampton Court so that he could hear different shades of opinion. To his horror he found that there was a group of Independents who wanted to dispose of both the prayer book and bishops! They wanted to choose their own ministers and form of service. No changes came from the conference, but James ordered a new translation – to be known as the *Authorised Version of the Bible.*

Conspiracies

The Roman Catholics were bitterly disappointed that they had not received royal support. Of the various attempts to force changes, the best known is the *Gunpowder Plot.* Some young, impatient Roman Catholics devised a plot whereby they would hide gunpowder in the cellars at Westminster and ignite it just as James was opening the new Parliament. The events which today take place each 5th November are to commemorate the failure of the plot and the capture and burning of conspirator Guy Fawkes.

The Puritans*

There were still many people (especially in Bedfordshire) who
wanted to reduce the power and income of the bishops and to use
some of their estates to improve clergy stipends. They also
wanted to encourage educated preachers to leave the cathedral
and university towns and go to more rural parishes. this group
may have been frowned on but were not persecuted. However
the much smaller group of Independents mentioned above were
regularly fined and threatened with prison. Some individuals
slipped away to live in Holland and in 1620 a larger group
(known as the Pilgrim Fathers) sailed for America.

Settlement in America

In 1607 a permanent English settlement was created in what
became known as Jamestown, in Virginia. This made it easier for
other settlements to be established and greatly encouraged trade.
The Pilgrim Fathers made a small settlement which gradually expanded at New Plymouth in New England. During the next reign
settlements with Bedfordshire names appeared across Massachusetts.

Charles I (1625–1649)

James' eldest son, Henry, died in 1612, aged nineteen. His
younger son, Charles, would become the first English king to be
brought up and educated in the Church of England.
Unfortunately his tutor, the Bishop of London, William Laud,
influenced him against the Puritan movement. Charles became
convinced that the Independents were not only a threat to the
Established Church but that their behaviour verged on treason.
Additionally, apart from the fact that he caused offence by
marrying a Roman Catholic, he still treated his Catholic subjects
very harshly.

---

*   The name 'Puritan' can also be used to cover the Independents. They are
then given different specific names dependant on dates and circumstances.
In this book, the name is used for the reformers, for simplicity.

He Tried to Rule Without Parliament

In those days Parliament only sat at the invitation of the King and when he felt that the business was complete, he closed the session and the members returned home. One part of the work of the Commons was to discuss national and the more serious of local problems. If necessary new laws were passed to cover these matters, but these laws had to be approved and signed by the king. The other part of their work was to discuss with the king the anticipated expenses for future military campaigns, diplomatic journeys and domestic expenses for his various households. The level of future taxation was then negotiated from this information.

As the gap between king and country widened, the Commons became increasingly reluctant to grant Charles' tax demand. Charles retaliated by sending them away and attempting to rule without summoning Parliament.

More Problems for the Church

In 1633 William Laud became Archbishop of Canterbury and immediately began a campaign against both Puritans and Independents. King Charles strongly supported the Laudian Church.

More Causes for Discontent

Because Charles was unable to draw income in the traditional way, he had to resort to taxes which were offensive to both business people and landowners. The most serious of these was the so-called Ship Tax.

The 'Ship' Tax Brings Matters to a Head

Apart from the subject of religious dissent, many of the other grievances affected the rich more than the poor, but in 1634 this new tax united everyone. Charles had decided to revive the ancient Ship Tax originally intended for the defence of the coastal counties.

In August 1635 the sheriff of Bedfordshire had to collect £3,000 which had been assessed as the value of a fully-fitted warship. This large sum had first to be divided between the towns and villages and then shared between the householders. Each year the deficit grew bigger and so each new sheriff had a larger sum to aim for. By 1639 a large number of people were refusing to pay and eventually goods were impounded instead of taxes.

The Outbreak of War

As resistance grew to the Ship Tax and punishments became more severe, a Buckinghamshire member of Parliament, John Hampden, refused to pay and was sent to prison. When he was released he continued to organise resistance, so on 4th January 1642 Charles himself took armed men into the House of Commons to try to arrest Hampden and four others. This inflammatory behaviour united the Commons and Charles was forced to leave both the House and London. He did not return to the capital again until the time of his execution.

Charles flatly refused to negotiate on the subject of his role; Parliament was to work for him, not share authority with him. By June both sides were openly recruiting. Royalist Sir Lewis Dyve, of Bromham and Sewell, recruited in Bedford and narrowly escaped when Parliamentarian Sir Samuel Luke, of Cople, tried to arrest him. On 29th August 1642 King Charles raised his banner at Nottingham and war could no longer be prevented.

Just as with earlier civil wars, the two armies moved about the country challenging each other's castles. there was a small Parliamentary stronghold at Bedford and a large one at Newport Pagnell. the first terrible battle was at Edgehill (Warwickshire) on 23rd October. It has been estimated that at least five thousand men were killed. This came as a terrible shock to both sides and negotiations were re-opened. During December a petition was sent to both Houses by the people of Bedfordshire asking them to open negotiations with the king. Another petition from 'divers of your Majesties loyall subjects inhabiting the County of Bedford amounting to the number of 3800' was sent to Charles asking him personally to re-open negotiations. Both failed and in the spring fighting resumed, continuing on and off for over two years. Eventually the battle which took place at Naseby on 14th June 1645 was a conclusive victory for Parliament. Charles retreated to Oxford and surrendered on 5th May 1646, not to Cromwell but to the Scots. Nine months later he was handed over and moved to Holdenby House in Northamptonshire.

Two years went by and many changes took place. Senior negotiators retired and new spokesmen from more idealistic groups became influential. On 28th December 1648, the House of Commons began to plan Charles' trial. The result of this was a charge of guilty to being 'a public enemy to the Commonwealth of England'. With mixed emotions the court ordered his execution, which took place on Tuesday 30th January 1649.

The Levellers and Diggers

Two of the extremist groups which came to the fore during this period were seriously disappointed to find that Cromwell was not levelling out the social hierarchy. *The Levellers* were aware that while many ex-soldiers were living in poverty, not having received their pay-off money from the army, the rich were apparently richer. While Cromwell was worrying about and raising an army against Royalist support in Ireland, he was being attacked by speeches, pamphlets and demonstrations from extremists in his own party.

There was no way during the first few years that he or anyone else could dismantle the social system of power and land ownership. *The Diggers* were more practical in their approach. In nearly every county there were areas of land left uncultivated while people without work and with no land on which to grow food were suffering from malnutrition. The landowners (who were desperate to protect their parks) would not release land, so in April 1649, a group gathered at Walton-on-Thames and began digging up some common land to create allotments. They were eventually dispersed by troops, but the movement continued in a small way in different parts of the country including Bedfordshire.

The Commonwealth 1649–1653

There was great confusion after the death of the King: the brutality of the act sharpening emotions and opening up divisions within the victorious party. It was no longer followers of the King versus those who desperately supported the rights of Parliament. Those who had fought against the King had many different reasons and they all expected to see different, conflicting reforms. In addition as the Prince of Wales had been declared king in both Ireland and Scotland, Cromwell felt obliged to try to take military control of these countries. Finally there was a serious and violent disagreement between Parliament and the now extremely powerful army.

The Protectorate 1653–1659

The army proved to be more powerful than the sitting Parliament so that latter was dismissed. Efforts were then made to form a Parliament of faithful and God-fearing men selected by the army and representatives of the Independent Church [The Barebones Parliament]. This proved to be quite unworkable and eventually Cromwell agreed to become *Lord Protector*. Parliaments were to be called at least every three years and were never to sit for less than five months. During the next five years England was at last given the opportunity to recover from war and to rebuild and develop trade.

When Cromwell died in 1658 his son, Richard, hesitantly agreed to become Protector. He was not strong enough to control the *Military Council* and within a year he resigned. For the final year before the Restoration, England was ruled by this council or their representatives. It soon becae obvious that they were heading for disaster and even families who were strong Parliamentarians voted for *the Restoration*.

Charles II 1660–1685

Charles received a tumultuous welcome and expectations were very high, but events soon proved that, like his father, Charles would be very high-handed. The country was critically short of money and was already divided; although he had hoped to heal some of these breaches, he found it very difficult. During the previous twenty years, many of the Royalist landowners had been deprived of their estates; bishops, some judges and clergy had been deposed and there was a great deal of bitterness. The regicides (those men who had signed the death warrant for Charles' father) were themselves executed, which in many cases caused yet more bitterness.

Religion Divided the Country

Roman Catholics were feared because their religion was associated with the traditional enemy – Spain. It therefore caused concern when yet another Stuart king married a Roman Catholic. Although this reign included events which have gone down as key subjects in England's history: the Great Plague, the Fire of London and naval attacks by the Dutch, it was the subject of dissenting religion which dominated life in Bedfordshire.

Religious Persecution

Towards the end of the civil war and on through the Protectorate it was legal for men who were respected by their communities and with the gift of biblical teaching to preach quite openly, even though they were not ordained. After the Restoration they were arrested, fined and/or sent to prison. Before long even people caught listening to unordained preachers were treated the same harsh way. John Bunyan (see below) is the well-known example of these events. people and preachers alike went to great efforts to get round the laws. *The Corporation Act* which continued for the next two centuries made it illegal for any member of a corporate body, e.g. the Quarter Sessions, to sit without first receiving communion according the the rites of the Church of England. *The Act of Uniformity* required that every minister should publicly declare his assent to everything contained in the Book of Common Prayer or be deprived of his living. As a result, many clergymen, especially in Bedfordshire, lost their living without compensation. *The Conventicle Act* threatened with imprisonment any person who attended a religious meeting not held according to the Established Church. *The Five Mile Act* forbade the ejected ministers to come within five miles of any town except when travelling.

These Acts continued for many years and led to harsh fines, imprisonment and even transportation. In 1672 a *Declaration of Indulgence*, issued by the king, was intended to bring tolerance. John Bunyan and others like him were freed from prison. This Act was withdrawn the following year and Bunyan was returned to prison. It was while he was in prison that he wrote his world-famous book, The Pilgrim's Progress.

The Royal Succession

As the years went by and fears grew concerning the prospective Roman Catholic King the *Parliamentary Test Act* was passed. This forbade any Roman Catholic, other than James himself, from attending Parliament. Twenty Catholic peers and their descendants were deprived of their seats until the Catholic Emancipation Act of 1829. By 1681 both Charles and James were so unpopular that once again there was talk of violent plots.

The Rye House Plot

In 1683 a group of extremists tried to kill both Charles and James as they passed Rye House in Hertfordshire. The conspirators were caught and executed and because some were friends of Lord John Russell of Woburn, he was also executed. Some years later King William III gave the Russell family a dukedom to show that a mistake had been made and recognising that the family were really exceptionally loyal.

King James II 1685–1688

Two years later King Charles died and his fifty year old brother, James, Duke of York, was proclaimed king. He retained the existing ministers and issued a manifesto which stated that he would respect the civil and religious liberties of his subjects. However, Parliament soon became aware that he was planning a Catholic revival and in 1687 he declared an indulgence for both Catholics and Non-conformists. This was very unpopular and like the other Stuart kings, he alienated one group after another. The only hope was that both of his daughters were married to Protestants. When his second wife had a healthy baby boy in 1688, a group of representatives from all parties approached the Prince of Orange.

The Coming of William and Mary

James' eldest daughter, Mary had married what was known as the Stadholder of Holland. He was also Prince of a small area in western France called Orange. They were firm Protestants and very concerned about matters in England. Until the birth of Prince James (who would one day be known as 'the Old Pretender'), Mary was heir to the throne of England. Secret discussions had already taken place and so William and his army sailed for England and landed in Torbay. Having declared that the object of his arrival was 'the defence of the liberties of England', William and his army moved very slowly towards Exeter. As a result James brought his army down into Wiltshire, but realising the hopelessness of the situation, returned to London and after a series of adventures, succeeded in escaping to France.

In the introduction to this chapter it was divided into four sections with the Civil War dividing four Stuart kings. Queen Mary was also a Stuart, but the events which opened her period on the throne introduce such a major change that it is more suitable to place it as an opening to the last quarter of the millennium.

Part Two
Dunstable in the Seventeenth Century

The previous chapter closed with a reference to the innkeepers who were ready to receive a great rush of travellers. During the first forty years the industry consolidated but there was no spectacular growth. This was to come after the Civil War. It also closed with a reference to the Reverend John Richardson and his struggle against the Bishop's court. This theme continues during this century.

In previous centuries Dunstable played an important part in the nation's economy as a centre for wholesaling and exporting, as a suitable place for important meetings and as a place to rest during difficult journeys. It may be because of these same roads and the high quality inns which attracted educated and controversial visitors to the town that, in this century, the people of Dunstable became leaders in the fight for freedom of worship.

John Richardson's first recorded court appearance was ten months after the death of Queen Elizabeth. There were further summons and eventually he gave in and agreed to conform but left Dunstable soon afterwards. In 1609 the name Edward Alport appears as minister at the Priory Church.

The Reverend Edward Alport

Nothing is heard about his relationship with the town until 1616. It is possible that he was especially chosen to counteract any relaxation of church dogma put forward by Richardson. Whatever the intention there was obviously a complete breakdown between minister and congregation. He must have been desperate to have exposed his problems in public, such that it is still possible for us to read about them today.

He Took His Parishioners to Court

In 1616 he took twenty-six men, four ladies and 'others yet unknown' to the court of the Star Chamber. A group of tradesmen, small innkeepers and farmers had responded to their intransigent minister by attacking him in his role as clergyman and also when he was at home with his wife. The events which took place, together with potted biographies of the people involved, can be found in 'Dunstable in Transition'*.

They Baptised a Sheep!

The most serious accusation was that, infuriated by the lack of good teaching sermons, two of them had taken a sheep up to the font, baptised it with the name Edward Alport and then put it up

---

* Evans, V. Dunstable in Transition 1550–1700, published by
The Book Castle.

in the pulpit and told it to preach a sermon! This outrage, which must have taken place a year or two before, was too blatant to ignore and the culprits admitted that they had been severely punished. However, far from solving Alport's problem, matters then became worse. On one tack he was accused of not carrying out his duties efficiently and that he sometimes left them on Sunday with no one booked to take their services. He retorted that he did provide a locum but that the church-wardens turned his appointee away, inviting in one of the non-conforming lecturers instead. On the other tack, his accusers terrorised him!

After the beer-houses had closed, a large group would gather under his bedroom window and share a barrel of beer. They frightened him with their rowdiness and, what was worse, they taunted him and his wife to get them out in the road. Sometimes they warned him that someone was cutting his green corn and the rowdy mob then followed him to the empty field. On other nights when Alport refused to come out, they went up to the field and cut his corn before it was ripe.

A whole series of accusations were made on both sides; the suspicious thing being that although he had reported them to the strict Anglican Justice, nothing had been done. Serious as it all sounded, there is no record that the protagonists were punished. Apart from the fact that they invited some un-named lecturer(s) into the Priory Church, there is no reference to their chosen form of religious worship. Later evidence suggests that they were one of the first groups of potential Baptists in the country.

The group which Alport described as 'the Confederates' must have been relieved to get away without punishment and for a few years Dunstable faded from the news.

A Non-Conformist Minister at the Priory Church

Although James I was very supportive of the prayer book services, there were places where people were quietly preparing for more informal services. At St. Antholin's church in London a group of businessmen were financially supporting a scheme to train clergymen for this type of service. In April 1625 they bought the 'Impropriation pertaining to the Priory Church of St. Peter, Dunstable' for one of their students called Zachary Symmes. When Symmes arrived he found that the chancel was in such a bad state of repair that it was necessary to pay £25 for repairs. The society also rented a big house in North Street as a vicarage. This later became known as the Manor House. Symmes must have been the ideal incumbent for Dunstable and all was well for nearly seven years.

The Reverend Symmes and Family Went to America

Archbishop William Laud has been mentioned in the first part of this chapter. In 1633 he closed down the London committee which supported Zachary Symmes. In the summer of 1634 he ordered the Bishop of Lincoln to arrange a visitation. By the time that the inspectors reached Bedfordshire, Symmes and his family had already departed for America on the ship 'the Griffin'!

Symmes Was and Still Is Greatly Respected in Boston USA

Zachary Symmes, his wife Sarah and his large family arrived in Boston in mid-September. They were made very welcome and admitted to the Baptist church at Charlestown. He was 'elected and ordained teacher' [preacher] and started a second church in Boston. A few years later he encouraged the building of a baptist church at nearby Woburn.

He was both respected and loved in his new country and his family married and settled down there. When he died on 4th February 1670, a memorial stone was erected which records that:

> 'a prophet lies under the stone:
> His words shall live tho' he be gone'.

It is no wonder that the congregation at the Priory Church of St. Peter worshipped so peacefully during the ministry of this educated and respected minister.

Other Dunstablians Went to America

Archbishop Laud and the stricter of the bishops made it extremely difficult for the Non-Conformists. In twos and threes families and individuals sailed for America. Some Dunstablians sailed to Boston with the Symmes family while another party went to Charlestown and to other parts of Massachusetts.

Dunstable, Massachusetts

Mary Sear from Dunstable and her husband the Hon. Edward Tyng are thought to have founded this flourishing town. William Tyng, probably Edward's grandson and Elizabeth, his granddaughter together with her husband, were greatly involved with the settlement of that area of Massachusetts. When Mrs Pat Reeves was Mayoress of Dunstable, England, she contacted Mrs Lucy Kennedy, local historian of Dunstable, Massachusetts. Thanks to the friendship of the two families, contact between these two towns is firmly cemented.

Events Leading Up to the War

As far as Dunstable was concerned, damage to trade and illegal taxes were probably the main complaints, apart from matters concerning religion.

Religious Belief

The Symmes family had left Dunstable in 1634 and according to later evidence a William Pedder who then 'intruded himself' into the church left soon after the outbreak of war to become a Royalist chaplain.

Lecturers at Kensworth
Little is known about Pedder's relationship with his congregation, but it appears likely that many of them made a habit of slipping out of the town and attending religious meetings on the Downs

near Kensworth. Because they were not ordained, the Non-Conformist preachers were referred to as 'lecturers'. Lady Anne Bacon of Gorhambury financially supported some of them and the Lord of the Manor at Hemel Hempstead was also supportive. Some of the congregation at St. Mary's Kensworth were dissatisfied with their vicar. They were very pleased when, after the outbreak of war, parliamentary officials expelled him from the living. Their new vicar, Edward Harrison, was far more tolerant and went with them to hear the lecturer at Hemel Hempstead. He became convinced that those who dissented from the prayer book services were truly devout. He left the vicarage but, at the wishes of his congregation, stayed on at the church.

This is all very relevant to Dunstable because, after the Restoration, when the dissenting congregation which Harrison had built up were obliged to meet once more out on the Downs, they were joined by many people from Dunstable.

A Panel of Lecturers for Dunstable
After Pedder had left the Priory Church, the congregations were supplied with ministers from a panel of experienced lecturers chosen by The London Committee.

The Ship Tax

A high proportion of the households of Dunstable resisted this tax. Wealthy people who owned one or more inns, e.g. John Briggs, John Plott, Anne Fossey and Henry Montague, the business families, e.g. the Finches, Chapmans and Metcalfs and the small businessmen, e.g. William Element, the brazier, Edward Chester, the baker and Thomas Foxton, the butcher, all refused to pay. There were many more people on the list. The highest taxpayer was John Briggs (thirteen shillings [65p]) but the majority owed three [15p] to ten shillings [50p], while several were only taxed at one shilling [5p]. If a shilling is equated to a working man's wages for two days, it can be seen to be quite high.

The Civil War

As always Dunstable suffered badly not only from passing soldiers but also with groups sent out to buy or impound food and horses. The local Parliamentary leader was Sir Samuel Luke and the local Royalist leader was Sir Lewis Dyve. Both of their war diaries have survived and have been published as volumes of the Bedfordshire Historical Record Society. From these it can be seen that supplies sent to Newport Pagnell were brought as far as Dunstable, where they then waited for escorts from the garrison to accompany the final leg of the journey.

It was a difficult time for most Dunstablians; shops and the market were robbed, crops were damaged in the fields and food was compulsarily purchased for the king or his soldiers, leaving the townspeople hungry. Prices rose and so did taxes! The inns were short of food and labour, the roads became progressively worse as each year passed. However one of the worst effects for Dunstable was the shortage of horses. Some inns expected to make more income from hiring out horses than by supplying accommodation.

Murder at the Red Lion

At the outbreak of war, horses were requisitioned for the use of soldiers. As Bedfordshire was officially supporting Parliament, Dunstable had to regularly contribute to the county allocation of men, money, food and horses. According to the Parliamentary newspaper A Perfect Diurnall dated Monday 24th June 1644, information had been received that the Royalist forces were continually raiding Bedfordshire, Buckinghamshire and Hertfordshire 'committing many great and cruell outrages . . .'. On the previous Sunday the King has passed through Hockley in the Hole [Hockliffe] on his way to Bedford. His soldiers had plundered Leighton [Buzzard] and sent another party to Dunstable where they 'entered the Towne when the people were at church, not contenting themselves with plunder, but made a great disturbance, cutting and slashing the people in the [Priory] Church and shot a case of pistols at the minister in the pulpit, but missed him; and afterwards abused him very inhumanely'. This is a true story and the door, peppered with bullet holes, can still be seen at the back of the church!

Before they committed this outrage they may have been drinking heavily in the Red Lion on the crossroads. There were very few horses left in private ownership and the soldiers had heard that Mr Platt, the landlord at the Red Lion* still had some. They paid him a visit to try to requisition the horses, but when he recklessly went out to prevent them, he was shot dead in his own stable yard.

King Charles Rested at the Red Lion
After the battle of Naseby (Northamptonshire) in June 1645, the defeated king and his cavalry took a roundabout route back to Oxford via Stamford, Huntingdon and Bedford, spending the night of the 26th August at Woburn Abbey and riding on to Dunstable, arriving at 2.00pm. It is not known who was the new owner of the Red Lion but that is where Charles chose to rest before swinging west to Oxford.

The Eleanor Cross was Taken Down
The Parliamentary army also passed to and fro through the town. On 25th July 1543 'John Plant ye servant of the Earl of Essex [the Parliamentary army leader]' was buried at the church. This may have been the occasion when the dispirited army was returning from defeat at Roundway Down near Oxford. It may also have been the occasion when, incensed by the crosses and other carvings which they interpreted as religious superstition, they took down the Eleanor Cross, which stood at the start of North Street approximately in the middle of the crossroads. These soldiers were of the extreme independent side of the religious spectrum; they would have approved of the 'lecturers' who were appointed to take services at the Priory Church. On the other hand, the Royalist soldiers who fired a case of pistols at one of them were at the other end of the spectrum.

---

*   By this date the earlier name 'The Swan' had been changed.

123

At Last the War was Over

It was some years before all the fighting was over but Dunstablians were grateful for the more settled period which followed the Battle of Naseby. The changes which had taken place were probably more appreciated here than in most other places. Economically the greatest event which occurred during this period was the start of the stage-coach industry. In 1657 the first long distance stage-coach rumbled through the town on its way from London to Coventry and Chester. This event would bring economic benefit to Dunstable for the next one hundred and seventy-five years.

A Change of Religious Practice

During these years of recovery those who followed the independent form of religion were in control of the country. Many Dunstablians appreciated the freedom 'not to conform' to the Established Church and to enjoy bible-based services without being forced to use the Book of Common Prayer. They handed over the parish register to a secular clerk, Thomas Perkins. he appears to have lost his entries as there is a particularly long gap in the Dunstable register. Some couples in this period preferred marriage in the market place and preferred not to baptise their babies. These same couples may have been amongst the Dunstablians who went out to Kensworth each Sunday, where the church had moved on to embrace Believer's Baptism. This usually meant the baptism of adults. In the north of the county John Bunyan's church preferred but did not insist on re-baptism, but at Kensworth it was essential.

Some Dunstablians Became Baptists

Thomas Hayward, a local unordained preacher, had taken over from the Reverend Harrison. He realised that his scattered 'church' could become very isolated, so the Dunstable Baptists (as part of the Kensworth Group) joined an organisation known as the Abingdon Association. The local branch met in Dunstable in

1658 and it is of interest that the nationally-famous preacher Benjamin Coxe was present.

The Quakers Come to Dunstable

During the year 1654 Quakers from the Lake District and north Lancashire were travelling around the country spreading the news of this new personal form of religion. They believed that God's truth came more clearly when a group of friends waited on Him in silence.* They also felt strongly that there was no need for intermediaries, such as priests, sacraments and sermons.

At the end of 1654, a Lancashire farmer called Richard Hubberthorne was travelling north out of London. He stayed at Markyate and formed a group there and then came on to Dunstable. Edward Chester, who was a baker at what is now 2–4 High Street North, was impressed with his teaching and invited him to stay. By the time that Hubberthorne left the town Chester was leader of Dunstable's first group of Quakers.

So towards the end of the 1650s there was a Baptist group and a Quaker group, both of whom had separated themselves from the congregation at the Priory Church. This left behind a more moderate congregation of Anglicans.

A Resident Minister for the Priory Church

Although the lecturers on the panel were respected, educated men they were not resident. In 1656 the parishioners sent a petition to Oliver Cromwell. This included the information that the living had been empty for fourteen years, that there was no vicarage and that the stipend, glebeland and the small tithes added together, only came to £35 a year**. They asked for another £45 to be added to the stipend. As a result the *Reverend Isaac Bringhurst* (who was a graduate of Jesus College, Cambridge) was appointed. It is likely that he was awaiting ordination and that later on he was able to buy the rectory. In

---

*   Today they are known as the Society of Friends.
**   The great tithes had for many years been separated from the church. Before the war they were owned by City businessmen. They would then have been impounded by parliament. After the war they were in dispute.

1660 the Independent minister at Kensworth was evicted and the value of the vicarage greatly increased. Bringhurst then managed to get that living as well. As rector he was entitled to the great tithes of corn, calves and lambs. He had difficulty collecting these and there was a court case. This may be why he lived at Kensworth and appointed a curate for Dunstable. The curate had the unusual christian name of *'Bishop' Lyster*. Bringhurst then gave up the Dunstable rectory which Lyster decided to take. When Bringhurst left Kensworth, Lyster took that living as well. Within the next few years several other ministers also came and went.

The Restoration

More Trouble for the Nonconformists

Once again it was illegal to attend any religious meeting not held in the parish church and led by an ordained minister. However good a preacher or teacher a man was, it was illegal for him to preach in public if he was not ordained. By the winter of 1682 the parishioners of the Priory Church had had enough of the frequent changes to which they had been subjected. Thirty of them sent a testimonial to the bishop praising Kensworth's latest vicar *the Reverend John Lord*. They pointed out that the Reverend Bishop Lyster had held both livings and that the two livings together provided 'but a bare competency'. The two church wardens signed the petition and then there were two long lists of 'inhabitants'. John Lord was installed as rector of Dunstable on February 11th 1683. Although he mainly lived in Kensworth, he served the Priory Church for forty-five years.

Persecution of the Dissenters
There may be a connection between the general sympathy felt in Dunstable for the dissenters, the frequent change of Anglican clergy and the fact that there were so few prosecutions within the parish.

It was on the 12th November 1660 that John Bunyan was arrested and from then on all meetings of dissenters had to be held in secret. Bunyan had decided that if he hid from the authorities and failed to preach in public, it would give people the idea that his beliefs were not really sincere. In the south of the county leader Thomas Hayard decided that it would be foolish to allow the authorities to arrest him – he must stay free to encourage and support others at risk.

The Conventicle Act

After 1664 it became possible for anyone found at a conventicle [secret meeting] to be fined £5 or sent to prison. However Baptists from Dunstable slipped out of the town and secretly met up with others from the surrounding villages. Thomas Hayward and others like him risked their own freedom supporting, encouraging and whenever possible, preaching to these devout but persecuted men and women. The Conventicle Act lapsed in 1668 and for nearly two years the dissenters could meet discreetly without persecution. In 1669 Archbishop Sheldon set up an enquiry about these conventicles. A [rough] figure of forty Baptists were recorded as meeting at Caddington with widow Rotherham as their leader and about thirty at Houghton Regis with Thomas Hayward as leader. However in May 1670 another Conventicle Act was passed; constables were encouraged to break into private houses and neighbours were bribed to report any illegal meetings. It is significant that no Dunstablians are recorded as reporting their neighbours. During the next fifteen years there were hopeful periods of toleration but always followed by longer periods of severe penalties.

A Declaration of Indulgence

In 1672 dissenters were invited to register their meeting places. The list which John Bunyan submitted for the north of the county has survived but we do not know which houses and barns were registered around Dunstable.

This was a very short period of tolerance and persecution soon returned. When in 1676 the clergy were asked to report on the number of Nonconformists in their parishes, Dunstable admitted to having twenty-nine. This was probably a conservative estimate.

The Kensworth Register

During 1675 the Kensworth group felt sufficiently safe to start keeping a register of their baptised members. Twenty-four Dunstablians were entered, fifteen of whom had been baptised by July 1677. Brother Finch of Dunstable was elected as elder of the church and Brother Chambers as a deacon. Many others would have been attending on a fairly regular basis but had not, at that stage, put their names forward for baptism.

The Suffering of the People Called Quakers

In addition to their different form of worship, the beliefs of these peace-loving people caused them to stubbornly refuse to attend their parish church. They also refused to give financial support for ordained ministers or for church buildings and were therefore persecuted more severely than the Baptists.

When they were brought into court they refused to swear on the Bible, to remove their hats or to treat the justices with the traditional show of respect. For these reasons they were given very heavy fines, most of which they were unable to pay and were left in prison while their families suffered financial distress. If the prisons became overcrowded they were released, but officials then impounded goods far beyond the value of the original fines.

Because they were so scattered, there was little help to be gained locally, so a London committee, the *Meeting for Sufferings,* was formed. Local correspondents sent details of hardship and then received and distributed financial assistance. Edward Chester was correspondent for this area and some of his reports are included in two large volumes published in the late 18th century*. They tried to avoid arrest by meeting out on the Downs and on one occasion Chester himself was sent to prison having been caught at a meeting with some Buckinghamshire Quakers. It was easier to prove their refusal to attend the Priory Church than to find their secret meeting places. So in June 1688 the Archdeacon excommunicated Edward Chester, William and Daniel Fossey (described as grocers), Thomas Halsey and Thomas Colard for

---

*   The Sufferings of the People Called Quakers 1652–1689.

their refusal to attend the Priory*.

There was another group being even more harassed in Houghton Regis and so on the 26th April 1678, the two groups leased a plot of land at Sewell, where they were less obvious than in the market town of Dunstable and they could occasionally meet without giving offence. The site also became their burial ground and once it was safe to do so, they built a small meeting-house. Edward Chester and other Dunstable Quakers who were buried there can be traced through the Houghton Regis parish register.

In the 1669 survey, John Crook, owner of Beckerings Park in mid Bedfordshire, was recorded as their leader. He was one of the few landed gentry to join the movement and was greatly respected. About forty Quakers were recorded at Houghton with a further forty at Sundon.

Who Was Running the Town of Dunstable?

It has been noted above that by 1500 the businessmen of Dunstable were playng a large part in running their own town and that the prior's steward, Adam Hilton, also became steward for the King. Other stewards came and went and each in their turn reported to the royal estate office at Ampthill. In 1677 Robert, Earl of Aylesbury, leased the Manor of Dunstable from the Crown. The records of the Manor Court have not survived, but his steward would have been responsible for the court, the market and the smooth running of the town. At Parliamentary level, Dunstable was included with the rest of Bedfordshire. For matters concerning law and order, there were Justices of the Peace, who were invariably country gentlemen and met regularly in Dunstable.

The general organisation of town life, i.e. the maintenance of roads, the care of the sick and elderly, the responsibility for poor and ailing travellers and day-to-day matters concerning the Priory Church were all the responsibility of officers elected at the Easter parish meeting. 'Gentlemen' within the town community appear

---

*   If strictly observed, ex-communication meant loss of work, customers, friends and even ostracism by one's own family.

to have been consulted about sensitive matters but, in practice, it was the innkeepers who were influential.

The Gentlemen of Dunstable

By the end of the Civil War the area around the Priory was no longer thought of as part of the church. After the Dissolution [the Priory Church of] St. Peter's had been given to the parish and people now referred to 'Church Street' rather than 'East Street'. Stone from the monastic buildings had long ago been sold or stolen and what we call the 'Priory Meadow' had become part of the pleasure gardens of Priory House. It probably looked similar to the way it does today. Priory Gardens (once the courtyard of the Priory) had been laid out as formal gardens.

Priory House and the Crawley Family
In the last chapter we noted the will of Elizabeth Aves, who passed on Priory House to her son. We then lose track of it until after the Civil War.

Top of the column of names of those inhabitants who requested that John Lord should be their next rector was [Dr] Robert Crawley. During the war he had been a doctor in the Royalist army and a member of the strict prayer-book party. He had then married Joanne Taverner of Hexton and settled at Priory House. In his will he left £1 to each of his children. His 'mansion at the south end of Dunstable' together with '5 acres called by name Pryory' he left to his wife. When she died five years later [1701], she left the house and what we call Priory Gardens and Meadow to their eldest son John. Both John and his son Thomas became doctors. Robert had left five acres of land to Joanne, but she only passed four acres to John. This is probably because she cut off an acre to the south of her house and garden to provide a separate house for her daughters.

John, who was in his thirty-first year at the time of his mother's death, had gained his BA just in time to take over his father's practice. The year after his mother's death he married Anne Symcott of Clifton in mid-Bedfordshire. Whereas his father had been a doctor in the Royalist army, her father had been one of the physicians who cared for the health of Oliver Cromwell. Robert's youngest daughter, Martha, married the Reverend John Lord's son who was rector of Toddington, so eventually the second house passed to Thomas. This house, the mansion and grounds stayed with the Crawley family until December 1752.

Kingsbury and the Marsh Family

At the top of the second column of inhabitants was the name Francis Marshe of Kingsbury. He was eighteen when the war broke out and is not recorded as having fought on either side. However, his memorial, which was once in the Priory Church, records his 'constant piety' and his 'inviolable attachment through life to God's altar and worship, constancy towards the English Apostolic Church [and] also his unfailing fidelity in, alas, most depraved times towards his King, the most holy Martyr, that most beneficient of all men, King Charles . . .'.

Kingsbury Fell Into Disrepair?

There is a gap in our knowledge of 'the Old Palace' during the second half of the 16th century. George Cavendish returned to Suffolk after the death of his wife c.1543 and died there c.1560. No doubt Kingsbury fell into disrepair. The travel writer William Camden failed to mention it when he visited the town around 1571, so the first written report is by William Stukeley c.1723. He wrote 'Kingsbury the royal seat over-against the church is now a farm-house'. By that time the Marshe family had been living there for well over a hundred years.

The Coming of the Marshe Family

In the year 1605* the parish register records the baptism of 'Daniel, son of —Marsh'. This is the first written record of the arrival of William Marshe. The family had for many years held land in Caddington and Kensworth. It is possible that William and his wife Elizabeth took down part of the old palace and

---

*   Actually 16th February 1606.

re-used some of the materials. They built a house which was suitable for a comfortably-off, 17th century country gentleman. Daniel, two other sons and a daughter all died early in life, but three other babies grew up and produced families, some of whose names are remembered in the town today.

Elizabeth, who was born in 1613, married a Dunstable haberdasher, Thomas Chew. John, born in 1617, trained as a lawyer and married Blandina Iremonger, whose father had a law practice in Leighton Buzzard. It was Francis, the youngest, born in 1624, who married Rebecca Briggs (whose father was one of Dunstable's wealthiest businessmen) and eventually took over the Kingsbury estate. They had six children, two of whom died very young. A surviving son, John, trained as a physician and returned to live at Kingsbury. It had six hearths (the same as Priory House) and was probably a small, comfortable house, suitable for a gentleman-physician. It was sufficiently 'high-class' to allow Francis to choose Dorothy Wolseley, a younger daughter of Parliamentarian, Sir Charles Wolseley, as his bride. As with the Crawley family, the divisions of the war were now forgotten. Her family was obviously happy about the match because she was allowed to entertain her sisters and other relations at Kingsbury.

Celia Fiennes Visits Dunstable

Dorothy's cousin, Celia Fiennes, travelled all over England and kept a series of diaries to record her journeys. She stayed at Kingsbury late in the summer of 1687 when Dorothy's sister, Bridget was also in residence. In her diary she included a most important piece of economic information. *'Dunstable'* she said *'its a good town as you shall meete with on the Road, its full of Inns'*. She added the interesting fact that the town comprised a long wide road with a great sheet of water like a large pond.

Dunstable was Full of Inns

Although they occasionally changed their names or the nature of their business, once opened, inns tended to trade over several centuries. Because of this, many of them will be included in later chapters. As Celia Fiennes rode up North Street and turned left into East Street and Kingsbury, she would have passed at least fifteen inns of various sizes. Of these, five near the crossroads were in business long before the Dissolution. By 1689 they were ageing and not all survived into the next century, so these have been included here, along with 'the great Dunstable mystery' and the witch story, which took place at the *Nags Head.*

The White Horse Inn
All that remains today of the great Tudor inn where Henry VIII used to stay are the gateways and the adjoining buildings. Inside is a Totternhoe stone fireplace which still has its carved Tudor roses. By the Restoration this inn appears to have been a little old-fashioned and run-down. The very large building which included the Abbey National Building Society [once the Town Hall] on one side of the archway and at least two businesses on the other would soon be broken down into smaller units. Sometime before 1680 the owner, Henry Sam, had registered the inn as Dunstable's Post Office.

The Crown next door, then called *The Raven,* was the victualling house connected with the *White Horse* and was originally used by coachmen, servants and local people.

The Red Lion
Across the road on the corner, jutting out onto East Street, stood the Red Lion. This inn was still called *The Swan* when wealthy entrepreneur John Grigge rented it from the Crown in 1578. His rent was £4 per year but it had been reduced by seven shillings and sixpence because of 'reparacyons' [restorations] which had been carried out*. In 1621 it was included in the rent list of Mr Wingate of Harlington and was known as *The Lyon.* For many years it was part of the Wingate's Manor of Lewsey. After the Restoration when coins were in short supply, several innkeepers and retailers issued their own Trade Tokens. William Fossey

---

*   By 1618 a 'Mr Grigge' owned the Crown.

(landlord in 1667) used the famous White Swan badge mentioned in the 15th century.

It was already *The Red Lion* when the Earl of Huntingdon stayed there on 1st January 1639. The Earl's bill included: roast and boiled mutton plus 'a hen'. These were served with bread, salads, fruit and a dish of larks.*

He paid for the luxury of a fire in his room and lights. The wine, sugar and lemon which were included in his bill were probably served in his room. In the morning he had bread, butter and eggs. As tea, coffee and chocolate were not yet available, he probably drank beer with his breakfast. When he departed he took three dozen larks with him, as a local delicacy. These were priced at one shilling and sixpence [7.5p] a dozen, the hen was two shillings [10p] and a lemon three pence [1.25p]. These prices give us something with which we can measure the tips which he left. the chambermaid received two shillings and sixpence [12.5p but worth 1.25 hens!] and the cook one shilling.

In previous centuries travellers gave money to the friars to use as alms; now it was customary to put the money in the poor box to help the authorities support poor travellers. The earl left one shilling and sixpence.

The White Hart

A little further down North Street the *White Hart*, which was about the same age and size as the *White Horse*, was still a high-class inn and was often used by the Earl of Bedford. Landlord Nathaniell Wimpew had a White Hart on one side of his trade token and a mitre on the other. This was to remind people that his father had been a prebendary of Lincoln Cathedral. As has been noted, stagecoaches began to run through Dunstable in this century, the *White Hart* becoming a link in this important industry.

The Bear

This small business stood to the north of the *White Hart* and was probably connected with it in some way.

---

*   This is the first reference that has been found to Dunstable larks.

The Lyon and the Peacock

By 1689 these two inns which stood back-to-back in the middle of North Street were over two hundred and fifty years old. *The Lyon* had been adapted as a private house and the *Peacock* had been let to a victualler selling food and drink.

The Medieval Wall Painting

A little way down North Street (once Charlie Cole's cycle shop and now the Nationwide Building Society) is a great Dunstable mystery. The wall painting in this building portrays an intricate hunting scene and includes what is thought to be the first English representation of a man smoking a pipe. It has been dated at around 1600. No written reference to the painting has yet been discovered. It was probably completed by a travelling artist and possible commissioned by an innkeeper. Not only was no inn standing there in 1542, but none has ever been definitely identified on the site. However, there are several references to a *Three Black Swans* in that part of North Street.

The Witches of Dunstable

The Nags Head was not opened until after the Civil War but there are two reasons why it must be included in this chapter. The first is that *Elkanah Settle*, eldest son of landlord, Josias, grew up to become a famous dramatist. He was raised at Hemel Hempstead by his uncle who paid for him to attend Trinity College, Oxford. Success came early and he left the university before acquiring his degree as his first play had already been staged in London. Although his work was popular and he was commissioned to write for the royal household, the political and religious unrest of the 1660s and 1670s caused problems of loyalty within the theatre and his popularity fluctuated. In 1691 he was appointed City Poet, writing scripts for and producing the City pageants.

Elkanah married Mary Warner from South Bedfordshire, but she died without having children; he himself died in 1724 while living in London and was probably buried in the churchyard of St. Giles in the Fields. Copies of his plays and pageants can be viewed in the British Library.

The other reason that the Nag's Head must be included in this chapter is that two of Josias' sons were involved in the *Great Witch Scandal*. During the spring of 1666 Elizabeth Pratt, a possibly sick old lady called at the Nag's Head asking for toast and ale. While Josias' wife was fetching it, Elizabeth wandered into the kitchen and stroked the heads of eleven year old John and twelve year old Josias. Two days later John 'was tooke with a strange distemper, groneing, scritching and crying almost continuingly night and day for forty days together until he dyed'. During the final days of his dreadful illness, John had torn at his nose and lips and shouted out 'murder, murder, I am bewitched, I am bewitched'!

This was the start of an amazing series of events. Two weeks later Josias sickened and he also became distressed and cried out just as his brother had done 'Ah! Father' [he cried] 'the widow Pratt has bewitched me also'. Josias senior took Elizabeth up to the boy's room and encouraged him to scratch her with a pin. When the boy refused, Josias himself scratched and stabbed her and because she failed to bleed, he condemned her as a witch. As the days went by her fever or fear caused her to talk wildly about other local witches.

Before long the two little Heywood boys were critically ill and Elizabeth was accused. She claimed to have attended a meeting amongst the knolls on Dunstable Downs where witch Mary Hudson had cast a spell on a piece of wool. This, she said, had been put under the children's pillow. Sure enough when Mrs Heywood looked she found an unexplained knot of wool tucked under the bolster. Whatever the cause, the story had a terrible ending because both of these boys and one of the Settles appear in the list of burials for March/April 1666.

This was all so serious that George Briggs and the two Elizabeth Metcalfes (mother and daughter-in-law), wealthy and respected innkeepers and stable owners, were sent for to act as witnesses. There were several more incidents but by far the most serious involved William Metcalfe senior. He had been alone in his stableyard with the door and the great gates shut and barred when he became aware that Elizabeth Pratt was standing behind him. Convinced that she had come in through the keyhole he called her a witch and ordered her out of his yard. Whether he let her out or whether she left the same way as she had come in we are not told. However, he later swore on oath that as a result of this encounter she had bewitched his livestock. Sixty-five horses and seventeen pigs had died! Anthrax causes rapid death in horses but is not so virulent in pigs. Adult human are highly resistant to the infection but if children succumb, one of the symptoms is unpleasant sores. These may be what caused the Settle boys so much distress.

Apart from the terrible loss of the children, a town which relied on travellers and tourists was in trouble, whether the cause was witchcraft or infection. Gossip had to be prevented, so a committee of innkeepers had Elizabeth confined and magistrates John Vaux of Whipsnade and John Rotherham of Luton were sent for. Throughout the whole proceedings there is no mention of a doctor being consulted, but the magistrates did ask a group of innkeepers' wives to search the bodies of the suspected ladies for witch marks. Elizabeth had already confessed; nothing was found on Ursula Clarke, while various pieces of 'flesh' were found on Mary Poole.

Elizabeth and at least two of the others were sent to Bedford gaol to await the king's travelling judges. Luckily for her, Elizabeth died before they arrived and the other ladies were released.

Forward into the Future

At the start of this century it was illegal to hold any form of worship not strictly based on the Book of Common Prayer. It was also illegal to absent oneself from the parish church. In Dunstable loyalties were divided both over national policy and within the organisation of the Priory Church. By the end of the century the united congregation at the Priory Church were all the happier for having meeting-places licensed for both Baptists and Quakers.

In 1600 there was no organised postal service for private individuals, but long before 1700 Dunstable had one of a handful of main post offices on the London to Holyhead road. Economically the travel trade had not only grown but had changed out of all recognition. Instead of riders and the occasional private coach, numerous private coaches now passed through the town every day and stagecoaches also expanded the market. In addition there was a new type of traveller coming into the town – a group who can only be described as tourists, i.e. men and women who were travelling for pleasure and education. The expectations of these travellers, whether they arrived on their own or on the public stagecoaches, were quite different from those at the start of the century.

As we have seen, the businessmen and innkeepers of Dunstable were ready to meet the challenge.

Chapter VIII

The Century of Endeavour, 1689–1800

Models illustrating the uniform of the Chew School, which until recently stood over the porch of Chew House, High Street South.

Overview

During the first few years of this century a major change took place in the government of this country. The change affected not only the relationship between the monarch and Parliament but also the monarch and the people. So great was this alteration that from this chapter onwards the style of the book will be different from those before.

The last chapter ended as early as 1689 with the future King William III and his army travelling slowly across Devon. When he landed in Brixham, the poor people had greeted his soldiers with apples and cider but at that stage the influential landowners stayed away. Four years before, the Duke of Monmouth (illegitimate son of Charles II) had also landed in the West Country, counting on popular support. It was because the landowners stayed away that his unsuccessful attempt had become known as the 'Pitchfork Rebellion'.

William had not come to start a war; before leaving Holland he had insisted that he was coming to offer support to the people of England. It was only when very large numbers rode in to welcome him at Exeter that he continued on his journey.

King James Leaves England

King James set out with a small army to meet William, but many of his soldiers deserted. When he got as far as Salisbury, he realised that William's support was too strong and he slipped away, back to London.

English support was imperative to William. Over two hundred years before, Henry VII had claimed the throne after the Battle of Bosworth. William, on the other hand, insisted that he would only be king if he was offered the title by the majority of those in power. So, slowly, he and his army and an ever-growing crowd of English followers made their way to London.

The actions of King James and his eventually successful attempt to flee the country and the discussions concerning the succession can be found in any appropriate text book. In brief,

Mary, the daughter of James II, arrived in London on 11th February 1689 and on the following day her husband William accepted the crown on behalf of them both.

The Coronation of William and Mary

In earlier chapters different kings have tried to ignore the 'customs of the country'. It was partly because King James was beginning to do this that the country had forced a change so, as the Earl of Nottingham warned, the House of Lords, whatever they did with regard to the monarchy, must be 'upon the foot of our ancient laws and fundamental constitution'. As a result of the Act of Parliament which accepted that King James II had 'abdicated the government and the throne being thereby vacant', William and Mary were jointly offered the throne – but with conditions.

The Declaration of Rights

Before the crown was formally offered to William and Mary, they agreed to sign a charter of practical liberties. This took the power of independent action away from the king and obliged both William and any future monarch to act in consultation with Parliament.

> Several issues which we take for granted were included in this list:
> Parliament should be held frequently; elections should be free [though not with universal suffrage]; there should be freedom of speech in Parliament and justice available to all and arbitrary fines were to be forbidden, as were excessive bail and tampering with jurors.

Two other very different items were included:

> Taxes could only be raised following a grant from Parliament.
> No Roman Catholic could be monarch of England.

By the end of the year this declaration had passed through Parliament as *the Bill of Rights*, so for seven centuries and seven chapters, life in England had been dominated by the wishes and behaviour of those sitting on the throne. It was the 18th century when Parliament took the dominant position of importance which it holds today.

Part One
England and Bedfordshire in the Eighteenth Century

King William and Queen Mary (1689–1694)

King William Alone (1694–1702)

William selected his Parliament from both parties but as the Liberals were in the majority and were mainly sympathetic to the Non-Conformist church, William was able to promote his policy of toleration.

When Mary, James II's daughter, died in 1694, his son-in-law, William, continued to reign until his death in 1702. As they were childless, the succession passed to James' younger daughter, Anne.

Queen Anne (1702–1714)

Overcoming severe bouts of gout and the after-effects of a long series of miscarriages, she took an active part in public life and was popular with the people of England. She reigned until her death in 1714 when, as her son had died in 1700, there was, again, no obvious successor.

Back in 1673 her father, James II, had re-married and in 1688 his wife produced a son, James, half-brother to Mary and Anne. In years to come he had wanted Anne to name James as her successor, but she knew that this might lead to civil war. As Anne's health deteriorated, James tried unsuccessfully to take the throne by force. George of Hanover (son of Sophia of Brunswick, granddaughter of James I) was offered the throne.

King George I (1714–1727)

George with his foreign ways, lack of English and at times lack of interest in England was not popular. There were riots and the Earl of Mar led a rebellion on James' behalf. This helped to unite the country behind George and when he died in 1727, his forty-five year old son was crowned.

King George II (1727–1760)

The King appeared even less interested in England than his father had been. He spent most of him time in Germany and saw little need to improve his knowledge of English. His son Frederick, Prince of Wales, had been born in England and liked both the country and the people. He became very popular, but also became a focal point for those politicians who were against his father. George turned him out of St. James Palace, so Frederick, together with his wife Augusta of Saxe-Gotha, made their home in Norfolk House, St. James Square. This happy family man was never given the chance to see if he could use his popularity to become a serious and responsible king. He died on March 20th 1751, aged forty-eight.

His father George II lived on to his mid-seventies, dying on October 25th 1760, by which time Frederick's son, George, was twenty-two. He had been nearly thirteen when his own father died and although his mother, Augusta, had previously taken no part in politics, she now had every intention of acting on behalf of her son. She turned to the Earl of Bute, friend of her late husband, for help and advice, encouraging him to take over the role of father-figure to the young George. Between them they totally isolated him from his grandfather, the King, and from most of the politicians. This caused both jealousy and suspicion and Bute and his family, as well as George and Augusta, became figures of fun.

King George III (1760–1820)

George was twenty-two when he acceded to the throne, keeping Bute as his advisor. Between them, mother and son persuaded him to take on the role of Prime Minister. He was not an enthusiastic politician and would have preferred to spend his time studying plants and trees. To escape from the stress and publicity, he purchased Luton Hoo and commissioned Lancelot (Capability) Brown to lay out the park and gardens. Some years later he encouraged Augusta to establish what became Kew gardens. The reign of King George III lasted for sixty years, running well into the next century.

The Age of Elegance and Culture
The nouns 'elegance' and 'culture' were certainly reflected in the country houses of Bedfordshire. Life at Woburn and Wrest Park rivalled the gentility and culture of other houses throughout England. Several other houses within the county were centres of culture and their owners patrons of the arts. Although Ampthill and Someries 'Castles' had been deserted and houses like Houghton House and Toddington Manor were losing their social importance, their position had been taken by Park House, Ampthill and Stockwood House, Luton, (after 1740). Houses like Luton Hoo and Southill Park were rapidly rising in social status.

The Age of Invention
However, in addition to elegance and culture, this was also a century of invention. Locally, the Monument in Ashridge Forest commemorates the third Duke of Bridgewater who, in 1760, set his engineer, James Brindley, to lay out the first of what would become a whole network of canals. It is said that as a result of these early structures the price of coal was nearly halved in industrial Manchester. The significance of the canals was not only that the price of coal dropped, but also that coal and other heavy commodities could be kept off the roads, despite the expansion of the manufacturing towns. It also made it possible for materials like Bath stone to be transported into Bedfordshire for building work at Woburn Abbey.

Canals Come to Bedfordshire

During the next century man-made waterways were used to improve navigation from the River Ivel. A network from the Ivel proved very successful in the Biggleswade area. A coal merchant from Biggleswade did such a good trade in Dunstable that he rewarded his customers with a 'coal dinner'. In 1805 the Grand Junction Canal, which linked London with Warwickshire, passed along the side of Leighton Buzzard. What was an important industrial wharf has become an equally important leisure and tourism attraction. A proposed new canal from the Grand Junction through to Bedford proved too expensive, as did a branch through Dunstable to St. Albans.

Another innovation which would be of great importance to Bedfordshire in the following century was James Watt's experimental work with steam engines.

More General Improvements

During this century Bedfordshire's roads were much improved by the Turnpike Trusts. Better roads meant better communications and gradually a degree of culture and comfort filtered down the social ladder. By the end of the century an awareness of the appalling conditions in which some people were living had spread beyond the areas themselves. Improvements were slow to come into the industrial towns and cities, but in parts of Bedfordshire, cottages were improved and more care given to the sick and aged. This part of England benefitted from not only the new and refurbished London hospitals but, above all, the introduction of smallpox innoculations. However, one of the effects of the success of these innoculations was a rapid drop in the death rate. This, coupled with a period of favourable weather at the close of the century, led to a gradual increase in population numbers, which although it was to cause most serious problems in the next century, meant more consumers and an expansion of trade and production in this one.

Throughout most of the century there were great fortunes to

be made in the City. Trade with the East Indies expanded and as England began to play a larger part in world affairs, there were other important centres for trading. Some City business-men bought country estates; in 1696 Samuel Ongley bought Old Warden. Also rich country families spent more time in town.

Agriculture Was Also Improved

The population of London grew rapidly and there was an increasing demand for fresh fruit and vegetables. By the end of the century there was a successful vegetable growing business in east Bedfordshire and meat and dairy-producing businesses in mid and west of the county.

Artificial fertilizers were not yet available but carefully selected seeds, improved drainage, the folding of sheep and a wider selection of crops in the rotations encouraged higher yields and better grassland. Wider use of turnips and the introduction of swedes made it easier and cheaper to over-winter livestock and so bring down the price of meat. It may have been in this century that the village people between Dunstable and Hockliffe began to produce ducks for the London market. This was often a sideline for the agricultural labourer who was struggling to support himself and his family. By far the majority were day-labourers and would be without work or pay on days when the ground was wet or frozen. However, apart from these lost days, for most of the century the rural labourers of Bedfordshire enjoyed fairly full employment.

The Methodist Movement Comes to Bedfordshire.

Out of this period of improved communications and if not education, a raised level of public awareness, a new religious denomination spread rapidly across the country. It was in 1728 that John Wesley began a new movement within the Anglican Church which had a simple and immediate appeal to working people. Everywhere he went vast crowds turned out to meet him.

The extent of his travels is well known and he must have crossed Bedfordshire on numerous occasions. One recorded example was in 1741 when he stopped in Dunstable for a hot cup of tea on his way to a preaching engagement in the north.

On February 16th 1747 he set out from home to preach at Potton. He and his friend were up at three in the morning and rode as far as Hatfield against a violent north wind. From then on the weather became even worse! Riding against driving snow and hail they eventually arrived in time to rest before his six o'clock sermon. The weather was not much better when, on March 6th 1758 he rode through Dunstable on his way to visit his friends at Sundon. This time a north-east wind blew torrential rain in his face so fiercely that he left the road at Dunstable and took a short cut across ploughed fields.

Wesley's Sundon friends were William Cole and his wife, of Sundon Manor. The year that William was High Sheriff he invited Wesley to preach the assize sermon. This was a very formal affair but most of Wesley's many visits were in small humble buildings, even in one case in a room over a pig style!*

At this time Wesley and his followers were seen as a break-away branch on the Anglican church and were not always popular. When he preached in Luton church the church wardens had the windows removed to a safe place in case there was a violent protest. However some years after his death his followers were recognised as a separate denomination.

Even the Calendar was Changed

A quite different 'improvement' that was introduced in 1851 was an Act of Parliament which brought in a 'New Style' of calendar. When Pope Gregory XIII introduced a new style of calendar in 1582 it was ignored here in England and the traditional Julian Calendar remained in use. From 1752 England joined Europe's Roman Catholic countries and started each new year on January 1st.

---

*   Miss Joyce Godber describes these visits in her comprehensive book about the county.

Bedfordshire's Towns Were Prospering

The Directory of Bedfordshire of 1785 records the prosperity of Bedfordshire's towns. Bedford, home of the tax and excise offices, the County Court and County Gaol was particularly prosperous. Barges could tie up near the bridge and there was a very successful business distributing 'sea' coal brought in from [Kings] Lynne. There were enough customers to support nine bakers, eleven butchers and every other type of shop – except a fishmonger. Fish was caught in the Ouse and kept in artificial pools near the bank. There were over forty inns and beer-houses listed! The market towns were all doing well and the larger villages had several shops and craftsmen.

Dunstable was still confined to its four hundred and fifty acres and four main roads. It had far fewer shops and other services than Bedford, but was, nevertheless, extremely prosperous. It had become a key site on the main road from London to the Midlands, (via Hockliffe and Stony Stratford).

Part Two
Dunstable in the Eighteenth Century

Success!

Past was the century when Dunstable's world really did turn upside down. The dominance of kings had given way to the Bill of Rights and the power of Parliament and the Protestant church accepted that there was more than one form of service acceptable to God. Now the people of Dunstable could unite and concentrate on exploiting the exciting new travel trade as it passed through their town.

The Roads Caused Trouble

Despite the prosperity of the travel industry, the roads (which were the key factor) were still cared for by local amateurs! It was comparatively easy for the surveyor (or stone-warden) elected at the Dunstable Easter vestry to collect the road-rates and supervise the care of the town roads. However, to the south of the town, Kensworth and Caddington were both responsible for miles of rural roads plus a share of their London road (A5) boundary. The parishioners of Houghton Regis had to raise the money and supply the labour to repair even more country roads, both sides of the Holyhead road (A5), as it passed through their parish, including the notorious Puddle or Chalk Hill. They even had part of the Luton road in their care. Further north, the villagers of Chalgrave and Hockliffe were responsible for the terrible mire through that village and the next steep hill was cared for by the people of Hockliffe and the few families who lived in Battlesden. So it went on – mile by mile; the magistrates encouraging and disciplining, the surveyors demanding a second and then a third set of road-rates.

Despite all this effort, there were some months when, even on the main roads, powdered chalk as fine as talcum powder rose above the level of the axles. At other times liquid mud disguised the potholes, leading to broken wheels and traces and strained and wounded horses. The system was inflexible. Even if a wealthy man like William Duncombe of Battlesden did leave money to repair the road from 'Puddlehill foot [to] Little Brickhill lane' it did nothing to stimulate the long-distance travel industry. However, once the network of *Turnpike Trusts* was established, things began to change.

The Turnpike Trusts

The first local trusts were set up in 1706; one was for the piece of Watling Street from Hockliffe towards Stony Stratford and the other from Hockliffe towards Woburn. These were followed by another in 1710 from Hockliffe back to Dunstable. However, there was difficulty in raising money and in buying or renting roadside land on which to mount the original pole or 'pike'. These sites had to be large enough to take future gates and eventually tollhouses. The section of road to be cared for by the trust had to be measured and registered and there were several false starts.

In 1723 a new committee started the Pondyard Trust from the Bull back to Shafford House, north of St. Albans. This is the low-lying area near where the cricket-bat willows grow today. The Act was for repairing and widening the road, which was described as being part of the 'post rode to Ireland'. It was said to be 'ruinous', 'almost impassable' and in places 'very narrow'.

South of Dunstable, Turnpike Farm marks the site of the first gate, but it was moved on more than one occasion as travellers discovered ways of evading the gate. The tolls charged at this gate in 1723 were:

Coach or chaise	3d (1.25p)
Wagon or cart	3d
Saddle horse (without a cart)	1d
Packhorse	1 halfpenny
Drovers with oxen	3d per score (20)
Drovers with hogs	1 halfpenny per score
Drovers with sheep	1 halfpenny per score

As the years went by, these prices would rise quite sharply. Gates higher up Watling Street which started at the same modest level had, by 1800, risen to one shilling and sixpence (7.5p) per coach, eight pence per cart and up to five pence for a score of sheep or pigs.

Even at the lower rates, these charges, which would soon be levied about every twelve miles along the Holyhead road, greatly added to the price of travel. This is why carters and drovers tried to find side roads whereby they could bypass the gates. Sometimes they tried to bribe the gate-keepers. In 1752 it was reported from the trustees of the Puddlehill turnpike that the takings had averaged just over £583 over the past seven years. After the death of the toll-collector, the new man was collecting £2 per week extra in the summer and £1 extra per week in the winter! However, they admitted that the expenses of running the toll-gate had risen from £46 to £83 per year. Both changes were due in part to the fact that they had decided to pay for two collectors. Toll collectors were not very well paid, so there must have been temptation to take bribes.

The Pondyard Trust filled in a gap between the toll roads from St. Albans back to London and from Dunstable north to Stony Stratford. There were still long gaps further north. Celia Fiennes reported in 1697 that the road called Hockley in the Hole was '. . . full of deep slows' [wet muddy patches] that in winter it must be impassable and that there was a 'very steepe chaulky hill from whence it has its name the Chalk Hill just as you enter Dunstable'. Celia Fiennes travelled through, thirteen years before the Act to set up the trust was passed. Fifteen years after the Act, the experienced traveller Daniel Defoe reported:

'upon the great Road there are wonderful improvements made and making . . . and we now see the
most dismal piece of ground for Travelling that
ever was in England, handsomely repaired; namely
from the top of the Chaulky Hill beyond Dunstable
down in Hockley Lane and thro' Hockley, . . .
such a road for Coaches, as worse was hardly
ever seen'.

Collecting tolls and employing a professional surveyor did not automatically lead to better roads. Unless trustees were conscientious, the surveyor capable and a good source of suitable stone available locally, the system could still fail. In general, the nearer to London, the better the roads.

The Earl of Egremont Visits Buxton
In 1744, the wife of the first Earl of Egremont was advised to take the waters at Buxton to help relieve her severe headache. Leaving London on April 23rd, they drove up to St. Albans where they spent the night at The Red Bull. The next morning they drove through Dunstable and had lunch at The George in Woburn. They continued like this up to Buxton where they stayed for several weeks. Unfortunately her headache did not

improve but when they heard that their daughter was soon to be 'lying in', they decided to return home. They slept at The George, Northampton on May 31st, ate lunch at Woburn the next day, slept at The Bull, Dunstable on the night of June 1st and on June 2nd, set off for home, stopping for lunch at Barnet. Luckily he kept a detailed record of his time-keeping. On the way out his journey from London to St. Albans was at four miles per hour. Driving from St. Albans through to Dunstable he managed three-and-a-half miles per hour. On some stretches north of Woburn his speed dropped even lower. He does not record if he had two or four horses, but most days he travelled between thirty-three and thirty-four miles, about two-thirds of these in the morning. These speeds are only a guide, but they do reinforce our knowledge of the hazards.

A local industry at the foot of Puddlehill and other steep hills was the stabling of the 'Cock Horse'. In practice the stable probably had a team of several very heavy horses. They were hired out to join the owners' horses in pulling coaches up and over the hill.

As a way of protecting the roads, Government policy occasionally changed concerning the number of horses legally allowed to pull coaches and the width of the iron coach wheels. On May 11th 1768 the trustees of Puddlehill tollgate announced that 'it is impracticable for wagons' with the weights announced by Parliament 'to be drawn up Puddlehill (the length thereof being [just over] 102 poles, and bounded by a post at each end) by the number of horses by the said Act allowed'. They therefore ordered that wheels nine inches broad may be drawn up the said hill with any number of horses not exceeding six. As Puddlehill delayed and put travellers from London to the northwest of England, Scotland, Wales and Ireland at risk, it would appear to have been a national problem, but in practice, it was now the responsibility of the Puddlehill Trust.

The Romans were the first people known to cut chalk from the top of the hill and to spread it lower down. This type of effort helped, but made little impression on the real difficulties and dangers.

A Circuitous Route

By 1780 there had been so many accidents and so many complaints about the delays and damage to coaches and horses that the trustees decided to implement a major change. In those days it seemed impossible to cut through the hill, so they decided to make a 'circuitous' coach road. Using a gang of labourers, they cleared a route from behind what is now Chalkhill Garage round to and across the road to Sewell and continuing round to what is now the area of French's Avenue. It was, 1,400 yards long in total, cost £16,000 (an enormous sum of money) and it would take several successful years of road tolls to recoup the cost. However, it was never really successful. It had a poor surface, was uneven and hilly and its particular disadvantage was that it added about half a mile to the route. Both roads remained open for people to choose which one they would use, leaving the trustees with the extra expense of keeping both in good repair. Despite all the work and expenditure, there was no real improvement until 1837, when Thomas Telford ordered a cutting to be made right through the chalk and a narrow road to be constructed at the present level.

Some More Dunstable Inns

In one way Puddlehill brought extra business into the town. Coming from the south, travellers preferred not to tackle the hill at the end of a tiring day. The risk of getting stuck just as it was getting dark was very frightening and apart from the general discomfort, there was a real risk of attacks from highwaymen. Travellers coming from the north were often in a nervous condition after tackling Hockley-in-the-Hole and Puddlehill. They were in need of a meal, a rest and a good night's sleep.

Dunstable was well-equipped to provide these services. Inns have been noted since the 14th century and in the last chapter we looked at some which were already becoming out of date. Now we shall look at some which started in the 17th and 18th centuries.

The Bull

There was a Bull Inn in South Street from about 1500 but this appears to have been closed well before the end of the 17th century. The deeds of the present Bull have survived and entries start in 1648, but there are references to two earlier names: *The Red Hart* and before that *The Prince's Arms*. The evidence suggests that the land had once belonged to Dunstable Fraternity, that the Wingate family had bought it, built a new inn and named it in honour of Prince [later King] Edward. By 1671 it was slightly bigger than The White Horse and The White Hart, but unlike these town centre inns, it enjoyed fifteen and a half acres of 'closes' or paddocks. At this stage in its history William Kitteridge was the inn-holder, but by 1678 he was getting into financial difficulties and borrowed money from Henry Earle (coachman). As Kitteridge was unable to repay the debt, Earle took over the business. The smaller 16th century Bull Inn having closed, Earle used the name. Economically this change of ownership was good for Dunstable as Earle wanted it for sound business reasons. (Continued below.)

The Stagecoach Industry

Earlier in this chapter it was noted that economically the great event of the last century was the start of the stagecoach industry. On 9th April 1657 an advertisement appeared in the newspaper *Mercurius Politicus* announcing:

for the convenient accommodation of passengers from and betwixt London and West Chester there is provided several stagecoaches which go from the George Inn without Aldersgate upon every Monday, Wednesday and Friday – to Coventry in 2 days for 25 shillings, Stone in 3 days for 30 shillings, Chester in 4 days for 35 shillings. Return on the same day with fresh horses each day.

This was the first long-distance stagecoach service and it stopped in Dunstable. Timetables were published, cross-routes were established and the standard of both roads and inns began to improve.

The Bull (Continued)

One of the entrepreneurs who started this new service was Henry Earle. As the years went by he established a chain of stables to provide a pool of spare horses and an opportunity to rest or rear others. The fifteen and a half acres of pasture extended from North Street round in a crescent to Leighton Gap in West Street. These would have been ideal for his thriving business.

For many years the success of the inn continued with various local tenants. However, when Earle's daughter, Sarah, married a Dunstable cutler,* John Wright, on May 4th 1713, The Bull passed to a less experienced owner. Financial difficulties built up and in less than a year they were obliged to sell. John and Sarah remained in Dunstable and between 1712 and 1720 baptised two sons and two daughters. The John Wright who was buried in 1735 may have been one of their sons because John Wright senior aged 'about sixty-five years' was still alive in 1737. At that date he was living in Middlesex, having left Dunstable seventeen years before. (Maybe his wife died when the last baby was born?) At this time anyone finding themselves in financial difficulties was by law returned to the parish of their birth, or to the parish where they had previously contributed to the poor rates. Wright swore on oath that he had once paid 'Parochial Levies and rates that were assessed upon The Bull Inn in Dunstable'.

After John and Elizabeth left The Bull nothing more is known about it until 1744, when the highwayman story recorded below confirms that The Bull was still a regular stopping-place for stagecoaches. There is then a gap until 1770 when Arthur Young (Secretary of the Board of Agriculture) called in as he started his six-month tour to the north of England. He noted that he had enjoyed very good mutton steaks for which he had been charged one shilling (5p).

Ducks were available at two shillings and each person paid tuppence towards the shared bread. Ten years later there was a new landlord, William Palmer. In 1785 Palmer's Bull was still of sufficient standing to be one of the four inns which were included in

---

* Someone who makes or deals in knives.

the Select Directory of Bedfordshire. This may be why, four years later, the famous gentleman traveller, Viscount Byng chose The Bull. At the end of his stay he wished he had ridden on to The Sugar Loaf. He and his friend had gone to visit the Priory Church and when they returned saw ducks 'dead and dying' in the orchard. To their horror, duck was later offered on the menu for supper!

Unfortunately there is currently no evidence to show when this important stagecoach inn was pulled down and replaced by a beer-house, now the popular public house, nor do we know what happened to the closes until, one by one, they were sold for building.

The Crown

During the Civil War, Michael Grigg was one of Dunstable's few Royalists. In 1618, a 'Mr Grigge' owned the newly-opened and prestigious Crowne Inn. At a later stage this was regularly used by the Earl [later Duke] of Bedford and his family. The Russell papers contain details of a hawking expedition in August 1689. After a day on the Downs he and his friends rode into the town and had a great dinner at The Crown. Trumpeters came out to lead the party, the church bells rang, musicians entertained the guests during the evening and people from miles around lined the street and loitered round the kitchen door. It was a very grand affair.

In the 18th century it was owned, for a time, by Jane Cart's charity and was known as *The Windmill* or *The Windmill and Still*. The 19th century owner was forced to go out of business when the railway came. The site is remembered as Warren's Hat Factory and is today occupied by Imagine and the buildings which lie behind it, near the pedestrian crossing.

The Cock

This inn stood next door to The Crown. In the Morton family wills of the 17th century, they described it as an inn, but it was a small house with little room for stables and by 1697, the family were describing themselves as victuallers and their business was selling food and drink. In addition, different members of the family were [straw] collar-makers or saddlers. Later in the century they sold the business and the premises as a saddlers' workshop.

This was a typical example of the versatility of Dunstable's businesses. It was not solely income from inn-keeping that kept the town economically buoyant. There was a blacksmith in the centre of the road by the pond and at least two nearby in inn-yards. Apart from the Moretons, there was another leatherworker near The White Hart and several other dependent businesses.

The White Horse
Henry Sam continued to run the post office until his death in 1703 although the inn itself was much smaller.

The Wrestlers
By the time that Celia Fiennes rode into the town, The Wrestlers had become a separate business at the northern end of The White Horse. It continued as a victualling house into the next century.

The Raven (later Crow, today Crown)
Once connected to The White Horse, this was one of Dunstable's victualling houses. The business was similar to the one that is running there today.

The Nag's Head
The connection with the Settle family has been described in the previous chapter. Elkanah returned to Dunstable in 1702 to arrange the sale of the property to George Knowles, who had opened a large drapery shop next door.

The Red Lion
This inn continued to stand out into Church Street until 2nd June 1963 when it was taken down to road widening. In the 19th and 20th centuries it was a popular town centre hotel.

The White Hart
This important stagecoach inn continued through the 18th century with a blacksmith in its courtyard and a saddler to the north, where *The Bear*, which in the future had several retail uses, had once stood. In the mid 19th century it was called *The King's Arms*.

By the end of the century travellers were expecting a much higher standard of comfort and 15th century inns such as The White Hart found it difficult to compete. Also as the roads improved, it became possible to travel further during the hours of daylight. From being first or even second night stop out of London, Dunstable was regarded by many people as a meal break, rather than an overnight stop. On 14th March 1786, it was described as 'formerly The White Hart' and had become a gentleman's residence. In 1795 it was still a private house but by 1804 it was owned by Thomas Burr, brewer, and had become a public house. Mary Nicholls was running the blacksmith's business in a newly-built workshop at the back. Her family name is recorded as Nicholas Way. The White Hart was finally taken down in July 1965 when the new shopping centre was built.

The Sugar Loaf

No date has been recorded for the opening of what became Dunstable's premier inn. The first written record is in the will of George Briggs in 1692, where it is not described as 'newly-built'. His tenant was Jane Lee and in 1671 a John Lee had a building with six hearths, i.e. the same size as Kingsbury and Priory House, but nothing like the size of Dunstable's older inns. Jane Lee was further up the social ladder than the average innkeeper's wife. George Briggs left her money for a mourning ring and she was a personal friend of the later owner, Jane Cart. When her son died in 1688, his burial entry in the register reads 'John Lee, innkeeper of The Sugar Loaf'. An earlier John Lee married Elizabeth Griggs, daughter of the Mr Griggs who owned The Crown, in 1596.

Sources such as The Sugar Loaf advertisement in the Dunstable Gazette during 1874 ignore the above evidence and state that the hotel had been established in 1717. After the death of George Briggs, his heir sold the inn to William Chew and 1717 is the date when Jane Cart bought the business. Her restoration was to accommodate the growing high-class trade. The Lee family continued as tenants and Eleanor Lee was postmistress 1765–1770; it was essentially an inn for private travellers and stage-coach travellers were encouraged to go elsewhere.

The Post Office in Dunstable

The registered post office moved on more than one occasion but was usually in a room (building) on the northern side of The Sugar Loaf. The post office licences were only offered after careful scrutiny and an official registration. The Sugar Loaf was lucky not to lose the licence in 1793 when the holder, Mr Oliver, 'sold' it to Mr Coates, the new tenant of the inn, without going through the formality of first handing it back to the Post Master General. Unknown to Mr Oliver, a London official had promised the lucrative position to Mr Ward, the local contractor who was responsible for the running of the mailcoaches and supplying the horses. The local post office representative was sent to interview Mr Coates and considered him to be suitable for the responsibilities involved. He recommended appointing Coates from 4th January 1793, at a salary of £24 per year plus approximately three shillings [15p] a week, calculated at the rate of one halfpenny per letter delivered. However, this undermined post office authority and was not acceptable. There were further discussions and Mr Oliver wrote that as Mr Coates had been his clerk [representative?], he was quite familiar with the business. A letter was then sent from the London office requesting sworn affidavits. These appear to have been received on January 4th, but they did not solve the problem of the promise made to Mr Ward. Eventually the officials decided that rather than accept Oliver's resignation, they would formally dismiss him and so remove the subject of Coates' purchase. They could then appoint Mr Ward without any argument, but five days later they learned that he had refused the position. When it was discovered that Mr Ward had never meant to actually do the work himself, but had intended passing it to the bookkeeper who managed his coach company, there was relief that he had turned it down. After some discussion, it was decided that Mr Coates had 'willfully' been endeavouring to secure the position for himself by mis-represenation. This freed Oliver of much of the blame, so dismissal was forgotten but a formal reprimand was issued and he was asked to continue running the Post Office, but 'in a convenient place in the High Street', not at the Sugar Loaf! The correspondence ends at this point and for a few years the Post Office moved from place to place. In 1840 it was run by Joseph Squires at number 2, Middle Row (one of the shops which once jutted out into West Street). By 1851 the main Post Office was back at The Sugar Loaf. Letters and parcels now had to be collected from the railway station and the postmaster had one or two sub-branches under his control.

After the coming of the railways (see below) The Sugar Loaf closed for a few months and then re-opened as a small modern hotel. The Johnson family were still there; John was in charge of the hotel and was licensed to sell wines and spirits. Thomas Coates Johnson, stationer, was in charge of the Post Office.

In the Post Office's 1862 letterbook, there is another flurry of correspondence concerning Dunstable. To put if tactfully, Thomas had 'muddled' the money he had received for stamps issued to his sub-branches. The officials were scrupulously fair and wrote letter after letter weighing up their desire to sack him and their hesitation about leaving him without income. Their final decision is not included, but in 1864, George Fisher Scroggs opened a new Post Office in his stationer's shop near the cross-roads. In 1912 it moved across the road to the first 'Old Post Office' building [DHSS] and the site of Scroggs' shop was bought by Barclays Bank.

Yet More Dunstable Inns

The Duke of Bedford's Arms – Later Grove House
There are various families connected with innkeeeping in Dunstable, several of them owning more than one inn and others who were intermarried. In 1747 Harry Norman was landlord of The Crown (ex Windmill), the high-class inn which was rival to The Sugar Loaf. Although the latter had a large site and access to paddocks at the rear, The Crown only had its yard and a field with stables near the Friary site in South Street. Norman was about to marry Ann Swindall, whose father had just built a new inn with access to a great deal of pasture (this became known as

the Duke's Close). At that time Swindall was living in his newly
built inn, The Duke of Bedford's Arms, but he moved out to
make room for his daughter and son-in-law. Their first son was
baptised Henry Swindall Norman. Norman managed both inns
and in 1751, Swindall bought The Saracen's Head. When he died
in 1759 he left The Duke of Bedford's Arms to his family and not
a lot more is heard of it. It was still an inn in 1762 when an
auction was held to sell a long lease of the Totternhoe Quarry.

This inn was probably built at the wrong time, trying to break
into the market just as there was a real improvement in
conditions on the roads and Dunstable had less need of hotel
bedrooms. John Miller, who owned the Duke's Closes, bought
the inn in 1773 and for some reason felt that it was more suitable
as a private house. He let it out to a series of tenants until 1813
when he sold it to Frederick Brown. The Brown family used it as
a family house. It was a most handsome property with a park,
lawns and pleasure gardens. Shortly before 1840 William
Frederick Brown decided to enlarge the house, divide the
grounds and let it as two private houses. The northern part was
called Grove House and the southern half, the Beeches. In 1890
the Reverend Canon Heyrick Macaulay MA, rector of Dunstable,
moved into Grove House, staying until 1903.

About this time a Mrs Mary Elizabeth Maulden from the Isle
of Wight bought both parts of the property. In 1906 she let
Grove House to Arthur Bagshawe (see below) and in 1914 he
took over the tenancy of the Beeches and united the two, buying
both properties on October 13th 1920. When he died in 1926,
the reunited Grove House passed to his eldest son Arthur William
Gerald Bagshawe, who sold the house plus five acres of land to
Dunstable Borough Council on July 9th 1936. He parted with
this valuable property for only £8,000 as he was 'of the opinion
that Grove House and gardens should belong to the town'. He
made this gesture of goodwill to the town and its inhabitants and
expressed a hope that the council would maintain the high
standards of care kept by himself and his father. I hope that they
are aware how well it looks today – I am sure they would be
pleased.

The Saracen's Head

This was opened by the Priory as an extension to their other sources of accommodation. Although there was once a severe fire there are still very old timbers in the roof and judging by the position below street level, it could go back to the 14th century. It is unusual to have an old building enjoying such a long street frontage and this is why the Saracen's Head is included in this chapter.

The building which we see today originated as at least two or maybe three units. The Priory opened The Saracen's Head (a name which was of obvious interest to early travellers) and also *The George*. In the 17th century Josias Settle of *The Nag's Head*, owned a second inn called *The Bell*, which he left to his daughter, Sarah. It was described as being between the 'Sarizenshead' and The George. The years went by and there were many changes. In the mid 18th century Robert Crouch, bricklayer owned The Saracen's Head and a cottage on either side; there was also a block of stabling on the roadside and a barn and more stabling at the back. He passed this potentially valuable estate to his son James. At that time the business was not big enough to support a family and James was also a bricklayer. His widowed daughter Hannah Cook, lived in one of the cottages and ran the inn for him. On the east of this estate was Priory Close and on the west was Fryars Pond, another Dunstable pond sited out in the road. In 1791 James Crouch divided the estate between his daughters. One daughter was married to John Gostelow who agreed to sell their share to Hannah for £125. She or her descendants owned it at the time of the Great Fire in 1815 and they must have rebuilt the surviving frames as one long building. There was no reference to the Fryars Pond when the Cook family sold the business to Daniel Twidell, of Totternhoe, in October 1834. It was probably filled in at the same time as those in North Street. Twidell sold it to Benjamin Bennett in June 1841 for £880. From Bennetts Brewery it passed to Green's Brewery.

Surviving Records

While some inns have very sketchy records others, such as The Bull, are extremely well-documented and their stories illustrate many different aspects of Dunstable life through the centuries. Some, like The White Horse in Church Street, which was opened c 1544/5, can be traced through a long succession of owners, but only became really interesting in the 19th century when the owner kept a receipt book. Dunstable is very fortunate that, thanks to Bedfordshire and Luton Archive Service, so many documents have survived. A specialist book is required to cover all these inns, as there are too many for a book of this size.

Some Smaller Inns such as *The Rose and Crown, The Swan with Two Necks,* once called *The Lion and the Lamb, The Cross Keys,* all in Middle Row, were trading in the 18th century, but have long since gone. These town centre inns without land were actually beer-houses, which sometimes had a licence to serve food. The landlords usually had a second source of income, e.g. the landlord of The Swan sometimes acted as an agent for long-distance carriers and by the end of the 19th century the landlord of The Rose and Crown combined selling beer, fish and fruit. *The Shoulder of Mutton* is not recorded until the 19th century, when it is shown as a bigger building, allowing the landlord to augment his income by taking lodgers. On the night of the 1841 census, there were seven lodgers, but in 1851 the enumerator recorded: the landlady, her sister, two female servants, two bonnet-sewers and seven men!

18th century inns outside or on the outskirts of the town, such as *The Woolpack, the Half Moon* and *The Cow and Hare* (which was rebuilt in c.1762 and renamed *The Wagon and Horses)*, all had several paddocks for grazing livestock. They were successful businesses, often used by drovers and carriers.

Highwaymen

There are many accounts of horses and money being stolen – most robberies taking place on the outskirts of the town, especially on the road near Markyate. A drover foolish enough to be seen counting his employer's money in a London beer-house had it stolen on this stretch of road. In the 17th century a Dunstable carrier had hats stolen from his wagon, in the 18th century a box of lace was stolen from the Bedford wagon. Just north of the town the driver of the Manchester wagon had his money, watch and horse stolen and there were many similar robberies. On the outskirts of Markyate a stagecoach driver was not only robbed in 1777, but was also thrown from his box and suffered a broken hip. He was within the Markyate boundary when this outrage took place, but rather than accept the cost of his recovery and the care of his passengers, the local overseer of the poor put the driver into the coach and drove them all into Dunstable. He then abandoned the injured man, at two o'clock in the morning, 'to the tender mercy of anyone who should find him'.

Over the centuries there must have been many highway robbers working in Dunstable, but below are just two examples. The first definitely involves *The Bull* and the second may have been either *The Bull* or *The Wheatsheaf* [now the Distillery].

Gentleman Harry

The author CG Harper recorded this story, which is supposed to have taken place in the spring on 1747.

Harry's surname was Simms and when the story opened he was an undergraduate at Cambridge University. However, before he had completed his course, he was tempted by wanderlust and decided to go on a walking tour, supporting himself by some mild highway robbery. He eventually drifted into the army, then into the navy but this was a very hard way of life, so when his ship put into Bristol, he slipped away and deserted.

Remembering his carefree days on the road, he then turned to highway robbery as a serious career – but he never used force. He worked his way across to Essex and then south to London. There he had a very frightening experience; he heard a scuffle, witnessed a rough-looking thief being arrested and discovered that the constables thought that they were arresting him! This was indeed a warning; there and then Simms vowed to give up robbery and look for a new career. He did not even stop to sell the numerous watches and pieces of jewellery which he had collected in Essex.

Deciding to ride along the Holyhead road, living off his considerable savings, he intended to cross to Dublin, where he could sell the valuables, using the money as capital for his future.

All went well until he got to St. Albans. Then, safely away from London and sitting comfortably in an inn, he drank more port than was good for him. This made him over-confident so that as he was approaching Redbourn, he rashly overtook and challenged three men. One of them hit Simms over the head with his whip, before all three rode off towards Dunstable. The blow did not appear to sober Simms as, having allowed them to get ahead, he caught them up, demanded and got their money (7 shillings [35p], 2 guineas [£2.10] and 17 shillings [85p]) and an old watch, before himself riding into Dunstable. Arriving at the outskirts of the town he was then foolish enough to hold up the Warrington stagecoach, single-handed!

Not knowing where it would stop in Dunstable, he took a chance and cantered through the town, choosing to enter The Bull, where he ordered a brandy. Then he was very unlucky; before he got the drink to his lips, the coach came lumbering into The Bull yard and to his horror, he watched as the passengers headed for the very room in which he was sitting. In a flash he rushed out of the back door, pulled his tired horse from the stable and urged it on over Puddlehill.

He rode through Hockliffe until he reached The Star, which had a useful back entrance onto the Woburn road. This time he shunned the main tap room and sat by the kitchen fire, drinking more brandy but ready to slip out of the door. At least, that was what he intended, but the long ride, the brandy and the heat from the fire soon lulled him off to sleep. Unknown to him, a search party had been organised and was calling at every inn and beer-house along the road. He woke to find himself looking into the loaded gun-barrels aimed by three young soldiers. He at once surrendered and appeared to hand over all the watches and jewellery that he was carrying. Full of brandy, he staggered upstairs, fell on a bed and pretended to sink into a heavy sleep. The three soldiers made themselves as comfortable as possible and settled down to keep watch. Eventually a plan formed in

Simms' mind; he sprang up and, grabbing some trinkets which he had hidden in his neckcloth, returned downstairs. To the amazement of the soldiers he threw the trinkets into the fire.

All three soldiers rushed to the fireplace to try to save what they thought were valuable jewels, giving Simms the opportunity to grab their pistols. What he did not know was that they were old and, to get the bullets to fly in a straight line, they had to be fired at a slight angle. He therefore aimed in the normal way and all three bullets went astray. This had been his last chance; the soldiers would not dare risk another escape. He was tightly bound and carried off to London, where soon afterwards he was hung at Tyburn.

Dunstable's Own Highwayman

Charles Lambourn in his *Dunstaplelogia* tells of a highwayman who committed his one and only attack on the boundary of Dunstable. One wild night a grand traveller with a red cloak and real gold lace on his hat entered The Wheatsheaf in Upper Houghton. He ordered ale for himself and food for his horse. The landlord's wife wanted to keep such a fine customer and tried to dissuade him from going 'over the hill' on such a wild, moonless night: she insisted on telling him horror stories of attacks on other travellers. He became impatient and kept looking at a gold repeater watch 'the size and shape of a turnip', and said he must get to the coast to catch a boat the next day. The locals, drinking in the next room, watched with interest. One old man who came to beg the price of a drink was, to his delight, given half-a-crown (nearly two days' wages). The traveller, having finished his ale, called for his horse and set off towards Puddlehill. After a while he realised he was being followed by a well-dressed young man whom he had seen drinking with the locals. It was not until the traveller allowed the young man to catch up with him that he noticed he was holding a pistol. Rather diffidently, the young man asked for twenty guineas and offered his cheap ring as a guarantee that he would repay. The traveller realised that this was no ordinary highwayman and offered him a purse of silver, but the young man insisted that he only wanted a loan of twenty guineas. The gentleman, a Mr James Clemitson

from Mincing Lane, London, reached the port and sailed away
for ten years. When he returned to London, Clemitson found
great excitement in the City; the manager of the silversmith's
business in Ludgate Hill was about to marry the owner's daughter.
At once Mr Clemitson recognised his highwayman and out of
curiosity went into the silversmith's shop and showed him the
cheap ring. To his surprise the man was delighted to see him; he
had searched everywhere and had even advertised to try to find
his benefactor. Ten years before, when he was an apprentice, he
had returned to Dunstable to visit his mother and to his horror
had found that she was about to be evicted for not paying her
rent. He only had a few hours to find the twenty guineas needed
and had been sitting in the Wheatsheaf in utter despair when he
spotted the rich traveller and planned the forced loan. He had
not heard his victim say he was going abroad and was desperately
worried when he had been unable to repay what had been
intended as a short-term loan. The story ended happily, but Mr
Lambourn would not name the young man because in 1859 his
family was still running the silversmith's business in London. In
some versions of the story, the young man turns out to be Mr
Clemitson's grandson.

The Manor of Dunstable

It would be many years before Dunstable had a Borough Council
and meanwhile several different agencies were involved in the
organisation. Many highway robberies can be found in the
Bedfordshire sheriff's records, but more serious offences were
often committed by men already wanted for other crimes. If
captured, these men might be taken straight to London for trial.
The magistrates' courts continued to handle local offences and to
oversee the work and book-keeping of the 'volunteer' Overseers
of the Poor and Road Surveyors or stonewardens.

Parish Officers
In many places uneducated and often unsuitable people were
'elected' to hold these positions but in Dunstable the innkeepers

appear to have acted as church wardens and to have kept an eye on the other organisations which were responsible for spending parish money.

The Care of the Sick and Elderly

Rich people paid the local doctors, but the poor were dependent on the Overseer. In 1751 Dr Crawley was employed by the Overseers to treat those who were seriously ill or injured. A Mr Henry Danniels had an injured foot which appears to have become poisoned. Dr Crawley's time was included in one overall fee, but his recommended treatment for the month of December came to nearly five pounds. The foot had to be regularly bathed and soaked with 'fomentation spirits' and the patient was regularly given 'febrifuge decoction' to bring down his temperature. He was purged at least once and each night he had a soothing mixture to help him sleep. These medications came to £2.16 shillings [£2.80]. Another man had broken his leg and broken bones were not included in the contract. His bill included:

'For setting his leg of a Compound Fracture, all Dressings and attendance [3 months] £3.17 shillings [£3.85]'.

The Role of the Manor Court

From the above we can see that the Manor Court had no control over the day-to-day running of the town. We have also seen that when threatened by a fear of witches, the innkeepers started by handling the matter themselves and then referred the evidence to the magistrates, who, in their turn, referred it to the King's judges. There is no reference to anyone consulting the Lord of the Manor's steward.

The Lord of the Manor

The position of Lord of the Manor had previously been leased from the Crown by the Earls of Ailesbury (Houghton House) but was now leased by the Dukes of Bedford. The *Manor Court* records are missing until 1740, but after that date are full of interesting information. The charges had nothing to do with crime but concerned the smooth running of the town and the collection of rents and dues. The Duke's 'gentleman steward' was in charge, assisted by twelve local jurors plus foreman and two affeerors who traditionally helped to assess the fines. If anyone was serving for the first time, he would have to buy a shilling's-worth of ale to be shared with his companions. First it was agreed to continue with the existing bye-laws and then small fines were registered and collected from any new tenants. Other 'fines' which had actually become mutually-accepted rents were concerned with the 'Lord's waste'. Any small piece of ground (other than the main roads or a measured and recognised piece in private ownership or tenancy) was regarded as the property of the Lord of the Manor. The fine for grazing tethered cows on the grass verges was five shillings. Innkeepers who erected signposts out in the road were fined one shilling, as were the owners of houses with porches. Anyone enclosing a yard, garden or orchard was fined slightly more, while those in-filling or building houses along the edge of the road were fined several shillings at each court. Some items, e.g. positioning woodpiles and manure heaps well away from the roads, went back to the original bye-laws of the early 13th century. Before the court closed, four constables, two ale-tasters, two men to check the quality of leather that was sold and a hayward (whose job was to ensure the good repair of hedges and ditches) were elected.

The Market

The end of High Street North which adjoins the present roundabout was once on a slope and was known as Market Hill. This was where the main stalls were laid out; the cattle market was in the Square and the sheep market was in West Street. It is not known exactly what goods were on sale, but the currier (leather-dresser) who worked behind The White Hart had a stall and no doubt there were stalls selling straw and plait in addition to singing birds in cages and larks (netted on the Downs) prepared for the table. Everything was strictly controlled by the rules of the Manor Court. Anyone who hawked or pitched in the market had to pay one penny or, if at the fair, two pennies. Those selling out of a hamper had to pay a rent of one penny, whereas those using a basket only had to pay a halfpenny.

Newcomers wanting a stall had to pay an entry fee of ten shillings and all stallholders had to pay tolls. For every horse or bull that was sold, the toll was four pence, for every cow twopence and every calf, hog or pig one penny. Sheep and lambs, however, were charged at eight pence for twenty. An important rule for any market was the strict supervision of weights and measures. At each sitting of the 'Manor Court' it was recorded that every stallholder had to check his equipment against the standard provided. Dunstable's standard weights and measures are in Luton Museum.

The Churches in the Eighteenth Century

This century more than any other was dominated by the roads and the travel industry. However we must not forget that behind all this bustle Dunstablians were living normal domestic lives and, in this century, going to their chosen church on Sundays. Travellers and townspeople alike now had a choice of places where they could worship.

The Priory Church of St. Peter
The Reverend John Lord stayed at the Priory Church until 1728. Three other experienced clergymen shared the rest of the century and although repairs may have been delayed, it was a quiet and settled century for the congregation.

The Quakers
The Act of Toleration which followed the arrival of William and Mary, gave the Quakers their opportunity to build a permanent meeting-house. This was at 15 West Street, near to where the buses draw in today. They had a small graveyard at the back but for many years they continued to visit Sewell on special occasions. This building was expensive to maintain so in 1797 they decided to meet with the Quakers in Luton.

The Baptists
It is not known when the first services were held in Dunstable but

it was recorded in 1696 that Sister Riggs was received into full communion 'at a church meeting in Dunstable'. Thomas Hayward had died in 1688, the same year as John Bunyan, but his (or his son's) house continued as the licensed meeting house at Kensworth. Following his death his duties were shared by Brother Finch of Dunstable and Brother Hardon of Wheathamstead. Thomas Hayward, who his friends described as a 'laborious servant of Christ' had managed to served and unite a group which covered such distant places as (Old) Welwyn, (South) Mimms, Berkhamsted and Brickhill. After much thought and prayer, the elders decided to support a full time 'preaching brother' who would be assisted by the two local men. Unfortunately the choice of this new leader caused a breach amongst the members. In 1694 sixty-five members, including some from Dunstable, followed Brother Marsom to a meeting place which he had provided in Luton. This division *may* have been caused by the desire to be less rigid and to occasionally accept members who had previously been baptised as babies. At a later date this group became associated with the Bunyan group at Bedford.

The gravestones which stand in an orchard at Thorn were once connected with a small meeting place associated with Marsom's group. The Baptist Church, now the West Street Baptist Church, came to Dunstable via Thorn and Houghton Regis. The Old Baptist Chapel, first built in 1708, was started by a group directly associated with Kensworth.

The Methodists

It has been noted in Part One that in 1738 the Reverend John Wesley began what he regarded as a new movement within the Church of England. At a religious meeting in London he became assured of the salvation which was offered to true believers and in the next fifty years he carried his message all over the country. He sometimes passed through Dunstable on his way to visit friends at Sundon and recorded a visit to the town in 1758. His ideas were not popular with many traditional church members and gradually his followers became a separate denomination.

It is not known when they first met for worship in Dunstable, but in 1801 John Darley of Dunstable was circuit steward for Bedford. By 1812 a group of Methodists were meeting in Darley's carpenters' workshop in Church Street. This quickly grew too small and they moved, first to 7 High Street South and then into the building at 15 West Street, vacated by the Quakers.

Once established in this meeting house they began planning and fund-raising to get their own permanent building. In 1831 they built their first chapel in the Square and although it was burnt down in 1844, they built a much bigger one in the following year.

The Charitable Families

The Priory Church is rich in brasses and monuments, but these are not of titled people. Because the Lord of the Manor lived elsewhere and because the geographic layout of the town meant that it had no country suburbs, it did not attract traditional 'gentry'. The richer members of Dunstable's population were in the travel or service industries, farmers or commuters. In the previous chapter we met the Marshe family of Kingsbury and their immediate descendants. Some of the male descendants stayed in South Bedfordshire as doctors and lawyers, while others went to London and joined City companies such as the Distillers. Elizabeth, daughter of William Marshe, married Thomas Chew, haberdasher [dealer in small items of dress], at the Priory Church on January 13th 1640. Although the Marshes were a local family three of their sons joined the London Distillers Company. Two of their daughters, Frances and Jane, married two other London Distillers, James Cart (who may have come from a Dunstable family) and William Ashton. By the time that these two gentlemen died they had become very wealthy. Their widows lived on in two adjoining houses in St. John's Street, London. The Carts had nine children, all of whom pre-deceased their mother and the Ashtons eight, seven of whom had also died. Elizabeth, the youngest and only survivor of Frances' children, was struck out of her mother's will for marrying against her mother's wishes.

Frances was eighty when she died and Jane was eighty-three, so they had very few remaining relatives. They therefore made numerous bequests to charity. Some of these were to London churches and associated charities, some were to set up small charities in Dunstable; but in both cases their main gift to Dunstable was the foundation of six almshouses.

The Ashton Almshouses
In 1715 these were built in West Street, on the corner of Ashton Street, now Ashton Square. They were for the benefit of six poor women who attended church [of England] every Sunday and who had been communicants in that church for at least two years. They were repaired in the mid 19th century, but by 1939 were in a very poor state and not considered suitable for the elderly. In 1969 they were replaced by new, purpose-built flats in Bullpond Lane.

Jane Cart's Almshouses
This is the terrace of six attractive brick houses in High Street South which were for widowed or unmarried ladies who did not have the means to run a home. She left 2s.6d (12.5p) for them to have a dinner once a year, £2 per person for fuel and £1.10s (£1.50) to buy a gown, petticoat, 2 shifts, one pair of stockings and one pair of shoes. Each one was also to receive £5.4 shillings to help with the expenses of maintaining and caring for their homes. They are still in use today.

Jane Cart's Gifts to the Priory Church
She gave many gifts to the Priory, including the pulpit cloth on show on the north wall of the building. A few years before she died, Jane gave a set of communion plate to the church and also a clock for the steeple [tower]. In her will she left £3 per year for winding the clock and another £1 per year for keeping it in good repair. Both Frances Ashton and Jane Cart left money to provide bread for those poor people who attended church on Sundays. The shelves at the back of the church, which once held the bread provided by Jane Cart, are now used for hymn books and the bread money is used as part of the Mayor's Christmas fund.

The Ladies' Lodge Almshouses

John Marshe, brother of Elizabeth [Chew] and Francis [who married Rebecca Briggs], was the member of the family who married Blandina Iremonger of Leighton Buzzard. They had six children (cousins of Frances and Jane). By 1701, both John and Blandina had died, leaving one son and two daughters. John instructed that money from his estate should be used to help the poor. The son, John, died in 1706 and daughters Blandina and Mary, who had married Thomas Lockington, shared his estate. Mary died in 1730 by which time both sisters had made wills instructing their executors to use part of their money to help the poor. Both left money to help various unmarried 'gentlewomen'. About ten years later Blandina (died 1741) outlined her intentions to found another set of six almshouses. These were not for the very poor but for 'six maiden gentlewomen . . . upwards of the age of 40 years . . . who frequented the Public Worship of the Church of England as by law established, and no other person'. The almshouses were opened around 1743 and are still in use today.

The Chew School

William Chew, younger brother of Elizabeth (Aynscombe, died 1711), Frances and Jane, became a successful distiller, but died unmarried and intestate in 1712. His estate, worth nearly £28,000, was divided between Elizabeth's son, Thomas Aynscombe and his two widowed sisters. In 1714 this was divided into three portions. However, as they were aware that William had intended to found a charity school, they decided to use some of his estate for that purpose. The Chew School, which will be included in the next chapter, opened in 1715.

The school and three sets of almshouses were each put into the care of a very responsible and capable committee, the almshouses still being organised in the same way today.

Towards the End of the Century

In 1780 a list was made of men eligible to be called as jurors, i.e. above the age of twenty-one years but under the age of seventy years and who held freehold land worth at least £10 per year.

Nineteen Dunstable names were entered, which was not a great number compared to other towns, but few inn-holders were likely to be freeholders. In 1782 only two innkeepers can be identified – George Fossey of The Red Lion and John Hickman; John Cook, victualler of The Saracen's Head and John Green, victualler were added in 1785. From the combined lists we find that the biggest group of freeholders were the four or five farmers. There was one lawyer, two surgeons and Edward Snoxell, master of the Chew School; a freehold-owning baker, butcher, grocer and draper can also be identified. The 1785 Directory of Bedfordshire included two other high-class grocers. Amongst the tradesmen were a shoemaker, a peruke- (wig) maker and, of most importance to Dunstable, Mark Brown, 'hatter'.

Straw Hat Making

Mark Brown was listed because he was a freeholder; in practice he represented a quietly growing second industry which was expanding to fill the gap left by the drop in demand for accommodation. Pennant's *Journey to Chester* in 1782 notes that 'the great passage of travellers' was 'the chief means of support' but he also noticed a 'small neat manufactory of straw hats and baskets and toys' that 'maintains many of the poor'. This very well sums up the position in the 1780s. The advent of the mailcoaches, followed by a new stagecoach timetable, carried passengers quickly on their way with no overnight stops. The improvement of the road surfaces, resulting from the work by the turnpike trusts, also helped travellers to get further out of London before the hours of darkness. Well before 1800 the Bull, The White Hart and The White Horse had all ceased to provide accommodation. In different ways they had become the equivalent of licensed restaurants and/or commercial stables with horses for hire. They then probably helped to push some of the victualling houses down the social scale to become beer houses, or if suitable, to become private houses.

However, help was at hand. The new class of tourist was

prepared to spend generously on souvenirs. In some months of the year larks were available, but increasingly the cottagers living around the great innyards were making hats, bonnets, baskets and other fancy items. If the innkeepers ever really got into financial trouble, this could be expanded into another prosperous industry!

Chapter IX

A Century of Change, 1800–1901

Dunstable's first police station, still standing in Icknield Street.

Overview

King George III (1760–1820)

The sixty year reign of George III, grandson of George II, continued for twenty years into this century. It might have been far more peaceful had he not inherited both ongoing wars and the mismanagement of the colonies. At home, this reign linked the old ways of the eighteenth century with the new exciting progress which would be made later in the century. Canals came into general use, James Watt began to demonstrate the commercial uses of steam power and in 1784 William Palmer gave a practical demonstration of the speeds in travel which could be reached by posting relays of coach-horses along a route, changing them every 10–15 miles.

King George IV (1820–1830)

Long before he officially inherited the throne, this fourth George had, on several occasions, been acting as king during his father's illness. His reign lasted for only ten years but during that period two important pieces of legislation were passed. Although William and Mary had insisted on religious toleration, it was still impossible for those who were not prepared to take communion in the Church of England to act as local justices or to hold other public offices. This Bill of 1828, repealing the *Sect and Congregation Acts*, made it possible for Nonconformists to hold these positions. The Catholic Emancipation Bill not only allowed Roman Catholics the right to hold public office, but also to attend university and sit in the House of Lords.

Quite apart from the aftermath of continual fighting overseas, the reign of George IV coincided with the start of one of England's great periods of distress. Trade had been damaged and taxes were extremely high. In addition, Parliament was gradually becoming aware that the rapidly growing population was leading towards exceptionally high rural unemployment.

King William IV (1830–1837)

Frederick, Duke of Cambridge, the second son of George III, had already died and it was William, Duke of Kent, who followed George IV. He was the first king for many years to enjoy a mainly peaceful reign, which gave various Prime Ministers the opportunity to introduce electoral and other reforms. In 1833, just before the death of William Wilberforce, slavery was finally abolished. In the same year *The Factory Act* limited the number of hours per day during which females and young persons could be employed in factories. Schooling was also to be provided for these young workers.

The Poor Law Act

This Act passed in the following year can be viewed in two ways. Its intention was to weed out those [if any?] who chose to be out of work and to receive very low sums from the poor rate, in favour of those who were in desperate need. A good idea in theory and popular with many ratepayers, in practice it caused both hardship and distress. No longer were those in need supported and assisted to remain in their own homes, nor was there any longer a complex chain of care in the community. Those who were in dire need of help had to present themselves at a large, impersonal building in the centre of a 'Union' of parishes. Husbands (and single men) were housed in one wing, wives and single women in a second, and children in a third, with the provision that, if they behaved themselves, they were allowed to see their parents on Sundays!

The Tithe Commutation Act

This Act phased out the much-hated giving of tithes which had continued from the very earliest days of this book. Tithes had started as a means of helping to maintain the parish church but after the dissolution of the monasteries, private landowners and institutions had bought the tithes. For centuries, those who grew crops or raised livestock had been forced to give a tenth, not for the direct maintenance of the church, but often to some distant company who might or might not help with church repairs.

Finally *The Marriage Act* enabled persons to be married otherwise then according to the ceremony of the Church of England. This meant that the Nonconformists could hold their own ceremonies, but such weddings had to be legally registered.

Although all of these Acts were of importance in Bedfordshire, some would lead to disputes. the phasing out of tithes would be greatly welcomed, as would the opportunity for the large number of Nonconformists to marry in their own place of worship. The other two Acts were more contentious. Dunstable enjoyed full employment and even the elderly and disabled could find a niche in the booming travel or hat industries. Therefore the parish workhouse was not as busy as those in many of the villages. In many places, the removal of an elderly person from his/her home of forty or fifty years, became a terrifying possibility. The thought of leaving a familiar supporting community of neighbours and to be shut in a ward with complete strangers was a frightening concept for those who were sick or elderly.

Had the Factory Act been strictly enforced, it would have been of great benefit to the children of Bedfordshire. In practice, the work was so seasonal that the hat sewers themselves resisted the law, in their anxiety to get as many paid hours work as possible.

Queen Victoria (1837–1901)

Both the happiness and unhappiness of Victoria's domestic life are well known. Three kings reigned during the first thirty-seven years of the century, whereas she reigned for the remaining sixty-four, dying in the first month of the following century.

The year that Victoria came to the throne was the year before Leighton Buzzard railway station was opened. Two years after she died Vauxhall, an engineering works from south London, opened in Luton. When she came to the throne there were only about a hundred and twelve day schools in the whole of Bedfordshire, each catering for only a very few pupils, but by the time that Victoria died every boy and girl in the county between the ages of five and fourteen was attending full-time school.

Industry

Earlier in the century the turnpike system of canals and railways, the introduction of steam-powered machines together with the introduction of gas lights and telegraphs all made it easier for the expansion and modernisation of England's industries.

The Great Exhibition
The Hyde Park exhibition of 1851 was held in a great glass 'crystal' palace, designed by Sir Joseph Paxton, who was born at Milton Bryan. It brought together trade exhibitors from all over the world and helped to give the English manufacturers a feeling of identity. It was so successful that another was held in 1862, this time in South Kensington.

The Census
In 1801 a house-to-house census was introduced and was repeated every ten years. Each time it was commissioned the questions became more sophisticated and it soon became possible to tell not only where there were pockets of industry and housing density, but also to predict where new factories, houses and schools would be needed.

Part One
England and Bedfordshire in the Nineteenth Century

Boards of Health

Towards the middle of the century, the government became concerned by the increasing outbreaks of cholera and other serious infections. So they set up a Central Board of Health and invited representatives from the towns and cities to apply for a licence to do the same. Many Bedfordshire people saw this as an unnecessary expense, as it was obvious that a new rate would be brought in to pay for it. An investigation at Bedford around 1859 reported that there were about three thousand cesspits in the town, many of which were sited far too close to the wells. Despite this, following an indignation meeting, the council voted unanimously that a public water company would be of very doubtful advantage and that it should withhold its support. In Luton it was 1870 before a reservoir was built on Hart Hill.

Dunstable's Board of Health added one shilling in the pound to the rates in 1863 – an annual return of £470. This addition was just as well, as an open sewer was located in 1868 by inspectors who had come to investigate the source of so many cases of consumption in the town. They also discovered the proximity of wells and sewers and the way that both were placed close to the open back doors of the sewing rooms.

Dunstable received its Charter of Incorporation from Queen Victoria in 1864. The new Borough Council backed the Board of Health, who enclosed this first and subsequent sewers, but the problem was where to drain the waste that the sewers carried away. It was decided to use a 'private pond' (at the back of Kingsbury?), but it was continually overflowing and at best was extremely offensive. Piped water was installed in 1873 but the town had to wait until 1902 before a proper sewage system was installed. Even then it simply involved carrying the waste outside the town! It was a problem which was not finally resolved until the new sewage treatment plant at Thorn was opened later in this century.

Plans for Modernisation

In the absence of government grants and county rates, local rate-payers had a great influence over any plans for modernisation. The way round this was for a group of the richer businessmen to form a Board and to invite subscriptions. In 1847 funds to build Luton's Town Hall were raised in this way, as was Luton's cemetery in 1854 and Dunstable's in 1863. In a more ambitious way the county families, often headed by the Duke of Bedford, funded hospitals, e.g. the Luton and Dunstable Hospital.

Starting with land donated by the Earl of Bute and a bequest from a Dunstable benefactor, a subscription list was opened and fund-raising events began.

In most towns businessmen were prepared to subscribe towards the introduction of gas. The plaiting and bonnet sewing rooms were particularly anxious to receive a source of artificial light. The Bedford Gas Company issued two hundred £30 shares in 1832. This provided first street lights and then lighting for houses. Two years later the Luton Gas Company raised £2,500 in £10 shares to provide forty street lights. Dunstable's first gasometer was built in Dog Kennel Close in 1836. The factories along the High Street were told to be prepared by the end of October 1836; it actually opened in 1837. An informal ceremony and the filling of the gasometer was to take place on Friday 28th October, so that the Mayor could officially light up the factories on Monday 31st. Hundreds of people turned up to watch the gasometer gradually rise and stand aloft. Once there was nothing more to see the crowds drifted away from the site (near the present Ashton Middle School) back into the town. Half an hour after their departure, at about 7.00pm, there was a violent explosion, wrecking the new installation and blowing two of the three men left in charge right across the road into The Bull Closes. Both were dead by the time help arrived, while the third was found among the wreckage, seriously injured. At the enquiry which followed it was decided that in the absence of the inspector (who had gone to have his tea) one of the workers had taken a candle too close to the hole leading into the gas tube. The above story, reported in a London magazine, appears to have been hushed up but was probably true.

When the gasometer was rebuilt it was on the other side of the road. In 1837 gas was being sold at seven shillings per 1,000 feet. Before long gas lighting spread from the factories to the private houses nearby and in 1865, there were ninety-four gas-lit street lamps. In 1871 it became known as The Gas and Water Company. Electric light was not introduced into Dunstable until 1905.

Bedfordshire County Council

As a result of the Local Government Act of 1888, sixty-eight councillors were elected to take over the administration of the county. They became responsible for two hundred and fifty-four miles of main roads and as the years went by, took over the checking of weights and measures and appointed first a part-time then a full-time medical officer. Some years later (1894) Rural District Councils became responsible for the local roads, drainage and sanitation. Any other powers which were still left with the church vestry were transferred to Parish Councils and the Quarter sessions (controlled by the local justices) were once again associated with law and order. School boards continued until 1903, when control of education was passed to the county and larger town councils.

Roads in the 19th Century

By 1800 a network of turnpike trusts managed the many main roads which ran north to south across the county. There was only one which went from east to west and that was managed by several different committees. It started as two roads from the north-east which joined Tempsford, divided again near Bromham and left the county with one branch heading for Lavenham and the other for Newport Pagnall. For travellers heading south there was an optional toll road just west of Roxton which went south of Bedford, where it joined the three main roads heading south. A plan to form a trust to improve the east-west route through Luton and Dunstable had failed to attract enough support. With so many committees, variable soils and local conditions, the quality of different stretches of the same road could vary. As the century progressed, some lengths of tollroad deteriorated and this discouraged travellers, but if the committee decided to compensate for the loss of travellers by raising the tolls, this could further reduce the number paying through each gate. However, one of the main problems which beset these committees was paying interest on the original borrowed capital. Sometimes they took out second and third loans just to balance their books. The loss of income when the railways took the trade from the stage and mail coaches was a serious blow. By the mid 1840s some trusts, e.g. the Pondyards, south of Dunstable, were suffering such severe financial losses that it was obvious that they could not continue much longer. The clerk to the trust wrote to the government requesting help in reducing their crippling debts. Meanwhile local people and local money were called upon to keep the roads passable. The Pondyards was not the only trust in financial difficulties and in 1862 the government brought in emergency measures to help. The Pondyard Trust was finally disbanded in 1877.

Rural Poverty and the Drift to Towns

Writing about the success of Bedfordshire's towns, it would be unfair to ignore the distress which swamped many rural families.

In its simplified form the various improvements enjoyed at the end of the previous century led to a growth in the population and the sharp rise in the period, 1800–1830, could not be absorbed. In counties further away from London, the poverty and distress was desperate but Bedfordshire was sheltered from the worst effects by its rural industries.

Lace Workers
Traditionally agricultural labourers had always been day [not weekly] workers and their wives were used to helping support the family. During the 18th century lace-making and lace-makers had gradually been organised into a profitable industry. It was an activity which could be carried on at home but involved highly skilled and painstaking work. To earn worthwhile wages it was necessary to work for a buyer who understood the demands of the market. The growing unemployment coincided with an increased demand for lace as a fashion item. The buyers (who also sold thread and patterns) mainly covered the area from Bedford to Woburn and into Buckinghamshire. At the start of the century many ladies in this area were working very long hours 'at

their pillow'. Although some very skilled ladies working ten or more hours a day might earn ten or twelve shillings a week, by the 1830s most of them were probably only earning four to six shillings.* As the farm labourer working six full days only brought home about eight shillings a week, even the odd shillings which the children earned were of great importance.

Straw Plaiters

There were lace dealers in the south of the county but not very many. Most of the village ladies and children (young boys as well as girls) were plaiting straw for the hat industry. Originally plaiting and sewing appear to have been taking place in both towns and villages. As the work became more specialised they gradually separated. The 1851 census shows that nearly all the women in Dunstable were sewing bonnets whereas in Houghton Regis, straw was being plaited. The work was seasonal and there were times when the market for plait was described as 'very slow'. However for several months of the year it more than made up for the money lost by the shortage of farm work. As with the lace, it was necessary to both keep the children out of the house and to start them earning as quickly as possible. Plaiting was not as intricate as working lace, so many three year old children were sent out to the plait schools. 'School' is hardly the proper word because some of the teachers could not write, read or plait! The children were taught at home and sent off each morning with their lengths of straw, bringing their work home at lunch time and returning in the afternoon with more straw. The so-called teachers were paid two or three pence each week to keep the child at work. When inspectors began to check on the hours and conditions in which the children worked, they were shocked to find how many were crowded into the tiny cottage rooms. Few of the children complained about actual cruelty at school or at home, but many of them said that any work not finished at school had to be completed at home before they were allowed to have their tea.

---

* Figures vary with the demand for lace and the skill of the worker.

Bonnet Sewers

As the industry became more organised and entrepreneurs began to establish factories, the demand for both lengths of plait and for bonnet sewers grew rapidly. When the demand for lace first began to dwindle, plait dealers would travel all over Bedfordshire. Unfortunately by the middle of the century good quality plait could be imported quite cheaply and the dealers did not have to travel so far. As a result more and more girls became lodgers in Luton and Dunstable and men who were useful in the building trades, such as handymen or carters, moved their families into the towns. Apart from jobs like maintenance, carting, box-making, warehouse work and other ancillary trades, very few men were actually employed in the industry. Making hat-blocks for the season's fashions, blocking (shaping), bleaching and dyeing were all very specialist skills. Because of its very tight boundaries, Dunstable was protected from speculative building. At Luton however, landowners around the town and its hamlets were ready to sell land for development, bringing a great deal of work for builders.

The Growth of Education

The rural industries which did so much to help the Bedfordshire families through the time of the agricultural depression held education back by many years. It was not the payment of the few school pence but the loss of earnings which created the problem. When this book started around the year 1000, such education as was available was based entirely on the religious houses. Although from time to time private and charity schools were founded, these were scattered at the will of their founders, whereas until 1540 monastic schools had been thinly spread across most of the country. Chaplains and secretaries trained in the monastic way or the occasional private school passed on basic education to the sons of their employers. Education at higher level was undertaken at the universities of Oxford and Cambridge. Increasingly, enlightened gentlemen began to open charity schools and Bedfordshire was very fortunate in this way. Local landowners and men who had themselves received education and then done well in the City set up endowments in their home towns or villages. Unlike the 'ragged' schools, this charitable education was not intended for the sons of the very poor. Most of the pupils were the sons of country landowners who might be expected to go on to study law and then return home to be of use in administering their county. A second form of charity school was for the sons of farmers and skilled tradesmen whose educated sons could help to administer the new towns and business centres.

The published work of David Busby has a complete list of Bedfordshire's early schools.* These include the smallest charity schools of the 16th century, right up to the 1870s and the coming of the Board Schools. Looking through this book, Bedfordshire might appear to be extremely well supplied with schools but in practice they were very small, usually excluded Bedfordshire's many Non-Conformists, drew their pupils from a tight geographic area and were not all open at the same time. The original endowment was invariably donated as land and its value fluctuated with the success of English agriculture. Another deciding factor was the way that the donor arranged for the appointment of trustees and how conscientious these men were. At times of agricultural depression, the schoolmaster might hold other better paid jobs and leave the teaching to an unqualified and unsuitable relative or older pupil. Sometimes when money was short these schools closed altogether. Also the type of school planned by the founder was not always suitable in the centuries that followed. Sir William Harpur's school at Bedford was supported by an endowment of paddocks and smallholdings on the northern outskirts of London. This land was supposed to provide enough income to run the school and to help to educate the poorer boys of Bedford. In practice it only just provided for the school and this gave an exclusively classical education, only suitable for the sons of the country landowners aiming for a career in law or the church. No money was available for boys in Bedford, so although it had a nationally acclaimed school, the

---

*   Bedfordshire Historic Records Society Vol. 67,
       The Bedfordshire Schoolchild.

county town had no provision for the sons of its business community. The situation was eventually saved when the leases ran out and the Duke of Bedford's land agent arranged for the development of a residential area. This extra income made it possible to open the Bedford Modern School and, much later, a school for girls.

Harpur's school had replaced the failing one originally run by Newnham Priory. At the other end of the county, the Houghton Regis school (opened as part of the charity of William Dyve) had closed completely. In the 1640s Thomas Whitehead (assistant to his father, who was headmaster of Repton School) endowed a new school in the village. A smallholding on the Green plus a package of other pieces of land were to be used to educate five poor boys from the village and five more from each of the two main hamlets. The house was to be converted into a school and school house for the master and the annual income from the land was to pay all the necessary costs of running the school. However, this income dropped seriously during the early 19th century, the only trustee lived in Cheshire and had no interest in the school. The master was running several other contract jobs from an office he had constructed in the centre of his house and the school was run by his family. Matters became worse and when challenged by the Charity Commissioners, the scandal which was caused closed the school for almost a year! However, it quickly recovered and is now the popular Thomas Whitehead Lower School. Like the Harpur School it is ready to move into the next millennium.

These two successful schools were very much the minority, many villages never had a charity school. It has been estimated that by 1800 only about twenty-five percent of Bedfordshire's towns and villages had any form of school available. Where there was a school, it might be limited to taking eight to ten boys free of charge and maybe another eight or ten whose parents were paying. In 1807 Samuel Whitbread of Southill presented a Bill to Parliament which included a clause to encourage the gradual establishment of a school in every parish. This Bill failed, as did the Parochial Schools Bill which followed.

Right back to when John Bunyan was a boy in the 1630s, some families paid a few pence for their sons to learn reading between the Sunday services. Skilled men like John's father may also have paid for him to be taught a little writing and arithmetic. The teacher would have been the vicar or someone appointed by him. As the years went by these 'Sunday Schools' became the basis of education in Bedfordshire. By 1818 there were seventy-seven Sunday Schools in the county, providing places for 4,728 scholars. During the next fifteen years an extra one hundred and twenty-one were opened, providing places for a further 11,180 children, between four and fifteen years of age. Sometimes older teenagers also went to Sunday Schools and in some places there were even classes for adults.

As attempts at getting government help for day schools failed, so voluntary efforts were organised. In 1808 the Royal Lancastrian Society was formed. This soon became known as the British [and Foreign Schools] Society which encouraged (and at times helped financially) schools whose religious and general education was Bible-based. It was non-denominational, did not use the prayer book or allow instruction in the catechism. Four years later a Church of England-based National Society was formed. The Bedfordshire Institution was established in 1815 to help church-based schools – these were expected to instruct children in the principles of the Church of England. The National and British societies, as well as an organisation run by the Wesleyan Methodists all gave help to start schools in Bedfordshire.

Despite all this prospective help, new day schools were slow to appear. These national movements were introduced just at a time when rural industries were expanding and providing paid employment for thousands of children. Nevertheless many Bedfordshire children of all denominations were taught by a method designed by Robert Lancaster, who experimented with a system of education which was then adopted all over England. The children sat in rows – new children at the front and the most experienced at the back. Lancaster himself taught a group of monitors each morning between 7.00 and 9.00am and from 9.00am to 4.00pm each monitor then instructed a row or 'form' of children. Reading schemes and other subjects were positioned around the room where different rows could visit them. Each row had attained a higher standard than the one in front and individual children progressed back from row to row (or form to form) at their own pace.

Bedfordshire was a county where there were very strong denominational loyalties. In 1839 the government arranged a scheme to award grants for school building and then to support and train pupil teachers. In many villages and small towns this would have meant having only one combined school. In 1843 a survey was conducted to see which counties had taken most advantage of the government grants. Bedfordshire was near the bottom but several villages had schools supported by Wesleyan funds, as did both Luton and Dunstable.

By 1869 every parish had at least a small school but the government was making plans to make education compulsory. This would mean providing a desk for every school-age child in the parish. Money would be provided for the extra schools or class-rooms, but the new schools would be inter-denominational with a religious, Bible-based training. Specialist denominational books such as the Book of Common Prayer would not be allowed. There was, therefore, a great rush to build and expand church schools.

The government allowed a short time and a little financial help to complete this rush of building but then said that any parish which had not made provision for every child must form a School Board. These Boards or committees, could then offer to take over a denominational school and modernise or expand it or the trustees themselves could apply for a grant to build a new school. Many British and Wesleyan schools were handed over to become Board schools. National schools mainly hung on to what they had and desperately tried to expand.

When the time came for a survey to be undertaken to discover how many more school places were required, the situation was very varied. The National and Wesleyan schools around the parish of Chalgrave had provided sufficient places. At Clophill there was no efficient school, at Eaton Bray the Wesleyans had a small school which the inspectors recommended fitting out with proper school desks and a certificated teacher, so that only a new infant school would be needed. Despite an enormous effort by the vicar, Houghton Regis just failed to find enough places. Dunstable, on the other hand, just succeeded.

Twenty-four Board schools were built by the end of 1874 and another nine during 1875. That still left more than twenty parishes where either there was a shortage of space or where the buildings used were unsuitable. Houghton Regis was forced to give in to forming a Board in 1878 but Eaton Bray's Board was not set up until July 1893. Once a parish had unofficially agreed to set up a Board, the next stage was to agree on who should sit on it. In some small villages it was difficult to make up the numbers but in towns like Luton and Biggleswade there was a great deal of bitterness before a final decision was made.

Once the schools were up and running, the next problem was to get the girls away from the plait schools and the boys away from the farms. Some teachers reluctantly allowed children to attend school as part-timers, while other teachers gave way and allowed for part-time plaiting sessions.

However, by the end of the decade there was very little demand for plait and, as the government inspectors became more strict, attendance improved. In 1898 a survey recorded that Bedfordshire had recorded the highest average attendance of any English county. At this time the children were paying a sliding scale of 0–3 pennies per week. This money was supposed to boost the small grants and make the schools self-supporting. Gradually debts were building up and in 1902 the Balfour Education Act was passed, resulting in the setting up, in 1903, of the Bedfordshire Education Committee. This was to maintain and keep efficient all public elementary schools in the county except in Bedford and Luton. These opted to become Part III authorities, responsible for their own elementary education. All school Boards were abolished and Board schools became council schools on 30th September 1903. Although voluntary schools were able to retain their voluntary status, the Local Education Authority became responsible for the secular education and for the payment of teachers.

So in one century Bedfordshire had changed from a position where only a handful of children received a very little informal education to a situation where all of its children were attending full-time school. An enormously important step before facing the rapid changes of the 20th century.

Part Two
Dunstable in the Nineteenth Century

As we begin the penultimate chapter of this book and talk about the nineteenth century, which will link Dunstable's Age of Endeavour with the century in which we live, we should perhaps pause to examine what the town of Dunstable was really like in those days.

Until the civil boundary changes of 1907, the amount of land which was included within the boundary was still less than five hundred acres. Walk just past The Bull in High Street North or a little way past the Priory Church in Church Street and strictly speaking you were in Houghton Regis. In West Street the land of Houghton Regis started on the northern side as soon as you passed Leighton Gap. On the southern side, the land of Kensworth joined Dunstable in the area of the present Catchacre allotments. Kensworth land encircled the south west quadrant and in High Street South came out north of the Half Moon pub. On the other side of High Street South (London Road), the piece of land where the Leper Hospital had once stood (north of today's Half Moon Lane) had been given to the town to raise money for the poor. South of that was the land of Caddington.

The estimated population of Dunstable in 1671 was around one thousand and the town had followed the national trend during the 18th century and had begun to grow. By the time of the first census in 1801, two hundred and ninety-six families were living in two hundred and forty-five houses and the population was registered as 1,296 men, women and children. As two houses were empty, the average works out at over 5.3 persons living in each house – rather higher than the figure which is used in earlier calculations [4.8].

At the start of this century, the entire town was still made up of four main roads, each lined by very large properties. Some of these were private houses, many having been sub-divided into shops, offices and workshops for craftsmen, but behind each one was a long, narrow piece of land. These strips usually started with a courtyard, surrounded by workshops and workers' cottages and then became a length of garden, orchard or paddock, some even becoming farmyards. An individual owner could use some of his land to build more cottages, but he was very limited because of the proximity of neighbours.

Most towns had one or two open fields which followed the traditional rural pattern, but in Dunstable the small Kensworth and West Fields were divided up between several owners or tenants and much of it was divided into paddocks for grazing. Deeds sometimes include very useful plans and from these we can tell that where Matthew Street stands today, there was once a private cart track. Mr Gutteridge, whose farmhouse is now represented by the solicitor's office in West Street, had his farm cottages along the west side of that track, his garden and orchard along the east side and his rick yard and buildings in the area of what is now the crossing of Matthew/Edward Streets and Edward/ Albion Streets. the house which eventually became the corner of Albion Street/High Street North had a garden and orchard running back to the farmyard. The present Albion Street entry to the Queen Eleanor shopping precinct (previously the concrete path leading behind the shops) was a strip of the orchard that an earlier owner sold to Mr Warren to make a cart entrance to his factory.

We left Dunstable towards the end of the last century facing up to the fact that their overnight bed and breakfast trade was rapidly disappearing. There was no government department, county or borough council to advise or help them. The main role of the Duke's steward was the collection of rents, but he would have prevented any new enterprise which might have damaged the town. It was up to the wealthy innkeepers to get together to help themselves. The economic reality was that if an inn wanted to continue to provide accommodation it must:

i) like The Sugar Loaf, provide superior accommodation which would attract private travellers;

ii) attract local customers who wanted to wait overnight, ready to catch the stage coaches in the morning;

iii) offer stabling and/or grazing for drover and wagoners.

Other than this, the obvious move was to forget accommodation and to provide reliable and clean food and drink. Just as today many different types of eating-houses survive side by side, so victuallers did the same in the previous century.

On the other hand it would be helpful if a new industry could be found to slot into the existing travel market and to share the existing buildings and courtyards. As we have seen, Pennant (on his journey to Chester in 1782) had noticed that behind the noise and bustle of the travel industry, the poor people were adding to their income by making hats, baskets and toys from straw. Back in 1689 when the feltmakers succeeded in bringing a Bill before Parliament to enforce the wearing of woollen winter hats, a local petition, said to represent nearly one thousand families, was presented against the Bill. The petition claimed that fourteen thousand people in an area which included Dunstable, Luton and twelve villages between Sundon and Redbourne and across to Edlesborough were dependent on the production of straw hats. This figure was, at best, a 'guesstimate' but it indicated that by this date there was a large organised rural industry.

The people who made up these large numbers were mainly women and children working in their own cottages. If Dunstable was to use the straw industry to make up the loss of income from the change in the travel industry, the hat industry must be both organised and marketed.

The Start of a New Industry

In 1780 when the list was drawn up of men who were eligible for jury service – Mark Brown was described as 'Hatter'. A man from a local family, he was beginning to convert a cottage industry into something more important and appears in both the 1785 Directory and the early jury lists.

In 1798 William Elliot was listed as hatter, joined by James Butterfield in 1800; by 1810 there were four names, including Robert Watts. In 1820 the constable who drew up the list was impressed by the quality of the men represented and ignored most of their trades and recorded 'Gent'. However, these jury lists (which began well before the regular trade directories) help us to recognise that some of the local men had adjusted to the new economic situation.

Deeds also demonstrate how the tradesmen changed to become hat-makers, e.g. the Oliver family bought The Cock and its saddlery business. It was still a saddlers in 1820 but in 1830 William was described as 'Straw Hat Manufacturer'. His widow (or daughter-in-law) sold the business in May 1850; it was auctioned at the Town Hall by John Mellor, achieving the highest bid from Benjamin Bennet, who paid a ten percent deposit of £70. Robert Watts (Gent 1820) had married the widow who had inherited The Wrestlers and in 1830 John Watts was recorded as 'Straw Manufacturer'.

A Typical Dunstable Family

Thomas Waterfield (born in Dunstable in 1786) was entered as cordwainer (shoemaker) in both 1800 and 1810, 'Gent' in 1820 and Straw Manufacturer in 1830. The Waterfields lived somewhere in the area of the present Woolworths and had a small bonnet-sewing room in Church Walk. By 1854 Waterfield and Co. had a factory north of The Sugar Loaf, now a pizza restaurant. When Thomas died, his widow Sophia carried on with the business; their daughter Sophia married William Milligan, an incomer from Scotland, who was a manager for Benjamin Bennet at what had been The Cock. Thomas' son Samuel became a plait dealer, living in West Street; he also had a bonnet sewing room in Middle Row, which was run by his sisters, Caroline and Elizabeth. When they retired, he and his wife, another Sophia, moved into the newly-built Icknield Terrace.

Dunstable in 1824

The jury lists were selective; Pigot's Directory of 1823/4 gives a more accurate picture of the state of the new industry. It includes nine straw hat manufacturers, a fancy straw manufacturer, a dealer in straw and a plait bleacher.

This was at a time when the coaching trade was nationally still at its height. It has been estimated that there were 3,300 stagecoaches in existence providing employment, in the widest sense, for 30,000 staff and 150,000 horses. The competition between companies was so strong that it was quite normal for a company to send three or more coaches to the same destination. One would leave very early in the morning, one at a more civilised hour and a third (with a name like 'The Rapid') would follow the most direct route at the break-neck speed of nearly 10mph. The complementary coach with a name like 'The Reliable' or 'Princess' would make various detours to popular watering places and travel at a safe and more comfortable 8–9mph.

The 1823/4 is one of the earliest and most brief of the directories. However, there were so many coaches passing through the town that it was noted that 'About fifty coaches pass daily backwards and forwards, amongst which are the London, Chester, Holyhead, Birmingham and Liverpool mails'. It is of interest that at that time, Dunstable had only two families acting as carriers, both running twice weekly services, one to London and the other to Luton and Leighton Buzzard.

After the Coming of the Railway

Within a year or two of the production of this directory, the Stockton and Darlington Railway Company began to carry a few passengers and in 1830, a passenger service opened between Liverpool and Manchester. Pigot's next directory, published in 1839, records the changes which had occurred twelve months after the London to Birmingham railway had reached Bletchley and shortly after it had reached Birmingham. Already the number of coaches was greatly reduced. Charles Lambourn (who had seen the records of the Puddlehill Trust) recorded that only twelve coaches a day passed through in early 1838.

The Last of the Coaches

By this time very few, if any, public coaches stayed overnight in Dunstable, but some stopped to pick up and put down passengers. Each day 'The Express' called at The Saracen's Head on both its outward and inward journeys to and from Leeds. The more comfortable but slower Courier called at The Crown and on its return it dropped off at four in the morning. The Crown was probably chosen because of its suitable accommodation. 'The Times' called at seven-thirty each morning on its way back to London, but took a different route on its way out. On alternate mornings it called at The Crown or The Red Lion. Passengers would have booked in for the night and been called by one of the servants when they heard the sound of the guard's horn at the entrance to the town. The Manchester coach called alternately at The Saracen's Head and The White Swan, the Northampton at The Saracen's Head and The Red Lion and The Wellingborough at The Crown and The Red Lion. The 'Union' coach to Leicester called at The Crown and these all turned off at Hockliffe, travelling through Woburn and Newport Pagnall. The 'Tally-ho' to Coventry and Birmingham called at The Saracen's Head, as did the 'Liverpool Star', both of which carried on along the Holyhead road.

So eight long-distance coaches per day were still calling on their outward journeys plus nine on their return, but there were no longer any mail coaches. This was a big decrease from fifty a day! A separate heading in the directory noted that Deacon's conveyances from The King's Arms went to and fro to Leighton Buzzard to meet trains from London and Birmingham.

The Carriers' Wagons

Deacon also had a team of 'fly' or fast wagons and each morning they would leave The White Swan for Leeds and for London. A man called Worcester had a smaller covered van which set out for London from The White Swan three times a week, while heavier wagons left The White Hart three times weekly bound for Birmingham and London. Meanwhile Ellis was despatching wagons from the Nag's Head three days a week and Richardson from The Swan with Two Necks twice weekly.

Two or three carriers specialised in local trade. William Kent's business was based in the High Street, with wagons leaving for Hitchin on Tuesdays and Fridays and those bound for Luton and Leighton Buzzard departing on Monday, Wednesday, Thursday and Saturday. In addition to meeting the Leighton Buzzard train, Deacon also sent wagons into Luton every evening from The King's Arms, while Worcester's vans left The White Swan every Monday, Thursday and Saturday, bound for Northampton. Toddington was served every Wednesday and Saturday by vehicles from Ellis' fleet at The Nag's Head, while Richardson's left The Swan with Two Necks *en route* for Towcester.

None of these were long-distance wagons calling in on their way to London. They were on independent routes set up by local carriers who had seen the opportunity to make a few pounds travelling to London, Birmingham and Leeds carrying hats. A separate network visited local markets and what were probably collection points for buying plait.

The examples of innkeepers changing to hat making and public houses acting as agents for carriers' carts (many of whom were collecting plait) illustrate that even prior to the arrival of the railway, local businessmen were turning to the new industry.

From Hostelries to Hats

Before continuing with the story of the Dunstable hat and bonnet industry, room must be found to illustrate what happened to some of the more important inns.

We have already seen how *The Duke of Bedford's Arms* had become a private house after a comparatively short commercial life. *The Bull* and *The White Hart* had closed and then re-opened to sell food and drink. *The Cock* had done the same with first a saddler's workshop at the back, then converting to a small hat factory. *The White Horse* had been divided into units, one of which, *The Wrestlers*, became a hat factory. Part of The White Horse became the handsome Garaby House which still stands today. The section nearest the archway in the early 19th century became *The Anchor* public house which was closed in the early 1890s and was taken over by Middleton and Gutteridge as a solicitor's office. At the rear of these buidings, Mr Bennet opened a larger hat factory. Later in this chapter we will discover that the building on the south side of The White Horse archway was replaced by the Town Hall.

The census records later in the century illustrate how the landlord of *The Crow* [today's Crown] was using his spare bedrooms to lodge girls who had come into the town to work with straw plait and that the landlord of *The Nag's Head* had a secondary occupation as a butcher.

A New Role for The Crown and The Sugar Loaf

The fate of Dunstable's two premier inns must best illustrate the commercial shock felt caused by the comings of the railways. Also two different ways of adapting to the new situation. In 1839 the original *Crown Inn* was still doing well enough to keep a selection of horses available for hire. Although it was never an inn where passengers disembarked from the stagecoach to spend the night, a new market was created around the needs of local people. Travellers from the surrounding area would stay there overnight to catch the London, Leeds, Leicester or Wellingborough coaches on the following day. However, although it was still operating in the early 1840s, it was eventually forced to close and to re-open in 1847 as *The Crown Hat Factory*

The Sugar Loaf (owned by Jane Cart and then by her trustees and tenanted by the Lee family followed by the Johnsons) became one of the top private inns along the Holyhead road. Mrs Cart's rent book from 1796 well into the middle of the next century has survived, showing an annual rent starting at £60 per year, rising to £80 in 1813 and £140 by the time that the railway came to

Leighton Buzzard.* In March 1839 £70 was taken for the half-year, but by the end of September the rent dropped to £50, while only £35 was collected in the spring and the autumn of 1840. Still unable to make a profit, the Johnson family had no alternative but to withdraw as tenants after many years trading. A new landlord took over at £50 per year and both the building and the business were redesigned and reorganised. On completion in 1847, the Johnson family returned at a rent of £70 per year. By this time it had become a modern, town centre hotel for local and private trade. During 1850 the owners built *The Sugar Loaf Tap* (now a shop), increasing the rent by £8 a year.

Charles Lambourn, writing in the 1850s, actually saw the balance sheets which were drawn up at The Sugar Loaf 1837–1839. Apart from the desperate drop in income, they illustrate the value of keeping horses for the 'post' or hiring industry. During the year 1837–8, the income from posting had reached nearly £2,500, while the following year it had dropped to just over £1,000. In the same two years, the income from accommodation dropped from £670 to £254. Again we are lucky to have evidence of the different types of trade carried on at The Sugar Loaf before and after the disaster.

The 'Housekeeper's Book' for 1829–33 has survived and was written when coaching was at its height; it reflects the 'high-class' trade which the inn enjoyed. On the cover and flyleaf are the addresses of their main suppliers. Food came straight from the London markets and bottled beer and spirits from London wholesalers. Looking-glasses and picture frames came from Fleet Street and upholstery was carried out by a firm in Newgate Street. Prices cannot always be broken down into unit charges, but the following are some standard charges:

Bed for the night	2s.0d
Wax light	2s.0d
Fire	1s.6d
Breakfast	2s.0d

---

*   The tenant was charged an extra £3.10s in 1824 as their share of the cost of installing a water-closet.

Tea	1s.6d
Tea with poached egg or bacon and egg	2s.0d
Welsh Rarebit and Ale	2s.0d
Gruel and biscuits	1s.0d
Apples and nuts	1s.0d
Writing paper (per sheet?)	0s.2d
Posting letter	0s.7d
Meat for dog	0s.6d

Although dinners were elaborate, some of the most popular dishes were roast fowl with bacon, roast beef, mutton with haricot beans and veal cutlets. On several occasions, larks, listed from 1/6d (7.5p), were taken away by customers, e.g. November 1830 – 2 dozen larks 12/- (60p). Many of the customers were titled, (e.g. Lord William Lennox, Sir William Ware, Lord Bradford) or army officers travelling in groups or with their families. Funeral parties were also a regular source of income, with a room being hired for the body, in addition to accommodation for the mourners:

December 28th 1829 – The Funeral of Lord Fitzroy

	Price	Approx. p. equivalent
Room for corpse	10s.6d	52.5
Refreshments for sitter-up	4s.6d	22.5
Fire and light all night	2s.6d	12.5
Plus food, drink and accommodation for 5 people		

Part of the reason for The Sugar Loaf's survival was because of its connection with Jane Cart's trustees; both they and the other family trusts would use the inn for many of their dinners and also their entertaining of the residents and tenants whose rents supported the charity. The account for their annual dinner in 1830 is indicated below:

Vegetables and butter	1s.0d
Peas and asparagus	6s.0d

Cucumber salad	2s.6d
Fowl roasted with ham	4s.6d
Fowl boiled with sauce	7s.6d
Fish with sauce	2s.6d
Leg of lamb	6s.0d
Tongue	5s.0d
Dessert	5s.0d
Bread, cheese and beer	0s.9d
Sherry (and snacks) before meal	1s.6d
Port and sherry with the meal	3s.0d
Sherry after the meal	3s.0d
Tea (for one)	1s.6d

The 'old ladies' dinner beer cost 14/- (70p) and with the tenants, they were greeted with port, sherry and claret £2.9s.6d and had a generous meal of roast beef, boiled mutton and caper sauce, pies, puddings and pastries which ended with bread, cheese and celery.

Customers like the Duke of Bedford's steward, when he came to hold the rent-collecting ceremonies and the Bishop of Lincoln or his representative on their visitations, would continue to stay at The Sugar Loaf when it re-opened as a commercial hotel.

An 1874 advertisement in the Borough Gazette described it as a 'family and commercial hotel . . . replete with every comfort and convenience'. The bedrooms were 'unequalled for size, light and ventilation'. Today we are accustomed to various traders hiring rooms in hotels and inviting in potential customers. The newly-opened commercial side of the hotel had a specialist room where salesmen could display their goods. A set lunch was offered on market day and both horses and vehicles were still available for hire. Dunstable had its own two stations, so The Sugar Loaf was an agent for both the London and the North Western Railway Companies. No charge was made for booking tickets and free transport was provided to and from the station.

A review in 1895 romances about the good old coaching days . . . 'no modern hotels can surpass these [coaching inns] in comfort and none are more pleasant to visit'. The Sugar Loaf had 'interior fittings and arrangements [which] are kept well up to standard of our advanced civilisation. Furnished throughout in accordance with modern ideas, with perfect sanitary arrangements and with all conveniences the most fastidious could desire . . .'. Downstairs there were smoke and commercial rooms and the bar. Upstairs there were private sitting rooms, bedrooms, bathroom [note not plural] and lavatories'.

Recovery was Round the Corner

Returning to the losses which The Sugar Loaf and the rest of the town suffered during 1838–39, Lambourn records that '. . . the people were panic-struck and dismay was visible on every countenance, the hope of their gains was gone . . . it was a fearful time . . .' He then went on to describe the depth of the piety of the people which carried them through. It was true, he said, that 'on this delightful town had long shone the sun of prosperity' but it had not weakened their manly strength: 'calmly and deliberately facing the evil they sought the remedy and were prepared to welcome George Stephenson, Esquire and listen to his proposition for railway communication'. This was 19th century language, but the message is true for any century. They had not allowed their success to weaken them and when their industrial base collapsed, they picked themselves up and looked for something else.

By this time the town had grown from two hundred and forty-five houses in 1801 to three hundred and eighty-six in 1841. This was a big rise but not as big as in some other towns. At this time, any spare land not privately owned or rented was the 'waste' of the Lord of the Manor. From 1801 cottages were built alongside the road in Church Street. Dunstable was so short of land that when the railway came to the town both Dunstable stations were officially in Houghton Regis!

The Railway Comes to Dunstable

Discussions started with George Stephenson in 1844. The main administrative problem was getting a Bill through the House of

Commons, while the main engineering problem was getting the line from Leighton Buzzard up and over the Chiltern Hills, the stretch of the line from Stanbridgeford to Dunstable needing a gradient of 1 in 40. The Duke of Bedford (no longer Lord of the Manor but still very influential) gave his blessing, the scheme was approved by the Board of Trade and the Bill got its first reading in Parliament on April 4th 1845. The new line, which opened on June 1st 1848, ran to Dunstable with one stop at Stanbridgeford, but did not continue to Luton as George Stephenson had planned. He met the people of Luton in 1844, but they objected to the potential loss of the Great Moor.

This line made it possible for passengers, hats and minerals to join the London to Birmingham line. In the 1840s the journey from Dunstable to London took one and a half hours (similar by bus and train today?) and cost (in current currency) 40p. This left Luton cut off and in 1861 it proved to be the largest town in the country not to have a railway line. Four years later it was agreed that a line should be built through Luton, linking Dunstable with [Old] Welwyn. The Luton to Dunstable stretch was opened on May 3rd 1858; Luton to Welwyn Junction followed on September 1st 1860. The whole line was eventually taken over by the Great Northern Railway. The site of the first or 'North' station was where the South Bedfordshire Council buildings stand today in High Street North while the second 'Town' station was to the south of Church Street. Both stations were then linked. By the end of the century there was an early-morning train which picked up passengers at North Station at 6.00am, Town station at 6.05am and arrived in Luton at 6.15am. The 7.10am service went on from Luton to Hatfield, arriving there at 8.05am. Six days a week there were eight through trains a day, plus another eight from Dunstable to Luton, two of each on Sundays. On July 13th 1868 a line was opened between Bedford, Luton and Moorgate (St. Pancras on 1st October). This meant that Dunstable passengers and hats had access to London, the Midlands and the north by two separate lines.

The Straw Hat Industry Expands

The report of the Chief Inspector of Factories and Workshops 'Presented to both Houses of Parliament by Command of her Majesty' dated October 1890 states that 'As you are aware, Dunstable is the mother town of all articles made from straw, or at any rate of all straw hat and bonnet work'. It correctly noted the making of bonnets; probably because of the coaches and the tourist trade, Dunstable specialised in fashionable, fancy bonnets. The coming of the railway and the sudden availability of space and spare labour attracted entrepreneurs from outside the town.

Craven's Trade Directory of 1853 lists 3 straw manufacturers, 11 straw hat manufacturers and 3 straw bonnet makers. There were 6 straw plait dealers, 2 straw plait manufacturers, and in addition to those employed by the big manufacturers, there were 2 self-employed straw bleachers and 2 blockers. Apart from 1 plait manufacturer who ran his business from the newly-built Icknield Terrace, 4 plait dealers in West Street and 1 straw manufacturer and 1 blocker in newly-built Albion Road [not yet 'street'], the rest were all in the High Street. John, James and George Cooper had come down from Manchester, bought the site of Burrs Brewery in 1847 and were soon employing three hundred ladies [near today's Bingo Hall]. On the other side of Albion Road there were about five hundred ladies employed in four separate factories but only about thirty men. There were two or three big factories on the eastern side of High Street North and at least two very large ones in High Street South. This does not include the smaller bonnet sewing rooms. There must have been well over one thousand people employed in this new industry.

The Coopers are said to have built the twelve small houses known as Manchester Place (Manchester Place path beside the Bingo Hall). In 1851 the twelve families included the Cooper's coachman, 4 blockers, 2 bleachers and 1 presser who shaped the hats. In those twelve small cottages there were 22 bonnet sewers, nine of whom were lodging to take advantage of the work. Humble as these cottages were, three of them employed young servant girls so that the mother of the family could go into the factory.

The Town Begins to Grow

A story has been passed down that the first house built on the waste in Church Street, in 1801, was a prefabricated structure, made by the bell-ringers at the Priory and carried triumphantly down Church Street. In this way they could get the roof on and smoke coming out of the roof before sunset and claim squatters' rights. At this time the Duke of Bedford was still Lord of the Manor and no doubt the 'fine' that his steward issued became an annual rent. By the time of the 1841 census, the population had risen from approximately 1,300 in 1801 to nearly 2,600, despite the fact that earlier in the year nineteen houses had been burnt in a fire on the corner of Church Street and High Street North. The only new residential development was houses built on the mediaeval lanes, i.e. Chapel Place (later 'Lane'), St. Mary's Street and Church Walk.

The rest of the increase had come from building on the waste and in-filling. In the 18th century there had been a small and probably squalid workhouse on Ashton Road (Square) facing Middle Row; this had been replaced by cottages. In 1836 the new workhouse in High Street South was also closed, the inmates removed to the Union workhouse in Luton and the abandoned building converted into four or five more cottages.

This was the way that development began, then in 1839 the Duke of Bedford's lease of the town came to an end and Dunstable became the direct responsibility of Queen Victoria's Department of Woods and Forests.

As we have seen, the coming of the railway in 1848 brought commercial disaster to the town, but the people pulled together and with the help of entrepreneurs from outside the town, were in a remarkably short time busier than ever. The demand for workers and for places to build hat and bonnet making factories became so urgent that new development began at last.

New Roads Were Planned

Once there was no further need to keep horses for the stagecoach industry, some of the Bull Closes became available. By the time of the 1851 census, the boundary path between Dunstable and

Houghton Regis had been laid out for building and named *Union Street*. Further south-west (but still on the Bull Closes), Burrs and one or two small builders were laying out *Mount Street* on a slope at the back of High Street North.

North of The Crown (a hat factory after 1847) was the Stone House and a row of seven cottages. Behind the most northerly of these seven were three more cottages. There was already a cart-track between the hat factory and the cottages, leading to a very large garden and orchard. These stretched from The Crown garden right across to join the land associated with Burr's Brewery (later Cooper's hat factory). Between 1847 and the census of 1851, maybe following the changes made to The Crown, the three cottages and five of the seven were pulled down. Two, a grocer's and a butcher's shop, remained and still stand today. The space where the five and the three cottages had previously stood, plus their gardens, part of the larger garden and part of the pasture land which led up to Mr Gutteridge's rick-yard, was being laid out as a new road called *Albion Road*. The only family given as living on that road, in the 1851 census, was that of John Limbrey, tin and copper manufacturer, who had taken a site on part of the rick-yard. In fact, the northern side had been built on, but the five new businesses were listed as High Street North. Dr Farr had the High Street corner house, with the coachyard and archway for his private coach (still there today). Then came a blocker, Henry Watson with his mother and three bonnet-sewing lodgers. Over the years we can trace this family as they open a bonnet sewing room and then a straw hat factory. Soon after this Edward Burr and others developed Mount Street until it met Albion Road. This end and then the whole road, became known as *Edward Street*. In 1850 Edward Burr sold the corner site to Frederick Burr who opened a beer-house called The [new] Crown. Once it had acquired its seven-day licence and could sell spirits, it became known as *The Borough Arms*.

By 1861 William Marshall, wheelwright, had taken over Limbrey's site (now recorded as Edward Street) and had built the corner house before either Matthew or (upper) Albion Streets had been developed. Set at an angle, it formed a link between (lower) Albion and Edward Streets. The yards and outhouses of Burr's Brewery originally came up to the east side of Edward Street, but by 1851, they had become Cooper's hat factory.

On the western side was the Congregational Chapel; next door at number 11 (today's number 23 and 25), Sarah Bass was the forewoman for Arthur Langridge's bonnet sewing room. At number 17 (now number 31), Edwin Johnson and his son John from Herefordshire, had started another small factory and on the corner opposite the Borough Arms there would soon be yet another small factory. In 1851 John Pickering was described as a warehouse manager. As the years went by he opened his own bonnet sewing room and gradually expanded from ten to fifty workers and his family stayed there to the end of the century. In total, nine out of the first thirteen houses in Edward Street were connected with the hat industry. Further along on the western side of Mount Street there were still gaps and much building went on between 1861 and 1881.

A terrace of a different class was built c.1850 facing onto the West Field – this would later become the start of *Icknield Street*. The original tenants were well-to-do craftsmen, but nevertheless their families were bonnet sewing. Mary Blake, a widow, had a bonnet and sewing school. Although she and her fourteen year old daughter were described as dressmakers, her four young lodgers were bonnet sewers and also lodging with her were four girl 'scholars' (apprentices) who came from near Hemel Hempstead and from various addresses in Buckinghamshire.

Off High Street South eighteen houses had been built in 'Britain Street', the sixteenth being the flourishing business of James Bowes, sawyer, who lodged four of his workmen and seven female bonnet sewers. This had originally been called *England's Lane* because it had been the headland around the 'inlands', i.e. back gardens and paddocks. In addition a terrace had been built in *Wood Street* and a second, still standing, called *Wellington Terrace*. These were occupied by working and retired shopkeepers or professional people. Their lodgers also tended to be business people but there were a few bonnet sewers. These developments, described above, were the start of modern Dunstable.

The Charter of Incorporation

When the Duke of Bedford's lease as Lord of the Manor of Dunstable came to an end in 1839, it was retained by Queen Victoria with the idea of working towards handing the town over to a locally-elected council. In the meanwhile, an increasing number of houses were built.

The Borough Council 1864–1974

Dunstable received its Borough status by a Royal Charter issued from Queen Victoria in December 1864 and elected 12 Councillors, 3 Aldermen and a Mayor in March 1865 to form the first Borough Council.

In October 1870 the Borough Council bought the Manor of Dunstable from the 'Lady of the Manor', Queen Victoria, for £750. This later included the rights to collect market tolls, rents and other forms of income. The group of businessmen who had collected over five hundred signatures for a petition and arranged for the Charter of Incorporation, not only kept Dunstable separate from Luton, but also provided an opportunity for modernisation and development.

Developing the Modern Town

The various services run traditionally by the parish, the care of the sick and elderly and the maintenance of the roads remained under their control but the presence of a Borough Council made negotiations for modern services possible.

On September 16th 1865 the Borough police were established and in 1867 a police station and house were opened at the far end of Icknield Street; a superintendant and constable supervised law and order within the town.

Back in 1803 The Lyon, The Peacock, and the old market hall, all of which stood in the middle of the road, had been taken down. In 1866 the new council bought the market hall as a place where meetings could be held and where the police court could meet and in 1869 a clock tower was added. When in 1870 they bought the market and remaining land and premises, they had complete control of the town. Their first development in 1872 was to open a corn exchange and plait hall at the back of the Town Hall.

In 1857 a new fire engine had been purchased. The existing 'engine house' was near the boundary of the town, just north of the Half Moon, opposite which was the pound and yet another pond. Now they could build a new 'engine house' right in the centre of the town, choosing a site by the corn exchange. It did not, however, occur to the planners at that time that one day the hall itself might catch fire and so prevent the engine getting out onto the road. This is exactly what happened in 1879 and the hall was completely destroyed, being rebuilt in 1880 and remaining a popular landmark until July 1966.

Modern Services Arrive in the Town

The railway's arrival in Dunstable had been a great boost to industry and the introduction of gas in 1837* was another innovation which encouraged entrepreneurs to come to the town.

The population was rising rapidly and there were urgent local improvements to be seen to. First they tackled the problem of the small town centre graveyard. In 1861 an entirely new cemetery was opened in West Street and its attractive entrance and mortuary chapel are still in use today. Then the problems of water and sewage were tackled. A Waterworks was opened in 1873, but as this could not handle the demands of the growing town, the sinking of a 175 foot deep well and pumping station were ordered in 1894, on the town boundary behind the Half Moon. Sewage and waste from the dyeing and bleaching works were still a major problem. In October 1892 the Corporation tried the temporary measure of buying a new sewage van and pump. This method and a limited sewer which flooded whenever there was a rainstorm was in no way sufficient for a town with a population which had risen to around five thousand by 1901. During the years 1901–2, a major sewerage and drainage scheme was undertaken.

---

*   See Part One.

211

Disaster Strikes Again – But . . .

By 1891 Dunstable was in trouble once more. Younger men were switching from straw boaters to caps and ladies were increasingly wearing felt hats and bonnets, rather than straw. With the dwindling market, manufacturers no longer needed two or more factories and several of them closed their Dunstable sites in favour of Luton, which was now connected with the main railway line to London. The people of Dunstable must have been very anxious as first the market was flooded with imported plait, then with imported hats and finally, as the fashion began to change, there was less demand for their straw bonnets. However, just as at the beginning of the century, a new form of industry was ready once more to provide full employment.

Waterlow's Printing Works arrived in 1891, followed two years later by Carter's Iron Works. Other firms were negotiating for sites and to encourage these new, exciting industries a private telephone exchange was established in 1897.

In 1898 the mayor of Dunstable was sufficiently confident of the Borough's future to provide a gold mayoral chain and badge of office. He contributed the badge and centre link and seventeen past mayors (or their relatives) gave one link each. Looking back, this was a fine way to end a century in which Dunstable had become an independent borough and prepared to enter the 20th century. However, before we move forward into that century, there was one other essential that new employers would be looking for and which Dunstable was well fitted to supply.

Education Is Needed

Little is known about the late 16th century, but there are several references to schools and schoolmasters during the 17th and 18th centuries.

The Chew School
It was noted in the last chapter that wealthy distiller, William Chew, had discussed with his family the possibility of starting a

school in Dunstable. When he died in 1712 his two surviving sisters and his nephew decided to start a school in his name. They found a site in High Street South and had a big enough house built to accommodate both a school and living space for the master. It opened in 1715 with the aim 'to make the poor content and to promote the doctrine of the Church of England'. The boys were carefully chosen from families who were practising members of the Church of England and, as at Bedford, the Dunstable boys had to be able to read and write before entering the school. The difference was that they were to be given a useful education. The master was to [attempt to] 'make them perfect in reading the English tongue and in the rules of grammar and in writing and accounts, so as to fit and qualify them for handycraft trades'.

All this would cost money and in 1724 an agricultural estate was built up of land from several surrounding villages. The income from this estate would pay to maintain the building, provide a salary of £40 per year (a very good salary in the early 18th century) for the master and clothes, books and fires for the boys. The master was to provide pens. The boys (who had to know their catechism before they entered the school) were taken to the Priory Church on Sundays to receive religious instruction, but were also given a good basic education. The curriculum was gradually widened and by 1847 they were also studying bookkeeping, geography, history, natural history and science. In summer they studied from 7.00am to 11.00am and 1.00pm to 5.00pm. In the winter they started an hour later, ending an hour earlier. When the master first asked for a rise, he was allowed to increase his income by taking six paying day-boys and four boarders. At a later date these numbers were increased.

The secret of the success of the Chew School was that the original founders carefully chose an educationally conscientious group of trustees from outside the town. Some came from London, most were local landowners and they took their duties very seriously. They raised no objections to the master extending the syllabus and once they thought it necessary, allowed the salary to rise with inflation. Therefore when there was a vacancy they were able to choose masters who had a good educational training and experience. Nor was there ever any difficulty in attracting boys to the school. Some of them were sons of farmers from local villages but most of the parents were shopkeepers and tradesmen (or their widows) from the town itself. It was a big financial sacrifice for these families because when their sons entered (maybe as early as seven) they committed themselves to leaving them in school until they were fourteen. An added attraction to the school was that both Mrs Cart and Mrs Ashton provided annual awards for a boy to receive a free apprenticeship, clothes and tools.

Until 1998 two models of the schoolboys in their uniform of (blue) coat, waistcoat, shirt, breeches, stockings, shoes and a black cap with a scarlet band and tassel could be seen over the porch. It is a sad loss to the town that they have now been stolen.

After the passing of the 1870 Education Act there was in Dunstable, as elsewhere, a panic to provide places for every child within the parish. So anxious was the Anglican Church to keep control over their schools that in 1883 the trustees began to build an adjoining grammar school [now the Little Theatre]. In 1888 this came into direct competition with the new Ashton Grammar School. Pressure was put on the trustees to use some of the charity money to help provide education for older girls but by this time they had overspent and would need help to keep going as they were. By 1905 new schools had been built in the town and the trustees decided to close the Chew School and convert the income from what became financial investments into scholarships and to help with apprenticeships. To this day an advertisement appears each year in the local papers inviting applications for these grants. Enquiries are handled via an office at Grove House and many young people have been helped in this way.

Sunday Schools

In the first part of this chapter it was explained that many of these were far more than a gathering of children who met to learn their catechism and listen to stories from the Bible. There are several references to Sunday Schools in Dunstable at the end of the 18th century. During the first half of the 19th century, these became larger, more organised and provided an increasing amount of help in reading and sometimes writing. In answer to an enquiry from the Bishop of Lincoln in 1818, the Rev. Mead of the Priory Church replied that the population of Dunstable was 1,616 and that the poor had 'sufficient means of education'! He listed the Chew School and a Sunday School for 110 boys and 130 girls supported by voluntary contributions and the interest on a bequest of £193 which the parish had received to found a church school. In answer to the question concerning other institutions he replied – None. In this answer he apparently ignored the small Sunday School which the Baptists had opened in their West Street Chapel in 1807 and the larger one which the Wesleyans had opened in 1812. Nevertheless he was exaggerating when he said there was 'sufficient' education available. Maybe the £193 which the church was holding made him feel safe in forecasting that they could keep up with the growing need.

The censuses of 1821 and particularly 1831 proved that Dunstable's population (including children) was growing very rapidly. By 1830 the government was planning to give financial help to provide new schools and another survey was sent out to check how great the need might be. By this time there were four free Sunday Schools attended by at least three hundred and sixty children. The Chew School was still providing free schooling for forty poor boys and eight other day schools had been opened: parents were paying for fifty-four boys and girls to attend two infant schools and for one hundred and nine boys to attend six small private day schools.

The National School

When applications were invited for grants, both the Anglicans and Wesleyans applied. After much discussion, the rector and his committee decided to hold the £193 bequest in reserve. They applied to the National Society for £85, the government for £85 and set out to raise a further £85 by fund-raising and sub-scription. These methods were all successful and in 1838 the foundation stone was laid for a National Sunday and day school on Church Green [now the church hall]. On Sundays the main teaching was reading of a religious nature but in the evening the young people were taught writing and arithmetic and gradually this school would begin to given lessons during the day.

Early in 1839 an inspector came to Dunstable to make sure that the grant was being used. He reported that there was 'an active and capable master' but that the accommodation was 'wholly inadequate for the needs of the town'. He then mentioned the large building which would soon be open as a daily school.

During the stone-laying ceremony for the National School, the rector and church wardens had led a crowd of five hundred people in the singing of the 70th psalm. It was announced that on Sunday the instruction would mainly be catechism and prayer-book based, but that the new day school would be open to young people of either sex and of any denomination, for which there would be a charge of one penny a week. He ended by saying that the scriptures would be taught in an unmutilated state, not in mere scraps to promote party purposes [but] the prayer-book would be used for devotional exercises. The school was opened in 1839; on Sundays the building was soon packed with two hundred and fifty children who were taught by ten male and fourteen female teachers. The weekday evening school quite quickly began to hold daytime classes and it is said that by 1855 there were more than a hundred attending during the day. However when the government inspector visited the day school in July 8th 1850 [haymaking?] there were only sixty-eight boys present. He was worried about the arrangement of the room where the bench/desk ends were mainly up against the wall, except for those used specifically for writing.* Because five of the classes were all in the same room and were under the control of five very young untrained monitors, both the instruction and discipline could only be described as moderate. He spoke very well of the headmaster but said he was obliged to spend his time with the elder children.

---

*   This sounds like the Lancastrian system and that depended for its success on highly-trained monitors.

Although the Anglicans and Nonconformists worked and co-operated fully within the business community, the latter did not want to share the educational provision made by the Anglicans because they felt strongly about not wanting their children to be forced to learn their catechism or to follow a form of education based on the Book of Common Prayer. Their Bible-based Sunday and day schools were open to everyone but in practice each denomination opened a school for their own children. Methodists, both Baptists and later the new Congregational church in Edward Street all started Sunday schools and, where possible, started day schools. Following their application, the Methodists received a grant for £100 and also raised money locally, aiming to build a new schoolroom at the back of their church.

The Baptist Schools

The Baptists, supported by the Quakers and others, did not apply for a government grant. They planned to start a day school on the British System at their own site in West Street. A subscription list was opened, fund raising began and they were able to open the new schoolroom in 1850. It was a long room, intended to hold up to two hundred children and cost £300. They had started to build on the strength of promised money without waiting until all the gifts were in hand. By the time that it was finished some of their members felt that it was an unnecessary expense, that it would be better to concentrate on religious instruction and send the children to the National School for their general education. More attempts were made to raise money but there was a strong feeling against the expense of having their own day-time school. In 1855 the sixty-five boys on the register were transferred to the National School.

This left the British School room free to be used by the group of girls who were at that time using the Temperance Hall. This was a great success, as they were fortunate with their choice of mistress and the numbers of pupils soon rose to one hundred. However the sixty-five boys (or as many as their parents would allow to attend) put a further strain on the space and the monitors at the National School.

The Wesleyan School

The congregation at the church in the Square took education very seriously and were prepared to make donations and hold fund-raising events to enable them to offer free education to those who needed it. Also both men and women were anxious to help in the school. When grants were offered they applied for and received £100 with the intention of building a school for two hundred boys and girls. On June 10th 1853 Mr Arnold, one of the most respected school inspectors, came to the school. There were ninety-seven children present and he reported that the buildings, furniture and discipline were all good. However, they were short of desks. Although there was no playground, land had already been purchased to create one. There was a good supply of books, sufficient apparatus and the instruction was fair.

The school was divided into two parts. Mr Arnold suggested that the infants receiving basic teaching would do better with a specialist female infant teacher and also noted that there was a room upstairs where the girls could be instructed in sewing. This school continued to provide a good standard of education for many years. An extension was added and as the years went by more subjects were added to the basic curriculum. By the end of the century there were about four hundred and fifty pupils.

Disaster struck on September 14th 1908 when the school was totally destroyed by a great fire. By this time full-time education was essential and the teachers and members of the church made every effort to keep the children together as one unit. A contemporary record noted that 'the Governors of the Chew's (Charity) School and the officials of the Osborn [Congregational] Hall willingly placed their respective buildings at the disposal of the managers'. Permission was given by the Education Committee for them to meet in separate hired rooms, providing that they remained with their original teachers and every effort was made to treat these scattered groups as one school. This was done and it appears that Chew School was used for the boys and Osborn Hall for the girls.

The Britain Street County Council School was opened on September 7th 1911, the headmaster recorded in a new log book,

'A memorable day – entered upon our new premises – boys and girls again together and we become once more a mixed school. Teachers and scholars alike delighted'. This had replaced the Methodist School.

The Ashton St. Peter School

Meanwhile the National School had become very overcrowded and it became obvious that a new school must be built. By this time some of the almshouse endowment of Mrs Frances Ashton had been sold and was bringing in a very high income. Permission was requested of the Master of the Rolls to allow the parish to use some of these funds to establish a Church of England school. Permission was given and the Ashton School in Church Street was opened in 1864. Ninety boys and ninety girls would be taught by two experienced and five pupil teachers. The pupil teachers were themselves receiving instruction, having to attend school an hour or more before the main lessons started and also having to complete homework. If they did progressively well over four years they would be given the opportunity to train for a certificate

Throughout the years the biggest problem was absenteeism. It was a continual struggle and although plaiting was forbidden, very occasional part-timers were allowed – usually because of a mother's poor health. Gleaning was a regular reason for absence, especially at the start of the autumn term; at the end of the summer term boys would drop out to work on the harvest. Due to the lack of effective medicines, an outbreak of measles or whooping cough would not only spread but might keep children away from school for several weeks. Other than these regular causes of absence, girls were often away because of 'household duties'. Outings to Ashridge and other similar places, arranged by different chapels tempted children to stay away, as did fairs and 'Wombwell's Menagerie'.

The Board School Act of 1870

After this Act of Parliament, the various churches in Dunstable had to either provide accommodation for every school-age child in the parish or arrange for the setting up of a Board. Great efforts were made and it became obvious that a specialist school for infants and more places for older children were needed.

The Infant School

The old National School building [the present parish hall] had been used for various purposes and it is likely that girls from the plait school and boys from the farms were still taught reading and religious education at a Sunday or evening school.

On January 7th 1873 the Rev. Hose admitted thirty-eight children when he opened Dunstable's first specialist infant school. The fee was to be two pence for the first child and one penny for any further children from the same family. The day started with a prayer and then there was a short talk stressing the need for cleanliness, punctuality and the importance of regular attendance. In most weeks there was at least one new enrolment and by the end of term the total had crept up to fifty-one. The average attendance was around forty-one, which was extremely good. By the beginning of February 1874 a permanent teacher, Alice Percival, had been recruited and the register total had risen to sixty; however possibly due to the bad weather, the average had dropped to thirty-nine. As with other Bedfordshire schools there was no difficulty in attracting very young children. The bonnet sewing mothers were only too anxious to be relieved of their young toddlers. The Rev. Hose stated that he definitely would not consider taking children under two!

By the end of the century this had become a settled and successful school. A Diocesan inspector of religious education reported on October 12th 1897 that in the Upper Division there were sixty-four children who were not only classed as 'very good' and 'excellent' in their test, but also repeated the 23rd psalm accurately and said prayers with great reverence.

The work of the thirty-eight children in the Lower Division (called 'babies' in 1899) was described as excellent and their prayers were repeated accurately and reverently. The final report could be summarised as teaching – very good, children – bright, intelligent and interested, singing – very good, school – excellent.

The Ashton Grammar School

In 1868 more of the Ashton endowment land was sold and again her Church of England-based charity had an embarrassment of funds. It would help the educational provision of the town if this money could be used for another school, and would make it unnecessary to have a School Board. This time it took many years for the Master of the Rolls to agree because various national commissions concerning charities became involved. Letters, applications, meetings and a four-day public meeting in the Town Hall took place. On August 12th 1885 Queen Victoria gave official approval and plans went ahead for a new day and boarding school; the foundation stone of the new grammar school was finally laid during 1887 and the school opened in 1888.

This school took over the central role once held by the Chew School. Many of the boys stayed on in Dunstable to hold positions in every part of the town's organisation and business. Other boys went on to work in different parts of England and abroad.

In 1971 when Bedfordshire changed to the comprehensive system of education, it was regretfully felt that the town centre site was too small for expansion. The grammar school was therefore closed and the Manshead Voluntary Controlled Upper School was built at the southern end of the town. However, full use has been made of the impressive grammar school buildings, now the Ashton Voluntary Aided Middle School.

The completion of the grammar school meant that Dunstable could move into the 20th century knowing that a full range of education was available in the town.

Chapter X

Dunstable Heads for the Millennium, 1901–2000

Street scene in High Street North. The buildings from Stevens back to and including the Prudential Insurance office stand on the site of The White Horse Inn.

Overview

So we come to the final chapter of this book. This is the century in which we were all born, of which we all have our own personal memories and which ends the second millennium.

For the purposes of this book it does not matter whether Jesus Christ was born exactly 2,000 years ago or not. From chapter one we have traced a chain of religious worship which started with a small Roman church, early in the first millennium, through to the present time.

It was also in the first chapter of this book and in the first century of the second millennium that England became united under one king, the county of Bedfordshire was established, Bedford became the county town and Houghton Regis became a wealthy household manor of the king. Even though twenty years after the Norman Conquest there was still no market in the village, long before the Conquest the residents were expected to pay their taxes in gold and silver. Although there is no written evidence, the conclusion must be that whenever it was possible, the people of Houghton Regis were trading around the important crossroads (known as Dunstaple) which made up one corner of their village. No doubt the various sheriffs accepted this illegal activity on the royal estate in return for a very high fine, which then became an annual rent. Even more trading was then necessary to pay the 'rent' and to make a profit.

The so-called 'Domesday' survey ordered by William (the first Norman king) exposed anomalies such as this, so when William's son, Henry I, set his officials the task of reviewing and improving the economy, they planted the new business town on the existing unofficial trading centre.

As we have seen, this happened in the first decade of the second century. By 1109 plans were far enough advanced for King Henry to be able to visit his new town and to stay in his new palace. By 1131, the Augustinian canons (whom he had invited to build opposite his palace) were sufficiently settled for him to hand over to them: the *town, the market, the schools* and various local and district forms of *administration*. From their foundation

it was taken for granted that the canons would be entirely responsible for the *health care* of the business community and its servants
and travellers. They would also be expected to provide *accommodation* for every type of traveller passing through the town.

The Medieval Town Today

Because of Dunstable's position on two main roads, its people
have always been aware of new ideas and 'business trends'.
Fortunately the various planners have kept pace with
modernisation while trying to maintain Dunstable's historic
centre. Most of the necessary modern developments have taken
place on the rapidly-spreading outskirts of the town.

The Royal Manor of Houghton

As the centuries went by, the village farmers profited by being so
close to Dunstable's market and inns. The Bull and one or two
small inns were actually in Upper Houghton and at the height of
the hat industry, several skilled male workers lived along the
main road. For many years the plaiters had a reliable market for
their work and when the hat industry began to fail, the Cement
Works arrived to offer employment. Rapid growth during the
second half of this century has resulted in Houghton Regis
becoming a town in its own right.

The Crossroads Brings Business

The crossing of these two busy roads (which was the reason the
business centre was originally positioned here) has always
brought problems as well as advantages. Over the centuries, the
nature of both have changed. A fear of unwelcome strangers, e.g.
soldiers, petty and more serious criminals plus the needs of the
sick and disabled has given way to a fear of traffic noise, pollution
and accidents.

The advantages, in particular income, generated via the roads
has also changed. During the early centuries, products were

bought locally, carried into the town, sorted and graded before being transported out again to distant markets or for export. In the 15th and 16th centuries commuters travelled out to London, but their presence encouraged the development of a thriving residential and retail centre. The 18th century travel trade relied on 'incomers' but the 19th century straw industry despatched wagon-loads of hats and bonnets out of the town.

A traffic survey on the crossroads in 1910 illustrates the way that Dunstable's industrial role was about to change. The twenty-four hour average of horse-drawn traffic approaching from all four direction was 911 vehicles, including twenty-six buses. There were also 119 handcarts and a flock of sheep. However, modern transport was represented by two steamrollers and 191 petrol-driven vehicles (including a heavy lorry and three trailers).

Gradually horses gave way to modern vehicles and the one heavy lorry increased to a steady stream. On August 6th 1978 the crossroads was adapted to a double roundabout, plus four pedestrian crossings.

Although Dunstable bonnets were no longer exported, as the century progressed, many other products were, and still are, despatched abroad. Paper was not manufactured in Dunstable, but several companies working with paper products carried the name of Dunstable around the world. Messrs *Waterlows* of London (who had arrived at the end of the last century) produced, at various times, passports, currency, cheque books and stamps for many different countries. This was only part of their work; they also produced well known magazines and many other products. Although the Waterlow factory has closed, they still have a small printing and binding unit (Polestar) on the Woodside Industrial Estate. One of the products which is produced there is the prestigious magazine, 'Country Life'. This is sold overseas as well as in this country.

In 1908 the New Industries Committee announced that *Messrs Cross and Co.*, a well-known manufacturing firm of London, had decided to build a factory in Dunstable. For around eighty years they made a variety of paper products which were exported around the world. The Dunstable Guide of 1935 described their products as: 'high-class stationery and goods, for the hygienic service of food'. In their advertisement, in the same guide, they described themselves as 'the largest Lace Paper Factory in the World' and listed: lace paper d'oyleys, embossed dish and plate papers, serviettes and many other 'articles for table decorations and service of food'. These products were not only produced in very large numbers for the home market and export but were also used on all the main sea-going passenger liners.

There were other firms working with paper whose Dunstable products were exported around the world. However, the firm best known internationally that started in Dunstable, developed in Dunstable and is still working in Dunstable today was originally known as the *Albion Press*. Sometime around 1850 James Tibbett started a printing press at the back of his stationer's shop in High Street South (now Moores). Three of James' sons worked as printers and/or publishers and under different names the family company expanded and built a large printing works at the back of their shop.

In 1853 James printed the first ABC Rail Guide; the years went by and this side of the business became a run-away success. Bus and rail timetables were in great demand and before long they were producing all the timetables for London Transport. They received so much new business that some of the printing was passed to Waterlows.

Orders came in from overseas and they soon had a section of their business which specialised in the production of timetables. During the 1920s the Tibbett family started the company known as *Index Printers*. Cyril Tibbett became the managing director and after the war he had the foresight to appreciate that air travel was going to become a very important business. In June 1946 he started the first ABC Air Guide. It had two hundred pages and cost 2s.6d (12.5p). The business continued to expand even more rapidly and soon it was necessary to build a new modern factory on the corner of High Street South and Oldhill. During the 1980s it was bought by an American firm, Ben Johnson. By the end of the decade it was closed and the factory taken down, but the section of the firm known as ABC Travel Guides was transferred to a new building on the Dukeminster Estate. It became part of the Reed Travel Group.

Publications in the ABC range now include: Atlases, Air Guides, Cargo Guides, Shipping Guides and an International Travel Guide which provides information concerning travel, health, passports and many other facts specifically for travellers. Although their name today is OAG rather than ABC, the publications still carry the name of Dunstable around the world.

Two other quite different companies who were once international names are *Dales' Dubbin* and Vauxhall's *Bedford Trucks*. John Thomas Dales established his business producing the leather dressing known as dubbin, in 1880, at East Dulwich in South London. He was attracted by the publicity of the New Industries Committee and in 1902 bought Tower House in High Street North. He also bought a disused factory in Tavistock Street.

The dubbin was made from grease which came in drums from the local railway siding. It arrived as a solid and was then melted in a vat. The recipe was kept secret but is thought to have contained vaseline, Australian mutton fat and castor oil. The tins were tightly packed in cardboard boxes, made by Parrot and Jackson, carted back to the railway and not only dispatched around England but also to countries as far apart as Africa, New Zealand and China.

Mr Dale died in 1934 and his daughter, Lucy, took over the business. As the years went by, the use of leather decreased and there was less need for preservative. The factory closed in the mid-1940s. The secret recipe is now produced at Winsford in Cheshire.

The best known name of all Dunstable's home and overseas trade, however, must be *Vauxhall's Bedford trucks and vans*. The engineering firm which moved to Luton in 1898 had taken its logo and badge from the arms of the man who had built the original Falkes' of Vaux's Hall. When the Vauxhall engine factory opened in Boscombe Road in 1942, the arms of the dreaded Falkes de Breauté (who caused so much trouble in chapter three) returned to Dunstable.

Increasingly during the last decades of this century an effort
has been made to bring more visitors into Dunstable. In the
earlier chapters of this book, pilgrims brought income into the
Priory and the town, In later chapters, a great deal of money was
to be made from the travellers passing through. Now, due to the
railways and motorways, this passing source of income has come
to an end and visitors have to be attracted into the town.

Dunstable Tourist Information Centre, and the various councils
which support it financially and with the Dunstable Mini-Guide,
are attracting an increasing number of short-break visitors; also,
thanks to the efforts of Bedfordshire Heartlands Tourism Association in producing their 'Days Out' leaflet, coaches now come in
increasing numbers to visit the Grade I (star) listed Priory Church
of St. Peter. It is hoped that this incoming trade will grow in the
future, to justify the plans for the founding of a Heritage Centre.

The Important Old Buildings

The Old Palace of Kingsbury

We traced this building (or buildings) from a royal palace large
enough to house the great royal Christmas courts, to a house (or
houses) where some of the king's wool merchants had their
headquarters. Although archaeological evidence is lacking, there
is written evidence that the palace (or part of it) became a
gentleman's residence, known in the 19th century as Kingsbury
Farm. However, soon after the First World War, Arthur
Bagshawe turned it back into a gentleman's house. In November
1959 the building was divided. The western end became the
private house of Dr (Gerald) Ashton and his wife Mary. Their
help and support for so many aspects of life in Dunstable will
long be remembered. This part of the building is now used as
sheltered housing. The eastern end was bought by Creasy
Hotels Ltd. and in February 1960 opened as *The Old Palace
Lodge Hotel*. A few months later the adjoining barn (once
Mr Bagshawe's museum) was purchased by Flowers Brewers Ltd.
of Luton. They enlarged it using contemporary materials and in
October 1961 opened *The Norman King* public house.

These two attractive buildings are well maintained and ready to continue playing an active role in town life and the tourist initiative into the next millennium.

The Augustinian Priory

Following the Dissolution and the delay while (eventually frustrated) plans were discussed for making the Church of St. Peter the basis for the new cathedral, the remains of the monastic buildings were at last cleared away. As for many centuries the people of Dunstable had paid for the maintenance of their church, it was eventually handed into their care without payment. We noted in chapter five that the parishioners had paid for a new roof and the carved figures; general maintenance continued with another major restoration in the last century and work still continues. The Friends of Dunstable Priory are actively involved with fund-raising and general support.

However important it is historically, a church is not a museum and the Priory Church is a much-loved place of worship, with people still liking to present the best of English craftsmanship. Of particular note is a fibreglass, modern approach to the portrayal of Mary, the Mother of Christ and her link between Man on Earth and her Son in Heaven. This was sculpted by Laurence Broderick and presented by William Gibbard, in 1970, following an exhibition of church art and craftwork. In the 1960s Mr and Mrs Clifford Flory began the rebuilding and refurbishing of the east end of the church in memory of their younger son who had recently died. Two large stained glass windows by John Hayward portray the history of the Priory. Since that date, the family have commissioned Hayward to design many more windows and the Priory Church now houses an important collection of his work.

The Priory Meadow

It is thought that much of the monastic building stone had been stolen before the site was officially cleared. However, Norman pillars were given stability with an infill of stone chips and quarry floor sweepings. The unevenness of this meadow and its height above the foundations of the church are due to the great depth of this rubble, covering the actual foundations of the Priory buildings. Although it belongs to Dunstable Council and the public is free to walk across it at will, it is a listed site where even shallow digging is strictly forbidden.

The Priory Gardens

This very flat area between the church and Priory House is all that remains of the Great Courtyard. The removal of an unsightly hedge in 1982 gave the Manshead Archaeological Society the opportunity to prove that the legend of the existence of a tunnel between the two buildings is unfounded. Although this is another site legally protected from any form of damage, the lawns and raised flower beds make a beautiful approach to the Priory Church and a very pleasant area in which to sit; there are plans to open up the views from both Church Street and High Street South. The Sunday band concerts which are held in the Priory Gardens each summer are extremely popular.

Priory House

Although originally built as a hostel or hotel for travellers, we have traced the later history of this building as a private house and a place where Dr Crawley could treat his private patients. In the late 19th century a Mr and Mrs Munt lived there, their neighbour to the south being a Mr Brown (hat manufacturer), who bought a strip of land between the two properties from the Munt family to provide a cart entry to the rear of his premises. A few years later the families pooled their resources and built a new factory – Munt and Brown, which continued until 1908 when it was demolished. Part of the front wall was saved as a boundary to the Priory Gardens. As a widow, Mrs Munt continued to live in the house but following her death, it was bequeathed to Dunstable Council. From them it passed to South Bedfordshire District Council. A great effort was made to have this building, which was actually used by the canons of the Priory and faced across the site of the Priory, used for a wonderful specialist museum. Backed up by a mobile classroom and tearoom, the site would have had great possibilities. However, it was not to be.

The company who bought Priory House restored it, exposed the fan vaulting and brought the stone Tudor fireplace into the front reception area. It now looks very much as described in the will of Elizabeth Aves.

Hospitality to Travellers

As we pass into the next millennium, Dunstable can proudly offer an even wider selection of food, drink and accommodation than was offered in the days of the Priory. There is a wide range of public houses (most of which sell hot and cold food), restaurants of many different nationalities and fast food outlets. Accommodation is offered in small private guest houses, large traditional hotels, motels and branches of the very large, modern hotel chains on the outskirts of the town.

The Inns and Public Houses of High Street South

If Priory House was Dunstable's first inn, then the *Saracen's Head* must be the second. Although a little of its history has already been included, it must be pointed out under this century, that it is probably the oldest public house business in Bedfordshire. Not only has it continued to serve food and drink throughout the centuries, but it has also kept the same name!

Although there are so many restaurants and fast-food shops nearby, most of the traditional public houses have survived and found their own share of a changing market. As mentioned before, Dunstable's inns and beer houses deserve a book to themselves. The (Kensworth) *Half Moon* had land, as did the *Woolpack*; both had been very successful but ceased to trade before 1900.

Any business nearer the town would automatically be short of land. *The Carpenters Arms* (now a dental surgery) was one of many Dunstable beerhouses which opened to serve a temporary need during the nineteenth century; a period when there was continuous building going on in that part of the town. This could explain the name.

The inns of Middle Row will be mentioned below. The reason that so many small and old-fashioned premises continued into this century must have been their proximity to the market. *The Five Bells* in Ashton Street survived for the same reason. One popular public house in this area which survived until the coming of the Sainsbury's development in 1973 was *The Foresters Arms* in Chapel Walk. When Charles Field was landlord in 1840 it was known as *The Cock* and he also ran a whiting works next door. On his death his wife continued to run both businesses, the pub re-opening as the Foresters Arms around 1880.

The Eastern Side of High Street South

The Saracen's Head was the most important of the inns in this part of the town but a few doors down, *The White Swan* could be almost as old. It was called *The Black Boys* in the 18th century, but not a great deal is known of its early history. The building is very old, but as a lively modern business, it is looking forward to continuing into the next millennium.

These inns and public houses clearly illustrate the adaptability of Dunstable's trade. The next two are typical of public houses which opened as 'locals' as the town began to grow. The exact opening of *The Star and Garter* on the corner of King Street is unknown, but there are no early references to its licence or name. Albert Henry Langridge of Duxford bought the building sometime before he made his will in 1888. He died in 1908 and his wife Elizabeth inherited what was then Numbers 61–64 High Street South and became 141/143/145 and beerhouse 147, in 1920. Elizabeth died in 1946 and her son Leonard sold it to Green's Brewery. Although there are so many public houses in Dunstable today, The Star and Garter, like most of the others had found its own section of the market for the turn of the century.

The Greyhound was another business which was put up as a 'community' beerhouse for the use of the builders and then for the new community. Although it is now a modern building [on the corner of Great Northern Road] the picture of Coronation Day 1953 by Bruce Turvey* illustrates it as a late Victorian-style house with bay windows. An inventory of January 1890 which

---

*   25 years of Dunstable 1952–1977.

may have been taken for the first tenant, described a house with five bedrooms, a taproom, bar and bar parlour. In addition to this there was only a scullery and wash-house so the so-called bedrooms must have included accommodation for the tenant. There was a settle around the taproom walls and a cooking range for heating the room and water. The bar had a stained deal counter, a wall-mounted settee by the fireplace and two pull-beer engines and piping. The rooms were lit by gas. Mr F. Howard of Berkshire let The Greyhound beerhouse to Mr Agate of Dunstable for a rent of £8 per year. He had to agree to conduct it in an orderly manner, not to open it out of hours nor to allow any intoxicated person to remain on the premises. He also had to agree to keep it as a public house and not convert it for private use.

The Highwayman started its commercial life as a detached house called Highfields, which opened as a tearoom. It was rebuilt as a small hotel and restaurant but in recent years the owners realised that the travel industry was once more expanding along the A5 and it is now a fairly large modern hotel.

The Wagon and Horses was a much older inn. It was called *The Cow and Hare* when records began in 1727 and the business probably dates back into the 17th century. In 1762 it was inherited by a relation of one of Dunstable's chief landowners, John Miller and it was this family who changed the name. Thomas Burr of Dunstable Brewery bought it in 1804 and the Barker family who were tenants for about forty years ran it as a type of licensed eating house. In 1847 it was bought by a surveyor, closed down and then sold to a bricklayer. When it re-opened in 1858 the present building was owned by Dagnall Brewery. The town grew and soon there were houses and businesses on both sides of the road ensuring the success of the what is now a very busy public house.

The Market

Dunstable's famous market grew from a collection of stalls which each Wednesday and Saturday were put up outside the Priory gate. This area became known as *The Market Square*; it quickly grew and soon spread out onto all four roads. Several of the early 13th century bye-laws, worked out by the Prior's steward and the businessmen, involved the market.

The Rules of the Market

The order to remove stalls 'at the end of the market day' had, by the 19th century, become defined as six o'clock on most occasions and midnight on Saturday.

The mediaeval instruction that 'butchers are not allowed to throw blood and filth of the animals which they kill . . . in the street as a nuisance to the neighbours of the market' also became more specific. By 1871 all litter, garbage, oyster-shells and rubbish 'arising from the sale or cleansing of animals, game, fish or vegetables was to be immediately put into 'a proper tub or basket which shall be provided'.

It is many years since carcasses were eviscerated and chopped up for sale in front of the customers, but there was a livestock market in the Square every Wednesday until August 8th 1955.

The Livestock Market

There were permanent metal stalls for the cattle and wooden hurdles, tied by binder-twine, erected each week for sheep and pigs. Don Kemp, who was once employed in the market by Mr Allcorn, the auctioneer, has recorded his memories of both the market and the fatstock shows.* He paints a colourful picture of drovers and cattle on the hoof, walking in from Hockliffe, Exmoor ponies arriving at North Station and running up Chiltern Road to the farm on Bull Pond Lane and the confusion caused when pigs or sheep escaped from their pens.

The Traditional Market

The market rules drawn up when the Borough Council took control allowed for the sale of: (1) Strawplait and strawplait goods, (2) Corn and farm produce, (3) Cattle and other livestock and then, near the end of the list, meat, fruit, vegetables and provisions.

---

*   Old Trades of Dunstable 2. Dunstable and District Local History Society.

The sale of straw goods continued well into this century. Corn was once displayed in the Corn Exchange behind the Town Hall and livestock continued to be sold in the Square, but the sheep auction in West Street had already been discontinued. In the mid-19th century there were private gardens along the southern side of West Street.

The Modern Market
The part of High Street North leading up to the crossroads was once called Market Hill. Until April 1st 1964 stalls were erected along the west side of the road each Wednesday and Saturday. After April 1st they were moved to the front of the Queensway Hall. In 1996 an extra Friday market was tried, along the pathway leading west between Wilkinson's and the Methodist Hall. This was very successful and towards the end of 1997, the main market was moved into The Square and along this pathway.

The Market Cross
On Monday September 7th 1999 work began on a modern representation of a medieval buttercross. There are seats, a covered area and a small tower with a clock, all providing a much-needed focal point for the market and the town.

The History of Middle Row

The original line of Middle Row (which the Priory referred to as 'Middle Rents') stood in the middle of the road separating two lines of traffic. The central roofline, following the direction of the road, contains roof timbers which date back to the 14th century; it may have been a market hall erected by the Priory.

The original number of units was the same as today, except for the two which once jutted out into West Street. They were taken down in 1911 to improve the approach to the crossroads. Some Dunstablians will remember the public lavatories which were built at the back. Because the design had a castellated wall, they were nicknamed Boskett's Breezy Battlements, after the then mayor. Because the narrow row of medieval shops gradually extended out

236

into what is now Ashton Square, it is difficult to realise that traffic could once pass on either side. From the time that these buildings were built, passageways were created leading down to the Priory.

The Twentieth Century

It is a proud piece of Dunstable's history that these shops have continued trading from the 14th century until the present day and will continue to trade into the next century and beyond. Starting from the crossroads, what was sometimes known as No. 189 High Street South was also known sometimes as No. 2 Middle Row. *Number 2, The Rose and Crown* was described in 1900 as being 'very old with low roofs', 'in a fair state of repair' and 'clean', it was tied to Green's Brewery in Luton, the lessee being Benskins and Co. of Watford. It closed just before the First World War, was partly rebuilt and let to Ernest Edwards, who ran a ladies' dress and underwear shop. The newsagent, Mr Keep (who gave his name to the corner shop) opened his business in the mid-1920s. Mr Stark and his successor continued the news-agency until 1985. Since then it has been occupied by Chiltern Sports and is now a branch of Taylor's estate agents.

Number 4 (188) had been a butcher's shop for over sixty years when it was bought by Mr George Costin early in this century. Better known for his work with horses, Mr Costin lived here and continued the butcher's business before moving into what became the Blacksmith's Arms in West Street. However, the name which will be remembered in connection with this shop is Tilley. The present Mike Tilley's grandfather bought the business in 1926, at which time there was a slaughterhouse in one of the lanes at the back. The late Mr Vic Tilley remembered delivering meat on his bicycle in the 1930s, when a weekly order of ten shillings (50p) was greatly respected, although a three to four shillings (15–20p) bill was a more usual amount. When Mr Mike Tilley retired it became a busy bakers and confectioners, known as 'Use Your Loaf'.

Number 6 The Shoulder of Mutton

This inn was described as being in 'a fair state of repair'. Nevertheless, it was difficult to make a profit. Benskin and Co.

closed it on April 5th 1903.

The reason that this building has a different appearance is that in 1959 the old building became unsafe. At that time the future of the whole row was at risk and the new, front, single-storey section was to be removed, if necessary, for road widening. During the early years of this century it was taken over by Blindells, the shoe retailers, but around 1938 there was a change of ownership and it became Burgess Stationers and Office Equipment Centre, remaining until replaced by Audiovisual in the 1980s. For a time it was known as Ashton Audio, but then T & P Stationers moved in from number 8 with a large and very varied stock for private and commercial customers.

Numbers 8–10 The Swan with Two Necks

T. Parsons of Princes Risborough owned this inn, leasing it to Adey White of St. Albans. In 1903 it was described as 'very old and inconvenient'. However it struggled on for a few more years, not closing until 1913. It was a hairdressing business in the early 1920s but by 1927 it had become a confectioners and sub-Post Office, well remembered for the Kunzle cakes and high-class sweets to be bought there. By 1966 it had completely changed and Halfords were claiming to have over a hundred bicycles in stock. Both Burgess and T & P were at one time in this building but for some time it has been a branch of Ladbrokes.

Number 12 (185) – now demolished

This shop frequently changed the nature of its business. It was a fish shop at one time and then Sanders Bros. turned it into a grocery business, before it was demolished in 1978 to improve the alleyway.

Number 14 The Cross Keys

This building was once part of the estate of Mrs Frances Ashton and was never a proper inn but a combined grocery business and beer shop. It continued to sell groceries into this century, but no longer held a beer licence. In 1911 Percy Lester opened a jewellery business in the shop and continued trading there until it was transferred to Walkers. After the new archway was constructed it was divided into two separate shops. The Dogs' Bowl pet shop has been there for many years. In the late 1960s it shared the building with Penny's Fashions; in 1999 it shares with the RSPCA.

The Great Fire of Middle Row

At 5pm on Boxing Day, Tuesday 26th December 1893, the lamp-lighter spotted smoke coming from the cellar of number 20 Middle Row. Having warned all the occupants, he hurried to summon the Fire Brigade who, although arriving quickly, could not apply enough water due to low pressure, allowing the fire to get out of control. The following day's edition of the Dunstable Gazette described the 'terrifying and disastrous conflagration' which was 'fed by old timbers'. The remains of numbers 16, 18 and 20 were later bought and rebuilt by a single owner, explaining their similar appearance today.

Four years later the Gazette reported another fire at number 20. Mrs Vater, wife of the upholsterer, was sewing some blinds when she accidentally knocked over the paraffin lamp. Once again there was a shortage of water and the building was severely damaged.

Number 16 (183)

Although this shop was not actually burnt in the fire of 1893, it was severely damaged by smoke and water, but was repaired by 1900 to become a grocery store. A later owner, P. G. Rennie, remained there for many years. In the 1960s it was a branch of Copyright. At a later date it housed one or more property agents but for the last three years the section facing Ashton Square has housed The Book Stop with the phone shop, Talk of the Town, at the front.

Number 18 (182)

The Janes family (who had been tenants here before the fire) returned to run their greengrocery business well into this century, while Mr George Gadd had the business during and after the Second World War and is remembered for the queues outside his shop when bananas returned after the war. In more recent times this will be remembered as different types of café or restaurant. In the mid 1960s it was Bubbles Wine Bar; in the late 1980s it was an Indian Restaurant. It is now a take-away called Montanna.

Number 20 (181)

This is where the fire started. For many years before it had been the shop and workshop of clock and watchmaker Alfred Barcock. He passed the business to the Sketchley Dye Works who purchased the building in 1925 and stayed for several years. By the end of the 1980s is was Pickfords the Travel Agents, but earlier it had been a branch of Reject China Shops. After that it was used by one or more Double Glazing concerns. However for the last ten years it has been known as Lunaria Designs. There are flowers and accessories here for the person who wants a simple display for the house or who wants to undertake more complicated decorations for a wedding.

Number 22 The Britannia Inn

This had only become licensed property during the preceding century. It stood next to the second archway and suffered badly during the fire. The Harpenden Brewery put the 'highly desirable Building Site' up for auction at the Sugar Loaf on April 8th 1893 when it was purchased by Cornelius Vater, upholsterer and furniture dealer, for £162. It was his wife who started the second fire, but luckily they were well insured and were soon back in business. In 1935 they sold to Mr A.E.F. Stott* whose popular town centre furniture shop will long be remembered. This building has since been divided into two separate stores. In 1985 the estate agent, Treasury of Homes, was on the upper floor but for many years it has been Bless the Bride. Since 1986 the ground floor has housed F. L. Moores (Records) Ltd.

Number 24 (179)

This had once been a small bonnet sewing room, but after the fire it was bought by Mr Thompson Smallwood. During the First

---

* Mrs Stott tells me that the frame, slightly charred from the second blaze, is still encased within the building.

World War it was let to the Misses Gaisford who sold clothes for ladies and children; when they retired it was purchased by Mr E.J.Buckle who converted it into a gentlemen's outfitters. Although his son, Mr Philip Buckle, has now retired, Mr Butterton runs a similar business in this shop.

Many of these buildings have been in continual use since the medieval period, but in this one, part of the early timber-frame can actually be seen. One of Mr Buckle's bills for 1937 has survived. A new suit cost £4.10s, a shirt ten shillings and sixpence (52.5p) and a bow tie to go with the shirt, two shillings (10p). At about this time he was offering overcoats from £2.5s and leather coats from £4.10s!

The deeds of the building contain an interesting item concerning the history of Dunstable. As the tenants of the Priory managed to become free of various traditional services, these were converted into small annual fines or 'reliefs'. They continued for hundreds of years and were regularly collected at the manor court. Even after Dunstable Council bought the market and tolls in 1870, forty-seven people had to continue to pay their customary dues. Their value at that time was scarcely worth collecting and in 1882 the town clerk offered to purchase them at an estimated twenty-five year value. These were gradually paid off, but when Mr Buckle bought number 24, he found that previous owners had been paying an annual relief of just over one shilling for over five hundred years.*

Number 26 (178)

When Saxby's bought the shop in 1914, it already had a very long history as a butcher's business but two years later the shop was sold to Eastman's and remained with them for many years. During the 1960s it was a centre for home beer and wine-makers, known as 'Brew-It-Yourself'. It then became the well-known and popular 'Bag Shop' before becoming 'Cooks Collection'. At that time the shop was stocked with every type of tool and utensil to do with cooking. Since the beginning of August this year it has

---

*   I am grateful to Mr Philip Buckle for allowing me to see these deeds.

become The World of Enchantment and is now packed with gifts, candles, books and ethnic crafts.

Number 28 (177)

This grocery shop, which had stayed with different branches of the Young family throughout much of the 19th century, was owned by Mrs Paxton Young during the early years of this century and when she died in 1921, it became the much-loved Hootens Penny Bazaar.

Amongst many other things, it sold dolls and many small toys (including penny dolls and a collection of clothes at a penny each). When Mr Hooten retired in 1936, there was a complete change; Mr Sewell opened a fish shop. He is remembered for carrying ice back from Luton station in the basket on his bicycle and for the smell of the haddock in his Back Street smoke-house, where, having soaked it in brine for half an hour, the fish was then hung up to drip dry in the smoke house.

There is a story that a chimney cracked during the severe winter of 1947, exposing a bricked-up cupboard. To his surprise Mr Sewell found a long black dress with a high boned collar, but, once exposed, the silk material fell into rags. During the 1980s it was a hairdressing salon known at different times as Mimosa and Blow Your Top. It is now called Beards and Barnets.

Number 30 (176)

Early this century the Singer Sewing Machine Company took over this shop, remaining there until the 1940s. A popular Wool Shop was there in the 1960s followed by a shop which specialised in children's clothes. It is now known as Outriggers and sells high-fashion clothes for men.

Number 32 The Magpie

Until 1864 this shop was often combined with a victualler's business where the tenant was serving food and drink. When the premises were renovated several old bottles were found under the floorboards. Charles Knight Boskett, hairdresser, traded for most of the first twenty years of the century, followed by several changes until 1934, when the building was bought by Brands the butcher and then A.E. Fisher took over for many years. In the 1960s Paraphernalia were selling a wide range of gifts and odds and ends. It has been a travel agency for well over ten years and is currently a branch of Going Places.

Number 34 (174)
Together with number 32, this was another unit which was once used in the hat industry. From around 1864 until 1911, it belonged to George Medcraft, hat manufacturer, and after his death his executors rented the property to George Perryman, hairdresser. Sometime after 1918, Henry Stoten and his daughter Lucy continued in the same trade until 1959, with Lucy running it alone for a time after her father's death. It was in 1933 that she advertised a lady's permanent wave for £1.

It was known as Fair Maiden in the 1960s when it was selling ladies' clothes and has been for some years Cambio Dry Cleaners.

Number 36 (173)
This building was sometimes used in connection with number 34 and sometimes number 38. During and after the First World War James Bareham ran what he described as 'a dining room'. By 1922 Francis Menear described it as a 'family restaurant' and it is said that it was patronised, at times, by executives from Waterlow's. The business closed shortly before the Second World War, when it was taken over by the army to be used as an office and occasional billet for soldiers. For the last eighteen years it has been a busy newsagency known as GB News.

Numbers 38, 40 and 42 (172–170)
The deeds of this building were housed in the estate office of Dewhurst House, Smithfield in the 1980s, when the author had the good fortune to be allowed to view them. Starting in the reign of Charles II, the evidence was that the building was a beer-house at that time, overlooking the cattle-market. Over the centuries it was the site for many different businesses – often two or three running at the same time. Mrs Paxton Young (of number 28) also

owned this property but her executors sold it to a butcher, whose family sold it to the tenant, the London Central Meat Company. Number 38 remained a butcher's shop until well into recent memory. What was number 40 (facing the cattle-market) is no longer a shop and number 42 was used for several different purposes. For several years now the whole ground floor has been used to raise funds for Cancer Research.*

Shopping in Dunstable

From early medieval times it has been noted that shopping was an important part of Dunstable's economy. Back in Chapter 3 (1297), it was the leading retail centre in Bedfordshire and evidence suggests that there had always been a good range of shops in the town. Nevertheless, research on Middle Row has proved that frequent changes in the ownership or position of shops is nothing new. However, one area where there has been some continuity is the crossroads end of High Street South. The Stott family business has been mentioned above but sadly Beverly Stott, who moved the family business back into Bull Pond Lane, died while this book was being completed. He himself was well-known for a range of excellent reproduction furniture but he told tales of the early days, when his father toured the villages taking orders and delivering any items of household ware for which his customers cared to ask. The family were also furniture removers and, as Dunstable began a new phase of expansion, their advertisement in Dunstable's Official Guide of 1935 advised the public to 'Remove to your new house the Modern Way'.

Three generations of the Tilley family ran the butcher's business at Number 4 Middle Row. The Costin family, who sold the butcher's business to the Tilleys, moved into West Street. While he was still a butcher in 1916, Mr E.G.Costin was advertising horses and various traps and wagonettes for hire. 'Traps for picnic and pleasure parties carefully arranged'. For those who preferred a more modern form of transport, he

---

* The History of Middle Row was included in the Chronicle series, published by Dusntable Museum Trust (1986).

offered 'Motors for pleasure and removals'. He also brewed beer and delivered it around the villages by horse and cart. When the author had difficulty identifying *The Blacksmith's Arms*, in West Street, his daughter, the late Miss Costin, explained that their kitchen was used in the evenings as a small beer house. Mr Costin's family built up a chain of motor-driven coaches which were eventually taken over by Tricentrol. Mr Keith Costin still owns coaches today.

Back in 1908 Mr Charles Moore opened a General and Fancy Drapery at 21 High Street South (now Family Affair). In 1914 he was advertising Made-to-Measure suits from twenty-one shillings. Three years later he moved the business to Number 11 (now 21–23) High Street South. In the 1935 directory he took a whole page advertisement to illustrate Durofront corsets. They were a halfpenny under four shillings per pair and although every effort had been made to make them look attractive they do not look very comfortable! Mr Fred Moore took over the business during the Second World War. As at one time he was a lay reader at the Methodist Church in the Square he is very proud to think that previous owners of Number 11 were members of John Darley's family – the founder of Methodism in Dunstable. Fred's daughter, Pauline Keen, is the third generation of the family to run this business. Theirs is now the oldest family business in the town. It has expanded into a traditional department store with a big selection of clothes for all members of the family, linen and Dunstable souvenirs.

A few doors down from Moore's what was the Victoria Bun Shop had been bakers and confectioners since at least 1870. In 1917 Joseph Andrews supplied wedding cakes for £1.8s, twenty-five wedding cards of 6/6d and cake-boxes for 2/8d. It was closed due to the ill-health of the owner.

Although not a family firm, Albion Buildings (now a branch of William Hill) was at the end of the last century owned by the International Tea Company. They originally let out part of the ground floor to William Francis, ironmonger, but early in the twentieth century they used the whole building as a branch of their International Stores. Originally they delivered with a horse and cart but later switched to motorised vans. When they eventually closed in the 1970s the building was used by yet another 'cheap and cheerful' branch of the company.

One of the features of shopping in Dunstable has always been the variety of shops. Among the names which are remembered with affection in High Street North is Charlie Cole's bicycle shop which proudly displayed the penny-farthing bicycle over the door. His advertisement in the 1935 Directory includes a photograph of Charlie holding a very large silver cup. He had received it for twice winning the Kettering Hospital Cup for a five mile scratch cycle race. He was already winner of over twenty cycle championships and as a veteran he kept racing well into his eighties. For a ten shilling deposit he would sell Rudge, BSA, Sunbeam and Hercules cycles. They cost just under £4 each! Tandems were built to order.

Nearer the crossroads many Dunstablians have happy memories of buying black lozenges, called Victory-Vs, or when they could afford it Edinburgh Rock, from the Confectionery Bazaar. This was run by Miss Rose Harlow and Miss Annie Omer; they started their shop early in the century and their young customers found them very staid and dignified. Nearby William Gibbard's corn merchants business continued well into the 1960s, at which time both he and his assistant still wore the traditional, long brown coat overalls. Inside the shop were open sacks of various foods for horses and small livestock. Although he still sold food by the sack, during the war many townspeople came in regularly for their 'balancer mash' for their chickens. By the end of the 1960s they were well adapted to cater for the needs of pet rabbits and guinea pigs.

Not in the High Street but back in West Parade, a 'Hat Renovating' service was offered in 1935. Ladies' and Gents' straws, felts, and velours could be remodelled to the latest fashion for 1/6d. In 1937 'Bessie's advert pointed out that one could see all the new Whitsun fashions in West Parade without going to London. In 1975 her shop was bought by Roy and Carol Smith. They opened as a greengrocery business called Farm to U. The popularity of this business quickly grew and although greengrocery is still the main section of their trade, both children and adults come from miles around to purchase food and litter for their pets.

Back in High Street North, the two chemists shops were of particular importance. One of the branches of F.E. Herrington's business was at 31 High Street South. His other branch was at 11 High Street North, on the corner of George Street. In 1916 Mr Herrington was advertising his Wild Cherry Elixir which should be sipped if one was bothered by coughing spells. It was offered at one shilling [5p] a bottle plus an extra three pence postage within Great Britain or a shilling if it was posted to France. He described himself as a Dispensing and Photographic Chemist. When Rosemarie Finch bought this business in 1984 two slot machines were found in the attic. One was free-standing and one designed to be mounted on a wall. Once a common feature outside a photographic chemist shop, they had held Kodak films. Customers wanting to purchase a film when the shop was shut put a shilling(?) in the slot and received a film in return. If they were anxious to see their photos, they put their used film, in an envelope, through the chemist's letterbox, for him to develop the next day. Many people will remember with affection and gratitude the work of Mr Eric Baldock who was pharmacist at this branch. His 'mixtures', 'elixirs' and advice were often preferred to the doctor's medicines. In 1987 Rosemary Finch moved the business into more convenient premises on the southern corner of George Street.

The other chemist was Flemons and Marchant. In 1881 Joseph Flemons of Leighton Buzzard bought the business of Thomas Coleash. He built up the business and was soon advertising 'Tasteless Dandelion, Chamomile and Rhubarb Pills'. Dandelion, chamomile and Mr Flemon's wild cherry are all common on the local chalk hills and Mr Flemons, later joined by Mr Marchant, developed a very large business drying, processing and preparing for use, local herbal remedies. Many young Dunstablians earned their pocket-money during the last war by collecting rose-hips. These were made into rose-hip syrup which was distributed to children all over the country as a valuable source of vitamin C. However this was just one branch of what became a big business.

The shop was on one side of The White Hart and there was space at the back where some derelict cottages once stood. Not just children but many village families supplemented their income collecting plants which were brought into the High Street North workshops. A detailed history of this business and several other important local shops and businesses are featured in the series of booklets researched and published by Dunstable and District Local History Society.

Other High Street North shops whose closure (usually due to the retirement of the owners) are greatly missed are: Anderson's, the gentlemen's tailors who supplied the Grammar School uniform, Monks, the haberdashers, Mr Bernard Stevens whose ironmongers shop not only supplied boxes of screws and nails and tools for carpenters, but also small quantities for the amateur and every type of tool and gadget for both inside and outside the house. However we must not forget the interesting shops which have opened more recently such as Imagine, which has been at the entrance into the Eleanor Precinct since it first opened and offers a wide range of high-class gifts; Anne Marie, which is in what was The Sugar Loaf Tap with specialist ranges of ladies and children's clothes and round the corner in Queensway, Lilies, who supplies not just fresh and dried flowers but full decorative displays for both the private and commercial market.

At the back of High Street North in the space once used by the hat factories is the small Eleanor Cross shopping precinct. The modern representation of an Eleanor Cross is by a local sculptor. The ladies' fashion shop, Gladrags, has been there since the precinct opened in 1985 and Eleanor's Gallery, the specialist shop for artists and those interested in pictures opened soon afterwards.

One other Dunstable firm which is missed from this end of the town is the Gas Board Showroom. The coming of gas and water into the town and the formation of the Gas and Water Company has been mentioned above. In 1935 they described themselves as 'The Housewife's Third Hand'. This was because she could receive hot water 'in her workshop – the kitchen . . . at any time for countless jobs, not only in the kitchen, but the whole house'. They also claimed to 'Banish Washday Worries. However big the family wash may be, the Gas Copper gets going at once'. The housewife pictured is apparently preparing for a party, because she is cooking in (surprisingly modern) strap court shoes and an attractive pleated black dress with a large white collar. On the other hand the kitchen which illustrates the advertisement in the Borough Gazette during 1937 is in chaos. The lady still wears the 'little black dress' but she is in tears. 'Who'll help Cinderella wash up?' is the question. The answer is 'Mr Therm' with his Ascot Sink Heater.

Shopping in Church Street was changed when the small family businesses were taken down to enlarge the car park near the Priory Church and to build modern businesses on the edge of the new shopping centre. One of these originals was J & W Baker who had shops on both sides of the road. They described themselves as 'Ironmongers and Complete House Furnishers' and advertised furniture, carpets and every type of floor covering. They were distributors of Slumberland products and also offered to remake worn bedding. They sold china, glass and earthenware, wire netting and garden tools and even tools for carpentry and engineering.

Near the crossroads at 4 and 6 Church Street, Gibbs and Dandy described themselves as 'Ironmongers and Builders' Merchants – Range and Grate Specialist'. Their stock included electric cookers and heaters, lawnmowers and rollers, paints, distemper and varnishes as well as domestic and farm utensils. They opened in Church Street in 1910 in a shop once owned by the drapers, Charles Lockhart and Son. This business cut across the corner into Numbers 3 and 4 High Street South. Many years later Gibbs and Dandy also bought this shop in High Street South and will be remembered for this L-shaped, double shop.

The most unusual looking shop in Church Street, Number 12, is housed in the Old Drill Hall. This was built in 1872 to train and exercise local volunteer soldiers. It became an antiques store-room and additional display area for Rixon's Antiques Shop at Number 26. In 1980 Mr Paul Bowes opened The Book Castle and in 1990 published 'Dunstable Decade', which illustrates life in Dunstable during that period. The publishing of this Millennium book will mark his twentieth year in the town. Not only does the shop sell a very wide range of new and second-hand books, they also sell maps, greetings cards, cassettes, videos and classical music. Under the same business name, The Book Castle, Paul Bowes has published over sixty local interest books.

Next door to the The Book Castle is Sweet Nothings, a shop full of beautiful lingerie and next door to that is the Vanity Box, with nearly-new ladies clothes. These two popular shops have their regular customers, some of whom travel a great distance.

Two of the oldest shops in Dunstable are Numbers 18 and 20 West Street. This important building was built as shops well before the closing of the Priory, but for many years it was used as a small inn or beer house. In the 16th century it was known as The Leaden Porch, then The Green Man. For a short time in the 19th century it was called The Maypole and the yard at the back is still known as The Maypole Yard. Its historic importance was identified in the 1970s by John Bailey, who can interpret the use and previous layout of buildings by the structure of their timber frame. He examined several of the old buildings in West Street and although there have been several good or bad alterations, this side of the road is still regarded as an important historic group of buildings. During the 19th and 20th centuries, Numbers 18 and 20 have been used as shops again.

In the 1980s the popular businesses which were here for some years were Pat and Ray's Fruit and Vegetable Shop and The Vanity Box (now in Church Street). In the 1990s there was a great deal of concern because a strong wind brought down the chimneys and damaged the roof. The rain got in and the building was at risk. Eventually it was completely restored and now houses Nightingale Wholefoods and a glass and china shop called Table Topics.

A little further along, in another of the old buildings, the Guard Room is one of the country's leading suppliers of military gaming, fantasy and science fiction games. Not only do people travel great distances to purchase authentic pieces of scenery or wargaming figures, but the business attracts a lively mail-order trade.

The Wool Shop and Jonquil Florists have also been trading for many years along this interesting street of shops, as has Unwins, the wine merchants. On the other side of West Street a new business, 'Lombardos', has attractively renovated one of the older buildings and has opened a fruit and vegetable shop plus a delicatessen. Also on this side, Ellis's the barbers, once a beer house called the Vine, was dismantled when the new shops were put up. This was another early timber framed building and is now safe at the outdoor museum in Buckinghamshire.

For many years now the very active Chamber of Trade has been working together with the Town Council to promote both home shopping and to attract shoppers from outside. A recent initiative has been a colourful 'Shopping in Dunstable' leaflet. This, with other initiatives which are in the planning stage, will help people to realise that the High Street multiples in the shopping precinct and the specialist and family businesses along the main roads and in the quieter side roads, together offer a wide selection of shops without the necessity of going out of the town.

Religion

In the days of the Augustinian Priory England was a Roman Catholic country. Although the break with Rome was forced through here in Dunstable, by the annulment of Henry's marriage to Catherine of Aragon, the 'Church of England' was not introduced until the reign of his son Edward VI. Even then no room was allowed for individual beliefs or for any variation in the form of worship. However as we have followed the struggle which took place to obtain freedom of worship we can see that Dunstablians played a very important part in its success.

We traced the arrival of today's two Baptist Churches and the Methodist Church in the Square. We have also seen that having played a major role in the right to introduce the Quaker movement Dunstable Quakers decided to worship with the Quakers in Luton. As soon as the first new housing development began, the Congregationalists built a church in Edward Street (1853) and the Primitive Methodists in Victoria Street (1862). The former building suffered from subsidence and the congregation, who joined with the Presbyterians and are now known as the United Reformed Church, now worship in what was their school hall. This was built in 1862 and was originally known as the Osborn Hall.

By the early 1960s the latter had joined up with their friends in the Square and no longer needed the second Methodist building. It stood empty for a short time and then in 1968 reopened as a Roman Catholic church for the many people in the area who were of Polish (or similar) origin. Before leaving the subject of Methodism in the town, the size of their congregation must be stressed and the important role that they played in the introduction of both education and welfare services. When a census of church attendance was taken, one Sunday in 1851, the congregation in The Square was even larger than that at the Priory. At about this time a Methodist Mission Chapel was built at the northern end of the town and this was so successful that in 1909 the permanent Waterlow Road Chapel was built. However in the last few years this congregation, like that of Victoria Street, preferred to worship with their friends in the Square and this chapel was also closed.

What is sometimes called 'the baby' of the Dunstable Circuit, is the Luton Road Church. In May 1927 a piece of land was purchased along the Luton Road for the use of Methodists living in the new area at that end of the town. At first only open air services were held but from May 1947 evening services were held at Evelyn Road School. The new church was opened on 2nd June 1949. Over the years the building has been enlarged and modernised and an enthusiastic group of worshipers meet there every Sunday.

As the residential areas spread further away from the town centre the Anglicans built a modern church at each end of the town. First, in 1959, St. Augustine's was built on the Downside Estate, to the south of the town then, in 1968, St. Fremund's was built on the Beecroft Estate to the north of the town. When the Katherine Drive area was developed the new United Reformed Church was built and dedicated to St. Katherine of Genoa. This now works in partnership with the Anglican Parish. As there are four churches in the partnership there is a Team Ministry made up of a rector, four vicars and several lay readers.

In the past, figures have shown that there were very few Roman Catholics in Bedfordshire. During this century numbers have grown and an increasing number of churches have been built. By the mid 1920s about sixty people from Dunstable were attending the Roman Catholic church in Luton. In 1927 a request was made to the Bishop of Northampton for a priest to visit Dunstable every Sunday. At first, Sunday Mass was held in a house in Regent Street but within a few months the Old Anglican Rectory had been purchased and services were held there while a new church was built on the West Street side of the rectory grounds. This was dedicated to St. Mary and opened in 1936.

However the number of Roman Catholics in and around Dunstable continued to grow quite rapidly. In 1957 Father Maurice O'Niell came to Dunstable and set out to oversee the building of a new church and presbytery. As a result a most exciting new church was built, thought to have been the first round church to be built in England for around four hundred years. It was opened by the Lord Bishop of Northampton on 15th March 1964. It follows the historic tradition of church building, using the best new materials and crafts of the day. The main material used for the walls was brick and for the roof copper. Inside the church use has been made of carved wood, stained glass and wrought iron and there is an amazing aluminium ceiling.

The Salvation Army has been working in Dunstable since the beginning of the century. In the 1930s they built a hall on the northern end of Bull Pond Lane. After the Second World War attendance at their services and the ever growing amount of social and welfare activities that they carried out in the town meant that this building was quite unsuitable. Fund raising took several years of very hard work but they at last opened their new church and community centre a few years ago.

Just as in years past, even with the number of different churches now available there are people who prefer a different form of worship. The Pentecostal Kings Mission has been in its own premises, in Lovers Walk, for many years and some house-groups have progressed to having their own buildings. The Evangelical Church in Langdale Road, follows a traditional design, while the Christadelphian Church in Kirby Road, has been gradually rebuilt following the layout of the original building. Several other house-groups meet in the town and at least three have reached a size where they hire buildings on a regular basis.

These and many other places of worship are set out on this book's end-paper, researched and designed by Omer Roucoux.

Churches Together
Some years ago members from the majority of Dunstable's Christian churches began to meet on a regular basis and from time to time enjoy shared services. Each year a Good Friday parade walks through the town before enjoying shared worship.

Hospitals

In the Middle Ages health care of all kinds, including research, was based on the monasteries and Dunstable was well provided for. Following the Dissolution, their hospital of St. Mary Magdalene continued as a hospital for Dunstable and district. After this closed, people probably turned to barber/surgeons like Josiah Settle. Although able to lance boils and tumours visible on the skin and to carry out bleeding if requested, internal operations were not within their ability.

As we have already seen, three generations of the Crawley family practised medicine from the mid 17th century and there was a Dr Marshe living at Kingsbury in the 18th century. In later centuries the prosperity of Dunstable attracted highly-qualified doctors to settle in the town.

Sometime during the 18th century an isolation hospital was built at the top of West Street, shown on Bowles' Pocket Map of Bedfordshire, c.1750, to have stood on the town side of the corner with the Green Lane. Before its apparent closure c.1784 it may have been used for smallpox patients. Although twenty-four Dunstablians signed a petition in 1766 to try to prevent Thomas Warren, the town's surgeon and apothecary, from practising innoculation, it had been accepted well before 1784.

The Priory Hospital

Even after 1900, serious outbreaks of 'fever' occurred quite regularly and in 1904 the Corporation bought Highfield House in Kensworth Lane (now Beech Road) for staff accommodation, building a new brick building for infectious patients. Being so far out of the town centre (actually over the Kensworth boundary), there were no modern services, e.g. piped water and sewage! In 1906 the Dunstable and District Joint Isolation Hospital was opened to take patients from Dunstable, Leighton Buzzard and the villages which comprised the Luton Rural District. By this date smallpox had been eradicated and the most frequent admissions were children suffering from scarlet fever and diphtheria, although there were occasional outbreaks of typhoid or paratyphoid, whooping cough and what have now become less serious illnesses, i.e. measles and chickenpox.

Even though the Medical Officer of Health was gradually controlling the more serious illnesses, continuing population growth meant that the hospital was always busy. By 1938 it was at last connected to mains water, drainage and electric light. This was just in time to help with the next rush of patients, caused by evacuees billetted in Dunstable and the villages swelling the numbers of children in the community. One Christmas the hospital was so full that the children were put to bed 'head to tail' and it took a matron, ward sister, two assistant nurses and five or six probationers to look after them. These young probationers had to work a thirteen hour day (including two hours of meal breaks) and had to cover night duties. Time off was restricted to one half-day each week plus one full day each month – all for £3 per month!

Miss Gertrude Dobson was the matron from 1920–1945. Having trained at the Derby Infirmary, she gave most of her professional life to Dunstable. Her successor, Miss H. Roberts, was only in Dunstable for a few years before a major change took place. In July 1948, the National Health Service was introduced and St. Mary's became part of the Luton and Hitchin Group Management Committee. As part of this group it was to have both a new use and a new name.

To take pressure off the Luton and Dunstable Hospital, it was decided to convert St. Mary's into a 'half-way house' for the elderly and long-term sick. They would spend time at what became known as the Priory Hospital before going on to a convalescent unit. Medical, surgical and orthopaedic patients were admitted and visited by their own specialists. However, some local doctors admitted and cared for their own patients.

During this period, extra rooms were added and in July 1976 the thirty beds became a specialist geriatric unit, administered from St. Mary's Hospital in Luton. This local facility was much appreciated and there was a general feeling of sadness when it closed.

The Luton and Dunstable Hospital

The story of Dunstable's St. Mary's Hospital overlaps the planning of the much larger and more modern General Hospital which was built between the towns of Luton and Dunstable. As Dunstable did not have its own cottage hospital and its residents were sometimes admitted to Luton's [also called St. Mary's], the people of Dunstable raised money to support that one. As the population grew, it became much too small and out-dated and suffered from the lack of an out-patients department.

In 1934 a ten acre plot of land was purchased from Electrolux and fund raising began. Back in 1917 a Dunstable grocer, Arthur Buckingham, had written on a brown paper sugar bag that he wanted his money (£4,436) to be used to found a cottage hospital for the poor and needy 'of Dunstable and district'. Welcome as this bequest was, it was hardly sufficient, on its own, to build a hospital so it was invested. Luton was able to sell the Bute Hospital to Bedfordshire County Council and so swell the building fund by £35,000. Dunstable's hospital money had been well invested and after an appeal to the Charity Commissioners, they could then add over £10,000. Local fund-raising efforts used many methods familiar today. In addition to mayoral appeals, fêtes and various entertainments, a list of patrons was opened, personal letters sent out, workers agreed to weekly contributions being taken directly from their wage packets, local papers gave help and publicity and a collection box for unwanted pieces of gold, silver and foreign coins was made available in Luton.

The opening ceremony was carried out by Her Majesty Queen Mary, the Queen Mother on February 14th 1939. From the formation of the sub-committee to the actual opening had taken seven years, but the time had been well spent. A hundred and seventy beds were ready for use and the layout was prepared for a further hundred and thirty. By the end of the year the war had started and the casualty department was soon overcrowded. Money was found to build a new large waiting room and the hospital was able to play an essential role in caring for and supporting the community.

With the creation of the National Health Service the hospital came under the North West Metropolitan Regional Board and part of Luton and Hitchin Group Hospital Management Committee. Since that time there has been continual building.

The medieval hospital of St. Mary was intended for the treatment of travellers as well as for the people of Dunstable. In 1963 a new wing was opened especially equipped to handle accidents and emergencies. A consultant was employed and a mobile X-ray unit was provided. This was primarily for the use of local people but has proved a life-saving unit for those involved in road accidents.*

Education

Schools

It is amazing to think that the earliest recorded non-monastic school in England was in Dunstable! The renowned scholar Geoffrey de Gorham opened his school even before the arrival of the Augustinian canons. In 1131 King Henry included 'the schools' in his gift to the Priory and from then on the canons were responsible for education in the town. Although no details are known there are various references to schools and school-masters during the 17th century. Then in 1715 the Chew

---

* For a detailed history of the local hospitals see Currie, M. Hospitals in Luton and Dunstable. An Illustrated History.

School opened; it was only for forty boys, but they were Dunstable boys and not outsiders. The education offered was excellent and each year there were apprenticeships available.

In the previous chapter of this book we noted the extremely rapid development of Sunday Schools. These became day schools and well before the turn of the century every child in Dunstable was attending school.

The Early Twentieth Century

Apart from the very small denominational ones, the rest of the 19th century schools continued into this century. However, the Chew School closed in 1905; it had played a most important role but its facilities could not compete with the new schools. The Chew Trust funds are still distributed each year in the form of scholarships and grants.

The buildings still stand and play an important role in the life of the town. Chew House contains the permanent offices of the Priory and other Anglican churches and its other rooms are let out to a wide variety of Dunstable societies. The second building, planned as a grammar school, became the town library (see below). When the present library was built it became the permanent home of what had been The Dunstable Repertory Company. In 1968 it became The Dunstable 'Rep' Theatre Club – affectionately known as The Little Theatre. Bernard Bresslaw performed the opening ceremony on October 5th 1968. Each play has nine packed performances.

Meanwhile the population was continuing to grow and Bedfordshire Education Committee had taken over responsibility for schools. In 1908 they opened Burr Street School (Icknield after 1952); in 1911, Britain Street Council Schools (Priory after 1947). The Methodist church was quickly re-built after the fire of 1908 but as other new schools were in the process of construction, it was decided to close the school. This school had also played a valuable role in bringing education to a wide range of boys and girls throughout the town. By 1920 the National Infants' School was in need of modernisation and repair. Back in 1882 the Houghton Regis school board had opened a school in

Chiltern Road. That, together with Burr Street, had enough room to take the extra infants and so the National School closed in 1922. This building re-opened in 1926 as the Priory Church Hall. Of the 19th century schools this left the Ashton St. Peter schools and the Ashton Grammar School. The former continued throughout the whole of this section and will continue on into the next millennium. Before moving on it should be pointed out that both before the Board School Act and before the founding of the Bedfordshire Education Committee, Dunstable was way ahead of other towns in the provision that it made for the education of its children.

The years went by and as the town grew schools were built in the newly-developed areas, e.g. following a large building programme to the north of Luton Road, a school was planned in 1936, for Evelyn Road. Later, in March 1952, when nearly five hundred houses had been built on the Beecroft Estate, the Brewers Hill County Primary School was built (Beecroft after 1952). Plans for the Downside Estate included the need for a primary school, opened in 1959.

The Northfield Estate was officially opened on May 23rd 1935 and by the end of the year a new senior school was under construction. The opening ceremony for Northfields Senior Elementary school took place on January 13th 1936. It was designed to take up to four hundred boys and girls and had extra classrooms provided for specialist subjects. The Dunstable Gazette described it as 'a model for the County' and 'a Monument to the advance of Education'. It pointed out that it was a 'monument to the emancipation of elementary education' and that it represented 'a style unique among the elementary schools of Bedfordshire'*. It is of interest that over forty-five years later, Northfields was selected to take part in a £4 million teaching pilot scheme – Technical and Vocational Education Initiative (T.V.E.I.). In 1945 Senior Elementary Schools like Northfields became Secondary Modern Schools. Two years later the school leaving age was raised to fifteen and that, together with the still rapidly rising

---

*   Northfields School, 1936–1986, (Dunstable Town Council).

population, made it necessary to plan for three new senior schools. In the meantime Northfields was given three 'huts' or temporary classrooms.

At the other end of the town, expansion had taken place at Britain Street School and in October 1947 it became known as Priory School. However there was still a great need for a Girls' Grammar School and at least one more Senior School. Nevertheless it was 1957 before Kingsbury Technical School opened. As with the grammar schools, selection for entry for both boys and girls was via the 11+ examination. This school was in the centre of the town and in the north of the town Northfields was getting increasingly overcrowded, but the other two new schools were still in the planning stage. The following year work at last started on a Girl's Grammar School and plans were drawn up for a Secondary School at Brewers Hill. The former opened in 1959 and the latter during 1961.

During 1963 another senior school was being built in Wilbury Drive. This opened early in 1964 and was called Mill Vale.

The Three Tier Comprehensive System
During the 1960s locally and nationally discussions were being held concerning the abolition of the 11+ system and to give all children the opportunity of a broader education. In 1969 it was agreed that Bedfordshire would work towards a three-tier system. All pupils would transfer from a Primary to a Middle School at the age of eight or nine years and then transfer to a Comprehensive Secondary School at the age of twelve or thirteen. The problem was how this could be arranged.

The Upper Schools
From the north of the town Northfields would need to expand from being a Secondary Modern School of six hundred pupils into an Upper School taking one thousand pupils!. It had sufficient ground to take extra permanent buildings and with its past successful history it could quite easily accept one more major change. The first stage was the building of a Sixth Form block to house one hundred and fifty students.

In the middle of the town it was not too difficult to merge the new Queen Eleanor's Grammar School with the nearby Kingsbury Technical School. This combined school opened in 1971 as the co-educational comprehensive known as Queensbury. However the Boys' Grammar School with its important historic buildings and traditions was trapped in its town centre position. Every available space had already been used to put up specialist labs and classrooms; there was no way it could accept what would amount to a new school within its grounds. After much discussions between the school governors, the Town Council, the Education Authorities from County Hall and the Ashton Foundation, it was decided to move out to a new site on the London Road. A Southern Campus Site was developed and in 1974 the Manshead Voluntary Controlled Upper School was opened to the public.

The Middle Schools

The buildings which were left vacant by the removal of the boys' grammar school were ready to become an ideal, town centre Middle School. This opened as Ashton Voluntary Aided Middle School. Another new Middle School, this time in newly-built buildings, was Streetfield Middle School on the Southern Campus. Brewers Hill became the middle school for the northern end of the town and Millvale for the area north of the Luton Road. Priory School underwent another change and quickly settled down as the Middle School for the central part of the town.

The Lower Schools

Dunstable already had a network of schools for infants and juniors. Of the very early schools Ashton St. Peter and Icknield schools were still both very popular. On the other hand, Chiltern Road school was desperately in need of modernisation. As it only had a small playground and was surrounded by houses it was impossible to make major improvements and it was decided to close it. For around seven years it was used as a Teachers' Centre but then became the headquarters of Chiltern Radio.

St. Christopher's, Downside, Watling and Hadrian had all been built in the 1950s and 1960s in response to the growth of the town. Ardley Hill and Lancot were both opened in 1969 and were ready, with the others, to form the basis of the Lower School network.

However still more schools were needed, so St. Mary's Roman Catholic Voluntary Aided Lower School was included in the new Southern Campus. It was opened in 1971 and three years later Lark Rise was built at the end of Cartmel Drive.

Into the Future
The three-tier system of education is now well established in Dunstable. In addition there are special schools, nursery schools and private schools. Mr Omer Roucoux has kindly supplied an end-paper map of the schools for this book.

Continuing and Further Education
In September 1961 the College of Further Education was opened in Kingsway to provide mainly post-secondary classes for those above school-leaving age. Throughout the years it has continually adapted to changing trends in education. The building has been greatly extended and covers a wide range of educational, vocational and leisure courses both during the day and in the evenings.

A Proud History of Adult Education
Many young people at the turn of the century left school with a good basic education but desperately wanting to build on this for interest and for career opportunities. Because very few of them had any hope of going away to college, any form of locally-based lectures were greatly appreciated.

As early as 1908 the Cambridge University Extention Movement were providing evening courses and by 1932 a branch of the Workers' Educational Association was formed. In 1935 they were offering two courses: 'Modern Books and Authors' and 'Psychology'. These subjects are still popular today although music, natural and all types of history are frequently requested.

The treasurer in 1935 was the late Mr Jim Leech and he continued to keep the accounts for fifty years. Mrs Leech, who was also a founder-member, still takes an active interest in the branch today. In 1991 the Dunstable branch of the WEA produced a booklet 'Henry VIII's Dunstable' and they were proud to dedicate it to Jim and Olive Leech.

The courses put on by the WEA are mainly for leisure; back in the 1930s Dunstable Evening School was offering career-based courses. It had three separate departments and over the years ran in different parts of the town. In one section a wide variety of commercial subjects were taught. In the second, five technical subjects useful for job opportunities in Dunstable. The third section covered practical subjects such as sewing, cookery, woodwork and physical training.

In addition to these formal classes, visiting lecturers were made very welcome and were greeted by very large audiences. This follows in the tradition of Dunstable Literary and Scientific founded in 1914. Members met in the Town Hall each Tuesday evening from October round to March; the hall was invariably 'full to capacity'.

The Libraries

In 1909 it was sadly recorded that the Dunstable Reading Room in High Street South, was unable any longer to sustain itself as a paying concern and was therefore to be closed. It was pointed out that what was required was a Public Reading Room and Library supported by the rates. However some years went by before a small library was opened in the 'barn conversion' at Kingsbury House. Mr T.W.Bagshawe (see below) converted the barn at the side of his house and part of it became the first Dunstable branch of the Bedfordshire County Library.

When Mr Bagshawe sold Kingsbury and its associated buildings, the library moved to 40 High Street North (now Oxfam). this building proved to be far too small and in 1938 it was moved to the building which is now The Little Theatre in High Street South. In the 1960s Bedfordshire Country Council opened a large new building to house many of their officers working in the south of the county. The new library was built alongside it and still stands there today. It is extremely busy and, having kept up with the needs of modern users, offers far more than just the loan of library books. In one corner of the library with a display window looking out onto the busy walkway and car park is the prize-winning Tourist Information Centre. This not only offers travel and other information for people in Dunstable who want to go on holiday outside the area, but plays an important role in attracting visitors into the area.

The Museums

In 1927 when Mr T.W.Bagshawe was living at Kingsbury, he converted the barn next to his house and fitted it out as a museum. He was a well known antiquarian and collector and in this way was able to share his important collections with the people of Dunstable. Some of his interests were in specialist subjects but many of them resulted in the preservation of in-valuable artifacts concerning Bedfordshire's economic, social and cultural history.

When the barn was sold in 1934, the museum was moved, with the library, into 40 High Street North. However, when in 1938 the library was moved to High Street South, the museum contents, including part of Mr Bagshawe's own important collection, went into the Luton Museum at Wardown Park. Under modern conditions it is extremely expensive to provide security, the correct temperature, humidity and lighting for a museum. The material from the old Dunstable Museum plus more recent material uncovered by the Manshead Archaeological Society can be seen in Luton Museum today. Items which are not currently on display can usually be seen by appointment.

Nevertheless many Dunstablians look forward to the day when Dunstable will get a museum or heritage centre of its own. In the 1980s the old timber-framed building, No. 26 Church Street, was standing empty and at risk. A group got together to raise money and to try and buy this historic building as a museum. They were not successful but thanks to the efforts of what became the Friends of Dunstable Museum, it was saved from destruction. It was restored and for many years has been an Italian Restaurant.

At the end of the decade the Friends made another attempt to get a museum. As mentioned above, Priory House became vacant and despite problems caused by its age appeared to be an ideal site. There is currently a feasibility study in progress concerning the layout of a brand new heritage centre, so it may not be too long before this is built.

The Local News

In February 1990 the Dunstable Gazette celebrated its 125th birthday by publishing a special souvenir edition.

The Tibbett family and their printing press have been mentioned in relation to ABC Travel Guides. James Tibbett tried a monthly and then a weekly paper but it was Daniel, James's son, who started the Borough Gazette on February 11th, 1865. He worked from a site on the eastern side of High Street North. Both Daniel and his wife died young and by the end of 1875 it was owned by Henry Ballans. Four years later he moved it across the road to what was then 39 High Street North, on the corner of Albion Street. With different proprietors and editors it continued to be produced from that building for one hundred and seven years.

At the end of the 1920s the paper was bought by the Luton News who had a modern printing press in Alma Street, Luton. As the years went by, improved print style and pictures led to an increase in circulation and the two papers shared the expense of increasingly modern technology.

The years have gone by, changes have been made and the Dunstable Gazette now shares offices and an editor with The Luton News. However the editor still lives in Dunstable and week by week the paper comes out packed with official announcements, local news and information about forthcoming events. This weekly newspaper not only gives pleasure but is a valuable source of past events and for recording the changes taking place at the present time.

The Growth of the Town

In some places, e.g. St. Albans and Bury St. Edmunds, the monastery was responsible for town planning and expansion, whereas in Dunstable the canons were given a town which was restricted to the four short roads. The small areas of agricultural land, e.g. the Westfield and Kensworth field, were already allotted to various businessmen.

The situation continued into the mid-19th century when on the death of Richard Gutteridge part of the town centre was sold to the British Land Company. It has been said that the company acquired in total over two hundred acres of land and laid out three miles of roads in the following few years. However, 'laid out' does not necessarily mean the immediate construction of houses.

Infilling the North West Quadrant

Starting soon after 1850, Albion Road was lengthened and became Albion Street, Mount Street was lengthened to become Edward and Matthew Streets; building on the Bull Closes and the boundary land between Dunstable and Houghton Regis gradually developed into Union Street. Street after Street was laid out and long before 1900, the corner from Princes Street to Union Street was filled in.

By this date two large employers, Waterlows and Harrison Carter's Iron works had arrived in the town and these put pressure on housing. Also, in the early 1900s a 'New Industries Committee' encouraged Bagshawe & Co's engineering works to come to Church Street (1907) and Cross & Co's paper works to come to London Road (1909).

New Estates Were Planned

As the years went by there was an even greater need for houses and new estates were planned. The two small fields south-east of the Priory Church (once known as Great and Little Inlands, but later known as 'Englands') were sold in 1877 when England's Close Estate was planned. Many houses were built in Priory Road/St. Peter's Road area between 1880 and 1910.

Bull Close Estate around the Clifton Road area was started just before the First World War, with Borough Farm Estate following a little later and developing very slowly. Small groups of private houses were built in Great Northern Road, and construction on the estate continued in the same piece-meal way. Only two properties were completed in Borough Road before 1910 and although a few were built in Downs Road and Grove Road from 1905, only sixty-nine houses on the estate in total were finished before the outbreak of war. Roads and plots (many priced at £25 to £30) were marked out and people bought them over a long period of time. Homes were either built for self-occupation or as an investment.

A New Boundary was Needed

Between 1885 and 1904 twenty-five new houses were built along the Houghton end of High Street North, and sixteen had been completed in George Street. In both cases more development was planned, and plans had been submitted for Houghton Road. The 1901 census had revealed how many Dunstablians were actually residing in Houghton Regis and showed that a total of three hundred and sixty 'Dunstable' houses were registered as being in Upper Houghton Regis.

During the year 1906–7 there was a local enquiry at the Town Hall, followed by discussions at a committee of the House of Commons. As a result, an Order was obtained for three hundred and fifty acres to be incorporated within the Borough. The 1911 census recorded 8,057 persons living in 2,081 houses, in comparison with 5,157 in 1,361 houses in 1901.

The extensive building programme had removed the pressure on the existing housing; however, because there was still a need for bonnet-sewers in the factories, there were nearly six hundred more women than men living in Dunstable in 1901 and seven hundred more in 1911. The next change came when, following the Local Government Act of 1929, the County Council was obliged to review all boundaries within their counties. By this time many houses had been built outside the town's other boundaries, so in 1933 the boundaries were moved once again.

Council Houses were Built in the Town

It was not long after the war that the Corporation began to build council houses. In 1921–22 houses were erected off High Street South in Garden and Periwinkle Roads and in 1925 at the other end of the town, at what was known as the Watling Street site. Construction started in West Street in 1926 and in Chiltern Road in 1930, new roads were laid out and the area was infilled. By 1934 when A C Sphinx Sparking Plug Company (later to become A C Delco) transferred their factory from Birmingham to the northern end of Dunstable, it was possible to start building at Northfields.

There were several more private developments but the next major development by the corporation was the Beecroft Estate in 1945.

Dunstable Town Council

Queen Victoria's charter which granted Borough status to Dunstable will be one hundred and thirty-five years old just as we cross over into the year 2000. The 1864 charter is displayed in the Mayor's parlour. The first Borough Council was elected in March 1865 and we have seen how they watched over the town as it grew, introduced modern services and encouraged new industry.

When Local Government re-organisation was brought in during 1972, Dunstable Borough Council was dissolved and its rights transferred to South Bedfordshire District Council. This caused great distress in Dunstable and it was decided that the fifteen District Councillors would be appointed 'Charter Trustees' (to preserve the town's charters) and that they would appoint one of their number to be 'Town mayor'.

In 1985 the District Council petitioned the Home Office to create a Parish Council 'for the area of the former Borough of Dunstable'. Since then there has been a Dunstable Town Council with twenty elected councillors who from their number annually elect a Town Mayor. This Town Council is responsible for providing local community and recreational facilities to support the strategic services provided by South Bedfordshire District and the County Councils. The council Chamber and offices are in Grove House. The attractively produced 'Dunstable Official Guide' describes all the different responsibilities undertaken by the Town Council.

Some of the major town events which are organised by Dunstable Town Council are the Charity Fireworks Displays, Community Carol Singing and various orchestral and brass band concerts. The population of Dunstable is now over 35,000 but thanks to its historic foundation it has not been possible for the town to become too large.

Down Memory Lane

During the course of this last chapter an attempt has been made to pick up the various threads of life during the medieval period and notice how they have progressed during this twentieth century.

Writing in this way has given me the opportunity to record the history of some of our schools, hospitals and churches. I have also spoken to many Old Dunstablians asking for their memories of shops, shopping and the market. Fred Moore in particular has shared his memories with me, not only of the shops which he knew about as a boy but about the pleasure that he and his friends got from local activities. The weekly dances at the Town Hall, the Operatic Society, the United Choirs, and the lectures given by the Literary and Scientific Society which all performed to packed audiences. Also like many Dunstablians he has the happiest of memories of visiting the Statty Fair on the third Monday of each September.

An Edward Street Childhood

One lady who has lived in Dunstable all her life and has an excellent memory is Mrs Dora Godfrey. When she was a child each residential area was like a small village; like Mr Moore she points out what an important role that the chapel played in her life.

In the early part of this century, Edward Street was a busy, thriving little community. Almost everyone knew everyone else, from the minister of the Congregational Chapel to the chimney sweep with his large family who lived at the other end of the street. There was always someone to chat to, always someone to listen and help in times of trouble.

There were people of many occupations living there and several shops. Two or three little grocery shops selling almost everything, a butcher's, a fish shop and two greengrocers. There was a shoe repairer, a tinker mending pots and pans, and a little haberdashery shop where the proprietors would have a paper of pins instead of a farthing or a halfpenny change. The shop was kept by two sisters, the Misses Roberts, whose brother kept a dairy at the back of their shop. There was a baker, a tailor, an upholsterer, a laundry, and of course, two public houses. A music teacher lived near the chapel, a Miss Westlake who was also the chapel organist on Sundays. Another occupant of Edward Street was a lark catcher who trapped larks on Dunstable Downs to send to London. He would go up the Downs very early, and hang his nets on the washing line during the day.

The Congregational Chapel was an imposing building, standing where the Osbourne House flats now stand played a large part in the life of the street. Sunday School and services were well attended, especially the annual Sunday School Anniversary and the Harvest Festival. Meetings during the week, the Band of Hope and Christian Endeavour were often quite educational. The singing at all services was led by an enthusiastic choir. The organ was operated by a 'blower' pumped by a blind man Frank Fox. The Anniversary was the time for new dresses, shoes and hats. New hymns were learnt especially for the occasion. At Harvest Festival a long table was placed across the front of the chapel, and groaned under the weight of vegetables and fruit always the best of the crop, and which would be auctioned the next day. Then there were the concerts and socials, always well supported. A concert would be given by pupils of the Sunday School, sometimes wearing dresses made of crêpe paper (my own particular memories are of being a forget-me-not and once a Roman soldier). At the adults' concert would be soloists, a violinists, a pianist, sometimes a magician, a comedian, and often a performer tapping two spoons on his knee.

For the annual summer outing the children would be taken to a nearby meadow or perhaps to Totternhoe Knolls for tea and games. They were taken by brake, an open cart with seats along the sides. One glorious summer, all the churches of the town combined, and a train was hired to take the children and their parents to Southend. The winter parties were eagerly looked forward to, with a splendid tea, followed by games, all very energetic. Some of the games were: 'Farmer had a dog', 'In and out the window', 'I sent a letter to my love', 'Winking' and 'Postman's Knock'. Everyone was eventually sent home with a bun and an orange, tired but happy.

Many tradesmen called at each house, coalmen emptying their sacks down the cellar grating; bread and milk were delivered by horse and cart, the milk in large metal churns and brought to the door in cans to be emptied into jugs. Gypsies called at the back door selling pegs or paper flowers and men would call to buy rabbit skins. The muffin man would walk along the street ringing on his bell, his muffin tray on his head.

Often a streetsinger would walk down the centre of the road, and children would rush out to give him a halfpenny or a penny. There was the rag and bone man, calling out 'Rags and Bones' as he went; the knife grinder and of course, the weekly dustman with his open cart of household refuse. In the evening at dusk, the lamplighter with his long pole would light the street gaslamps.

Children could play more safely in the street than is possible today. Games were played at their regular season each year. There was skipping and jumping, often with the rope tied to a lamppost, and games of marbles; brightly coloured spinning tops; hoops, wooden for the girls and metal ones for the boys; cigarette card spinning and hopscotch.

In the winter evenings most families were content to sit by a blazing fire, the women knitting or sewing, men perhaps smoking their pipes or reading. Often friends would call and Whist or Dominoes sometimes were played.

Into the Year 2000

So much has happened since Mrs Godfrey and her friends played hopscotch in Edward Street and the roads are no longer safe for children.

Dunstable was founded on a crossroads – in fact it was founded because of that crossroads. At the end of this century the traffic on that same crossroads appears to be overwhelming life in the town centre. Discussions have been going on for some time from Town Council level right up to Westminster. Numerous schemes have been suggested and sometimes it seems as if no improvement will ever be made. However if we look back through the past we will see that this is not the first century that has ended with a major problem. Each time the turn round has come quickly and unexpectedly – and it will happen again!

Meanwhile the Town Council and various groups such as The Chamber of Trade and The Town Centre Management Committee are working to promote the town and make it more attractive both for residents and for visitors. The traffic must be reduced but at the same time thought must be given to exploiting Dunstable's favourable position on the crossroads. The whole history of Dunstable is bound up with the roads.

We are all aware of Dunstable's role in the horse-drawn coach industry but it is not so well known that earlier in this century Dunstable was a major stopping place for motorised coaches. The Central Café and the Whipsiderry Café, standing in High Street North, provided refreshments and the shops near by benefited by the custom. As 'Wings and Wheels' is one of the themes already being marketed by Bedfordshire, Hertfordshire and Luton Tourism Ltd., a Heritage Centre based on The Priory, their visitors and different periods of transport would not only be of interest to schools and local visitors, but would bring coach parties into the town. Changing exhibitions covering Dunstable's travel based industries could also be a feature.

Twenty years after the London to Birmingham Railway severely damaged Dunstable's travel trade, Charles Lambourn praised the way that Dunstablians had found a completely new industry [bonnet making] and worked together to make another success. Twenty years from now I am quite sure that some other writer will look back and say the same.

Subscribers to 31st August 1999

Mr David Aldridge
Mrs Jenny Allen
David Amey & Maxene Miller
Mrs Shirley F. Ansell
Geoff Arnold
Ingbert Babst
Keith and Paula Baldwin
Jack A. Bannister
Neil A. Bannister
Angela L. Barnes
Norman & Maisie Bates
Mr J. Bolton
Celia Booker
Colin Bourne
Cheryl Brailsford
V. Brock
Christopher & Daphne Carey
Bill & Hilary Carter
David & Barbara Cheshire
Kathleen Clark
Mrs B. Clark
Sheila Colbeck
Vera & Jim Cook
Brian A. Costin
Tom & Shirley Crowley
Mrs Joan Curran
John & Margaret Currie
Tony & Anne Darby
Deborah J. Dennis
Roger Dixon
Mrs Olive Dodd
Nora, Michael & the Duffy Family
Trevor Evans
Mr & Mrs R. Frith
L. P. J. (Peter) Frost
Mrs Jenny Funning
Hugh Garrod
Mrs Ann Georgiou
Gareth Glover
Ryan Glover
Rose Gorman
Andrew Harries
Marilyn Harrison
Nicola Jane Hawes

Terence B. Headey
Paul Heley
Barry Horne
Dawn Hunt
Paul Hunt
Vincent Hunt
Die Familie Justen
Adele Kane
Jim & Roz Kearey
Stan & Pauline Kearey
Larry Kelly
Karl Kibens
Pat & Chris Kirk
Marion Lane
Matthew Lane
Mrs Olive Leech
Pat Lovering
Jeanette Matheson
Eileen E. May
Roy & Peggy Mepham
Patricia S. Morgan
Angela Morris
Maureen Pickles
John & Margaret Pilgrim
Audrey M. Rees
Miss H. Reglar
Omer & Jean Roucoux
Mrs L. Rovai
Maggie Shafi
Mr & Mrs C. G. Sieling
Derek & Joan Smith
Roy & Carol Smith
Bernard Stevens
Councillor Bill Stevens J.P.
Ken & Jean Stilby
David & Jean Thorne
Eddie and Edna Turpin
Miss J. Webb
Victor White
Mrs G. M. Whitington
Sandra Whitton
Mrs A. Wilson
Paul & Wendy Woodcraft
Y. V. Wooster

Books Published by
THE BOOK CASTLE

COUNTRYSIDE CYCLING IN BEDFORDSHIRE, BUCKINGHAMSHIRE AND HERTFORDSHIRE: Mick Payne.
Twenty rides on- and off-road for all the family.

PUB WALKS FROM COUNTRY STATIONS:
Bedfordshire and Hertfordshire: Clive Higgs.
Fourteen circular country rambles, each starting and finishing at a railway station and incorporating a pub-stop at a mid-way point.

PUB WALKS FROM COUNTRY STATIONS:
Buckinghamshire and Oxfordshire: Clive Higgs.
Circular rambles incorporating pub-stops.

LOCAL WALKS: South Bedfordshire and North Chilterns: Vaughan Basham.
Twenty-seven thematic circular walks.

LOCAL WALKS: North and Mid Bedfordshire: Vaughan Basham.
Twenty-five thematic circular walks.

FAMILY WALKS: Chilterns South: Nick Moon.
Thirty 3 to 5 mile circular walks.

FAMILY WALKS: Chilterns North: Nick Moon.
Thirty shorter circular walks.

CHILTERN WALKS: Hertfordshire, Bedfordshire and North Buckinghamshire: Nick Moon.
CHILTERN WALKS: Buckinghamshire: Nick Moon.
CHILTERN WALKS: Oxfordshire and West Buckinghamshire: Nick Moon.
A trilogy of circular walks, in association with the Chiltern Society.
Each volume contains 30 circular walks.

OXFORDSHIRE WALKS:
Oxford, the Cotswolds and the Cherwell Valley: Nick Moon.
OXFORDSHIRE WALKS:
Oxford, the Downs and the Thames Valley: Nick Moon.
Two volumes that complement Chiltern Walks: Oxfordshire and complete coverage of the county, in association with the Oxford Fieldpaths Society.
Thirty circular walks in each.

THE D'ARCY DALTON WAY: Nick Moon.
Long-distance footpath across the Oxfordshire Cotswolds and Thames Valley, with various circular walk suggestions.

JOURNEYS INTO BEDFORDSHIRE: Anthony Mackay.
Foreword by The Marquess of Tavistock, Woburn Abbey. A lavish book of over 150 evocative ink drawings.

JOURNEYS INTO BUCKINGHAMSHIRE: Anthony Mackay
Superb line drawings plus background text: large format landscape gift book.

BUCKINGHAMSHIRE MURDERS: Len Woodley.
Nearly two centuries of nasty crimes.

WINGRAVE: A Rothschild Village in the Vale: Margaret and Ken Morley.
Thoroughly researched and copiously illustrated survey of the last 200 years in this lovely village between Aylesbury and Leighton Buzzard.

HISTORIC FIGURES IN THE BUCKINGHAMSHIRE LANDSCAPE:
John Houghton.
Major personalities and events that have shaped the county's past, including a special section on Bletchley Park.

TWICE UPON A TIME: John Houghton.
Short stories loosely based on fact, set in the North Bucks area.

MANORS and MAYHEM, PAUPERS and PARSONS: Tales from Four Shires: Beds., Bucks., Herts., and Northants.: John Houghton
Little-known historical snippets and stories.

MYTHS and WITCHES, PEOPLE and POLITICS: Tales from Four Shires: Bucks., Beds., Herts., and Northants.: John Houghton.
Anthology of strange, but true historical events.

FOLK: Characters and Events in the History of Bedfordshire and Northamptonshire: Vivienne Evans. Anthology about people of yesteryear – arranged alphabetically by village or town.

JOHN BUNYAN: His Life and Times: Vivienne Evans.
Highly-praised and readable account.

THE RAILWAY AGE IN BEDFORDSHIRE: Fred Cockman.
Classic, illustrated account of early railway history.

A LASTING IMPRESSION: Michael Dundrow.
A boyhood evacuee recalls his years in the Chiltern village of Totternhoe near Dunstable.

GLEANINGS REVISITED:
Nostalgic Thoughts of a Bedfordshire Farmer's Boy: E W O'Dell.
His own sketches and early photographs adorn this lively account of rural Bedfordshire in days gone by.

BEDFORDSHIRE'S YESTERYEARS Vol 2:
The Rural Scene: Brenda Fraser-Newstead.
Vivid first-hand accounts of country life two or three generations ago.

BEDFORDSHIRE'S YESTERYEARS Vol 3:
Craftsmen and Tradespeople: Brenda Fraser-Newstead.
Fascinating recollections over several generations practising many vanishing crafts and trades.

BEDFORDSHIRE'S YESTERYEARS Vol 4:
War Times and Civil Matters: Brenda Fraser-Newstead.
Two World Wars, plus transport, law and order, etc.

PROUD HERITAGE:
A Brief History of Dunstable, 1000–2000AD: Vivienne Evans.
Century by century account of the town's rich tradition and key events, many of national significance.

DUNSTABLE WITH THE PRIORY: 1100–1550: Vivienne Evans.
Dramatic growth of Henry I's important new town around a major crossroads.

DUNSTABLE IN TRANSITION: 1550–1700: Vivienne Evans.
Wealth of original material as the town evolves without the Priory.

DUNSTABLE DECADE: THE EIGHTIES:
A Collection of Photographs: Pat Lovering.
A souvenir book of nearly 300 pictures of people and events in the 1980s.

STREETS AHEAD: An Illustrated Guide to the Origins
of Dunstable's Street Names: Richard Walden.
Fascinating text and captions to hundreds of photographs, past and present, throughout the town.

DUNSTABLE IN DETAIL: Nigel Benson.
A hundred of the town's buildings and features, plus town trail map.

OLD DUNSTABLE: Bill Twaddle.
A new edition of this collection of early photographs.

BOURNE and BRED:
A Dunstable Boyhood Between the Wars: Colin Bourne.
An elegantly written, well-illustrated book capturing the spirit of the town over fifty years ago.

ROYAL HOUGHTON: Pat Lovering:
Illustrated history of Houghton Regis from the earliest times to the present.

THE STOPSLEY BOOK: James Dyer.
Definitive, detailed account of this historic area of Luton. 150 rare photographs.

THE STOPSLEY PICTURE BOOK: James Dyer.
New material and photographs make an ideal companion to The Stopsley Book.

PUBS and PINTS:
The Story of Luton's Public Houses and Breweries: Stuart Smith.
The background to beer in the town, plus hundreds of photographs, old and new.

THE CHANGING FACE OF LUTON: An Illustrated History:
Stephen Bunker, Robin Holgate and Marian Nichols. Luton's development
from earliest times to the present busy industrial town. Illustrated in colour and
mono.

WHERE THEY BURNT THE TOWN HALL DOWN:
Luton, The First World War and the Peace Day Riots, July 1919:
Dave Craddock.
Detailed analysis of a notorious incident.

THE MEN WHO WORE STRAW HELMETS:
Policing Luton, 1840–1974: Tom Madigan.
Meticulously chronicled history; dozens of rare photographs; author served in
Luton Police for fifty years.

BETWEEN THE HILLS:
The Story of Lilley, a Chiltern Village: Roy Pinnock.
A priceless piece of our heritage – the rural beauty remains but the customs and
way of life described here have largely disappeared.

KENILWORTH SUNSET:
A Luton Town Supporter's Journal: Tim Kingston.
Frank and funny account of football's ups and downs.

A HATTER GOES MAD!: Kristina Howells.
Luton Town footballers, officials and supporters talk to a female fan.

LEGACIES: Tales and Legends of Luton and the North Chilterns: Vic Lea.
Twenty-five mysteries and stories based on fact, including Luton Town
Football Club. Many photographs.

THREADS OF TIME: Shela Porter.
The life of a remarkable mother and businesswoman, spanning the entire
century and based in Hitchin and (mainly) Bedford.

LEAFING THROUGH LITERATURE:
Writers' Lives in Hertfordshire and Bedfordshire: David Carroll.
Illustrated short biographies of many famous authors and their connections with
these counties.

A PILGRIMAGE IN HERTFORDSHIRE: H M Alderman.
Classic, between-the-wars tour round the county, embellished with line
drawings.

THE VALE OF THE NIGHTINGALE: Molly Andrews.
Several generations of a family, lived against a Harpenden backdrop.

SUGAR MICE AND STICKLEBACKS:
Childhood Memories of a Hertfordshire Lad: Harry Edwards
Vivid evocation of those gentler pre-war days in an archetypal village,
Hertingfordbury.

SWANS IN MY KITCHEN: Lis Dorer.
Story of a Swan Sanctuary near Hemel Hempstead.

THE HILL OF THE MARTYR:
An Architectural History of St. Albans Abbey: Eileen Roberts.
Scholarly and readable chronological narrative history of Hertfordshire and
Bedfordshire's famous cathedral. Fully illustrated with photographs and plans.

CHILTERN ARCHAEOLOGY: RECENT WORK:
A Handbook for the Next Decade:
edited by Robin Holgate. The latest views, results and excavations by
twenty-three leading archaeologists throughout the Chilterns.

THE TALL HITCHIN INSPECTOR'S CASEBOOK:
A Victorian Crime Novel Based on Fact: Edgar Newman.
Worthies of the time encounter more archetypal villains.

SPECIALLY FOR CHILDREN

VILLA BELOW THE KNOLLS:
A Story of Roman Britain: Michael Dundrow.
An exciting adventure for young John in Totternhoe and Dunstable two
thousand years ago.

THE RAVENS: One Boy Against the Might of Rome: James Dyer.
On the Barton Hills and in the south-east of England as the men of the great
fort of Ravensburgh (near Hexton) confront the invaders.

Books Distributed by THE BOOK CASTLE

Further titles are in preparation.
All the above are available via any bookshop, or from the publisher and bookseller,
THE BOOK CASTLE
12 Church Street Dunstable, Bedfordshire, LU5 4RU
Tel: (01582) 605670